Wily Modesty

Argentine Women Writers, 1860–1910

by

BONNIE FREDERICK

ASU Center for Latin American Studies Press

ARIZONA STATE UNIVERSITY

Published by ASU Center for Latin American Studies Press
Arizona State University
Center for Latin American Studies
PO Box 872401
Tempe, AZ 85287-2401

Published in the United States of America.

Cover art by Michael Grant Bronner, emMGee Graphics, Mesa, Arizona
Editing, book design, and typesetting by Evelyn Smith de Gálvez
Printing by Creative Press, Robert Ganz, President, Phoenix, Arizona

Library of Congress Cataloging-in-Publication Data

Frederick, Bonnie.
    Wily Modesty: Argentine women writers, 1860-1910 / by Bonnie
Frederick.
        p.   cm.
    Includes bibliographical references and index.
    ISBN 0-87918-086-2
    1. Argentine literature—Women authors—History and criticism.
    2. Argentine literature—19th century—History and criticism.
    3. Argentine literature—20th century—History and criticism.
    I. Title.
PQ7633.F74   1997
860.9'9287—dc21   97-40237
                                                            CIP

The ASU Department of Foreign Languages, Chair David William Foster, and The ASU Women's Studies Program, Interim Director Kathleen Ferraro, contributed to the printing of this book.

Wily Modesty

Argentine Women Writers, 1860–1910

The Author

B onnie Frederick (University of Arizona, 1983) is Associate Professor of Spanish and Chair of the Foreign Languages Department at Washington State University, Pullman, Washington. As a result of her research on this book, which began in Argentina while on a project funded by the Tinker Foundation, she has collected the largest library on nineteenth-century Argentine women writers outside Argentina.

Frederick's publications include "La pluma y la aguja: escritoras de la generación del Ochenta" (Feminaria Press) and "Women and the Journey," co-edited with Susan McLeod (WSU Press). Examples of her articles and chapters are "El viajero y la nómada: los recuerdos de viaje de Eduarda y Lucio Mansilla" in *Mujeres y cultura en la Argentina del siglo XIX*, edited by Lea Fletcher; "A State of Conviction, a State of Feeling: Scientific and Literary Discourses in the Works of Three Argentine Writers, 1879-1908" in *Latin American Literary Review*; and "Reading the Warning: The Reader and the Image of the Captive Woman" in *Chasqui*. A preliminary discussion of women writers of the "Generación del 80" appeared in *Hispania* under the title "In Their Own Voice."

Currently, Professor Frederick is involved with various innovative teaching projects, such as a video-based version of her Hispanic American Culture course that is broadcast nationwide, and a web-based tutorial on Spanish language and culture for veterinarians.

Dedicated to Lea and Lily

Contents

List of Figures

Acknowledgments

In 1982, I was in the old National Library in Buenos Aires, reading newspapers from the 1800s. The electricity went off, so, being a veteran of such blackouts, I pulled out a flashlight and began reading again. Perhaps because a flashlight creates a spotlight effect, a brief notice that I had passed over before, now caught my eye:

> La interesante novela de la simpática e inteligente escritora doña Josefina Pelliza de Sagasta, titulada *Margarita*, está haciendo furor entre el bello sexo. Sabemos que está por agotarse ya la primera edición de ese libro, que ha venido a poner el sello a la reputación literaria de que goza dicha escritora.[1]

> [The interesting novel, entitled *Margarita*, of the charming and intelligent writer Madame Josefina Pelliza de Sagasta is causing a furor among the fair sex. We know that the first edition of this book is about to sell out, which has sealed the literary reputation that the author enjoys.]

I had never heard of Pelliza or her novel. I certainly had no idea that women were writing best sellers in Argentina in 1876. I wrote down the citation and stuck it in the back of my folder. But now I had been alerted to mentions of women writers, and I began to see their names everywhere. As the stack of citations grew, it began to dawn on me that I had stumbled across a generation of women writers who were well known in their own time but virtually forgotten today.

Thus began a decade of searching for copies of these women's works, a process slowed by the demands of teaching and obtaining tenure. Having exhausted the resources in the United States, I returned to Buenos Aires in 1992. Doing research in Buenos Aires can be literally painful. One day, I twisted my ankle by stepping in a pothole dug by the phone company. I had been admiring the lovely wrought iron balconies on the *fin de siècle* houses instead of watching where I was going. As I hopped along, muttering curses on Telecom, I figured that the ankle was an omen. My research was not going well. The National Library was being moved from one building to another, and most of the books and periodicals that I had intended to consult were in boxes somewhere to be opened someday. Three weeks into my sabbatical, and all I had were sore feet and now a twisted ankle.

The bookstore I was looking for, Librería Alberto Casares, was on a

[1] "Conversación," *La Nación* (12 January 1876): 1.

narrow, crowded street in the old downtown of Buenos Aires. Dodging a homicidal taxi on one side and a man with an enormous briefcase on the other, I limped into the store, handed my list to the proprietor, explained my research, and waited for his "sorry, can't help you." Instead, he looked thoughtfully at the list, and said, "Yes, I have a few things that might interest you," and pulled off the shelf a bound copy of *La Ondina del Plata*, a magazine from the 1870s that published women's writing and sponsored polemics on women's rights. I had despaired of finding it, and now I held it in my hands. As Mr. Casares continued to pull books off the shelves, I realized that my luck was changing. Then came the day when Lea Fletcher placed in my hands a copy of *Margarita*. After ten years, I finally held the novel that began the research! It is not surprising that my hands shook as I opened the pages. That night I sat up till dawn, reading this novel from 1876, enjoying it, and wishing I could travel back in time to meet the author herself.

Carrying out research in Argentina requires many of the same skills as research in the United States—knowledge of sources, determination, and patience—but it also requires tough feet and sheer luck. In the United States, we are spoiled by our extraordinary library services: OCLC searches, interlibrary loans, printed and on-line catalogs, and (perhaps most of all) highly trained professional librarians. From Holland Library at Washington State University, I have been able to accumulate enormous amounts of material from all over the United States. But in Argentina's libraries and museums, there are virtually no computerized catalogues and few printed resource materials. The researcher must physically visit each collection to discover what is there—and Buenos Aires has *a lot* of libraries and museums. Moreover, the researcher needs to know that often the pre-1900 card catalog is stored behind the counter of the library rather than being in plain view. Knowing such tricks of the trade came in handy as I visited twenty-three libraries, seven museums, five private collections, three archives, sixteen rare book dealers, and countless used book stores.

Yet the painlessness of research in the U.S. has a price. Finding an item in an on-line bibliography is simply not very thrilling. It is satisfying, but it cannot compare with the excitement of finding in a dusty used bookshop a copy of a novel published in 1889, with the author's photograph and autograph tucked inside. Nor can a computer provide the kindness, generosity, and dedication of the human beings who helped me in my quest, such as the librarian of Ricardo Rojas' private collection, who said "But you don't have Echenique's book on this list." I said, "She didn't write a book." The librarian said, "Here it is," and stayed past closing time so that I could finish photocopying the entire book. And I will always remember the librarian at the Colegio Nacional de Buenos Aires who, after putting up with almost three months of my pleading, suddenly laughed and gave me permission to photocopy *El Búcaro Americano*, a women's magazine from the 1890s. Going home in a taxi, flying through the rainy streets, the driver and I sang to the tangos on the radio. I hit about one note in three, but I didn't care.

Not all personal contacts were so helpful, of course. It is hard to say anything about the personnel of the National Library without gritting my teeth. I will not describe my reactions the day they lost my request slip three times, told me that an index in plain view behind the counter did not exist, then closed the library because the one and only booklift broke down.

I admit that on that day I desperately missed the technology of the United States. The advantage of our system is that it is efficient and egalitarian, qualities I prize. However, I am also aware of how computers have made research largely impersonal. Research in Argentina, on the other hand, is painfully and delightfully *personal.* The human element is complicated, time-consuming, and often frustrating. At times, it is elitist, since some materials are inaccessible without the right personal contacts. Yet it can also be a joy. As I hold my copy of *La Aljaba*, the first Argentine newspaper founded by women (1830), I realize that it is not just an extremely rare document, it is also a souvenir. It makes me remember Lily Sosa de Newton, who introduced me to Lea Fletcher, who lent me her copy, which was copied by the good people at Librería Martín Fierro. Every book and periodical that I brought back from Buenos Aires makes me think of the people involved in its acquisition, and that is both the fun and the frustration of doing research in Argentina.

Quite literally, this book could not have been written without Lea Fletcher and Lily Sosa de Newton. They have spent their lives discovering Argentine women's works, collecting them, and bringing them to the notice of others. At least half of the original works studied here came from Lea and Lily. They unselfishly shared their libraries and knowledge with me in a spirit of collaboration, not competition. I am not only grateful to Lea and Lily, I respect them as scholars and love them as friends.

When the time came to write down my thoughts, Jennifer Jenkins became my best and toughest reader. She has an unerring eye for lapses in logic, awkward clauses, missing transitions, and my "Spanglish" prepositions. The rough parts of this manuscript are mine, the smooth parts are due to Jenni's good red pen. Her friendship is like her editing: honest and true. Others who have helped in this project include Birgitta Ingemanson, Jeanne Andersen, George Reid Andrews, Mary Berg, and Deborah Haynes. My dear uncle and aunt, John and Billie Kemplin, helped in the preparation of corrections. My adored mother, Kit Frederick, applied her good sense and intelligence to the first draft of the prospectus, and gently told me to rewrite it. As usual, she was right. I am grateful beyond words for the help of all these kind people.

The Tinker Foundation funded the original stay in Buenos Aires that led to my flashlit discoveries. Since then, Washington State University has supported the work with regular travel grants, a grant-in-aid, and a year-long sabbatical. In addition, my colleagues in the department and in the administration have encouraged me and waited with surprising patience for the project's completion. The National Endowment for the Humanities awarded a summer stipend that allowed me to read, reread, outline, and re-outline. A generous Fulbright grant allowed me to purchase the rare works studied here, works that too often are not available in libraries.

Last, but in no way least, I thank my family and friends for their support and good cheer. I am especially indebted to the Knitters, my anchor in high seas.

Introduction

On January 26, 1896, a group of women gathered at the Recoleta Cemetery in Buenos Aires to dedicate a plaque to Lola Larrosa de Ansaldo, a writer and editor who had died of tuberculosis at the age of 38. One of the speakers that day exclaimed:

> ¡Oh Lola! tú formaste parte de la legión de las escritoras de mi patria; tú, como la inmortal Gorriti, la esclarecida Pelliza de Sagasta, la Avellaneda de Sarmiento, Mansilla de García, Coronado que reposan en este recinto, has dejado grabado tu nombre en los anales literarios de nuestra patria.[1]

> [Oh Lola! you formed part of the legion of women writers of my country; you, like the immortal Gorriti, the illustrious Pelliza de Sagasta, Avellaneda de Sarmiento, Mansilla de García, Coronado that rest in this place, you have left your name engraved on the literary annals of our country.]

But her belief in Larrosa's literary immortality was wrong. Who today knows the name of Lola Larrosa or the other women writers of her day? Even the lovingly dedicated plaque and the remains of Larrosa herself were removed when the bills were no longer paid, and the relocation notation in the cemetery's records is too blurred to read.

This study recovers the lost memory of Lola Larrosa and other Argentine women writers of the second half of the nineteenth century. They were pioneers trying to break into all-male literary circles, frustrated by low pay and lack of critical recognition, but instrumental in accustoming the reading public to the appearance of women's names in print. Against all odds, these women formed a literary community, Argentina's first genuine female literary generation. They held literary salons, organized an eight-hundred-member women's intellectual society, edited periodicals, helped each other publish their works, debated social and political issues with each other, and even provided funerals for those who died in poverty. Later writers—especially the glittering generation of the 1930s—have overshadowed these authors, but the frustrations, spirited rhetoric, and personal contradictions of this first group of Argentine women writers anticipate themes found in women's literature today in Hispanic America and around the world.

Of the many women who were active in the second half of the nineteenth century, I have chosen to focus on nine: Elvira Aldao de Díaz,

Agustina Andrade, Emma de la Barra, María Eugenia Echenique, Silvia Fernández, Lola Larrosa de Ansaldo, Eduarda Mansilla de García, Josefina Pelliza de Sagasta, and Ida Edelvira Rodríguez.[2] These women were born between 1835 and 1865; thus their mature intellectual years occurred in the second half of the century. They defined themselves as writers of literature rather than of politics or history, and they considered their writing as more than a pastime or occasional exercise, since each published regularly during some part of her life. Each expressed ideas common in the female community of her day, while maintaining her own individual style and quirks; and each had a certain amount of popular success with her writing. These nine writers knew each other's work, and some of them were friends as well. The sense of community they shared was anchored in their common participation in women's periodicals.

These writers' principal years of productivity occur roughly between 1870 and 1910, with some works falling on either side of those dates. There is no simple term entirely satisfactory to describe that time period, which represents the critical years between the fall of the dictator Rosas and the celebration of the centenary of independence from Spain. Textbooks of Argentine history tend to call the period either the *Generation of 1880* (the *Ochenta*, in Spanish) or the time of *National Organization* or *Consolidation*. All of these terms refer to the 1880 political unification of Buenos Aires with the rest of Argentina, ending a long struggle that had violently divided the country. I prefer not to use the terms that refer to organization or consolidation, because they imply an orderliness that was not much in evidence during those years. Besides, they are more narrowly political than the Ochenta, which refers to literature as well as politics. Yet, the specific year contained in the term *Generation of 1880* implies a time span too narrow to represent the trajectories and vagaries of literary careers. Indeed, some of the writers discussed here did not begin to write until the twentieth century. For example, Elvira Aldao was born in 1858, but did not publish her first book until 1922. In contrast, Agustina Andrade, who was also born in 1858, published her first book in 1878. Still, since *Generation of 1880* is an established term in Argentine history, I will use it with the understanding that it refers to the first generation of writers to come to maturity in the post-Rosas years and that they share an acute consciousness of living between a turbulent colonial past and a future of material progress and political independence.

My procedure in studying women's writings has been to try to listen to what the women themselves have to say. There is certainly no shortage of men's opinions about women, but I have found it much more revealing—and often more disconcerting—to discover how women saw themselves. The exception to this procedure occurs in Chapter 5, which examines the reception of women's works by male critics and literary historians. In addition, the writers chosen for this study were those who published in commonly available sources. It is true that women's voices are also present in foreign-language immigrant periodicals, anarchist journals, and Afro-Argentine publications. However, by focusing on mainstream publications, this study is able to document that many women were *not* considered marginal writers in their own time; instead, their marginality today was imposed by later historians. Therefore, the primary texts studied here are conventional, middle- to upper-class periodicals with relatively large circulation.

These writers fall outside traditional literary notions of canon and master works; like Lola Larrosa, their names and remains have been misplaced and the record blurred. This study will bring them to the attention of scholars of Argentine and Latin American literature, as well as to readers of women's literature in general. However, restoring women writers to their place in literary history cannot be accomplished simply by inserting their names into chapters already written, since they represent a literature that is often at odds with that of their male colleagues. Edwin Ardener has said that "where society is defined by men, some features of women do not fit that definition."[3] In other words, where *literature* is defined by men, some features of *women's literature* do not fit that definition. In their writing, the women writers of the Generation of 1880 both *fit* and are *unfit*; that is, they frequently adhere to the dominant cultural patterns, but they also reserve a space for their own patterns. For instance, while men were employing the patriarchial family as their model for national reconstruction in the post-Rosas era, women were seeking broad reforms in traditional family roles. Even when women apparently shared a belief or experience with their male counterparts, they defined it and experienced it in their own terms, thus revealing the unspoken prejudices and limitations inherent in the men's definition. For example, scholars consider the Ochenta's travel memoirs an important source for understanding the elite's ideology, but these women's travel memoirs reveal additional aspects of that ideology, since the women were restricted by standards of female sexual respectability that men did not face. Moreover, the men of the Ochenta drew on literary influences that often were not shared by the women. The most significant example of this difference is *modernismo*, which was increasingly important among male writers after Rubén Darío's arrival in Buenos Aires in 1893, but which touched women writers hardly at all. Therefore, this study goes beyond biography and bibliography to include analysis of how these women writers both share and deviate from the male literary tradition.

In *Feminist Literary History*, Janet Todd identifies the primary dilemma of this project: the difficulty of reaching across time and culture to allow these women to speak for themselves. Todd captures the poignancy of the woman writer's life in the inevitable paradox of literary history: "The woman who wrote is no doubt in the end unknowable, but, at some level or in some gap, trope, or choice, she was working to be known."[4] In a sense, this study is a century late. Inevitably, information and documents have been lost to the passage of time, and some facts included here will appear of greater or lesser importance to today's readers than to those of a hundred years ago. This history should have been written by one of its subjects, but unfortunately the women studied here did not have control over the writing of their history. Instead, their role in literary history was distorted or even erased by men like Ricardo Rojas, Argentina's premier literary historian, who wrote about Juana Manso's face and Agustina Andrade's father instead of discussing their work. There were a few tentative efforts by women to document their own experience into formal history. For instance, Mercedes Pujato Crespo and Adelia Di Carlo, among others, wrote articles about women's journalism, which they knew from personal experience; but their occasional analytical insights were overshadowed by simple lists of journals and editors.[5] These lists provide valuable information, but they raise questions, too. Who were these editors? Where are copies of their journals now? What was said in those publications? Clorinda Matto de Turner's speech to the Ateneo de Buenos Aires in 1895 also mentions women writers from all over Hispanic America, but many of those names mean nothing now. The women and their works are lost to us.[6]

My task as an historian, then, is to listen to these women as best I can, recovering their voices, their audience, and their society to the extent possible from this distance of time and space. Writing this history of the women of the Ochenta has been like a visit to the San Telmo antiques fair in Buenos Aires: some of the objects on display are familiar and still useful, but others are unfamiliar. Turning a strange object in my hand, I wonder what daily routine required its services. Other objects are deceiving in their familiarity: that ivory-handled iron hook was not for crocheting, as it appears to be, but for buttoning boots. The yellowing lace in unironed heaps attests to women's long hours of labor with a needle; their pens and their books are nowhere to be found.

Necessarily, then, this history is firmly tied to a particular time and place, focusing on specific individuals rather than on "the feminine" in an abstract sense. It examines a group of texts that have the writers' gender in common, gender being understood as "the emotional and psychological attributes which a given culture expects to coincide with physical maleness or femaleness."[7] As the Seminar on Women and Culture in Latin America points out, the social construction of gender is influenced by class while also transcending it:

> On one hand, class hierarchies and relations of exploitation are reproduced within the gender system—for example, in relations between upper-class women and their female domestic employees. On the other hand, gender creates inevitable and significant instabilities in class hierarchies. It creates difference within class boundaries (upper-class women do not participate in society or culture in the same ways as upper-class men do), while it creates sameness across class boundaries (the experiences of upper-class and lower-class women have points in common).[8]

The women writers studied here felt kinship with women in general, though they were also bound by their upper-class ideology.[9] Significantly, the two middle-class women and one impoverished woman in this group identified themselves with the upper-class values that the other six were born to, thus muting any expression of an experience that the upper-class ladies could not know. Because the nine writers shared a class ideology, and because most of them had a father or brother who was also a writer and who serves as contrast, it is startlingly easy to see how gender overrides other factors in these women's literary identity. Such is the case of Lucio and Eduarda Mansilla. As brother and sister, each the favorite of the other, they shared an uncommon amount of life experience: family, socioeconomic class, education, personal tastes, etc. However, Lucio's military experience could not be shared by Eduarda. She, on the other hand, had six children—an experience Lucio was incapable of having. While Lucio's military life could be discussed in polite society, childbirth could not. Thus, a definitive experience that had repercussions for every aspect of Eduarda's existence was hidden away, referred to so obliquely that it could easily be missed or misunderstood by a reader who did not know the code. Eduarda probably shared more with her brother than with women outside her class, but even within her class she was set apart by gender. Indeed, this gender barrier is evident in the siblings' writing and its reception. Lucio's continuing place in the canon was gained by a book recounting a military-political journey to Indian territory. Eduarda's children's stories (the first in Argentina) and her memoirs of travel as an ambassador's wife merit her only a footnote in conventional histories.

This history is not meant to be read alone, but rather as part of a constellation of works that are redefining our understanding of nineteenth-century women writers. This study is, I hope, a part of the rebirth of women's history in Argentina. There, two women, Lily Sosa de Newton and Lea Fletcher, have inspired and encouraged investigations that form the complement to this one. I especially hope that the reader has close at hand *Mujeres y cultura en la Argentina del siglo XIX*, compiled by Lea Fletcher, and *El ajuar de la patria: Ensayos críticos sobre Juana Manuela Gorriti*, compiled by Cristina Iglesia. The observations found in my book are inextricably intertwined with these two collections of essays, which represent the current, exciting state of research in Argentina.

As for studies in the United States, I conceive of this book being read alongside the works of two other writers: Francine Masiello and Donna Guy. Masiello's *Between Civilization and Barbarism: Women, Nation, and Literary Culture in Modern Argentina* placed women's national imaginings in a coherent framework that has sparked others to seek out Argentine women's past. Where Masiello is more theoretical in her literary analysis, I follow a sociohistorical approach to the circumstances of women's authorship. Donna Guy, a historian, has provided the non-literary complement to Masiello's and my studies. Her rigorous investigations into women's work and their treatment by law, especially *Sex and Danger in Buenos Aires*, have unmasked the hollowness of the "angel of the house" ideal that has blinded historians in the past. This study is intended to complement Masiello's and Guy's works, forming a three-way conversation as well as reflecting women's new history in general. In addition to these two writers, many others—to whom I am equally indebted—are listed in the bibliography. Unlike the Argentine women authors of the 1800s, writers today can have no doubt that they form part of an enormous, international network of literature and history that will never let women's works be lost or minimized again.

As described below, the chapters of this study do not—and cannot—exhaust the possibilities for critical analysis of women's works. Instead, they are designed to trace notable and conventional features of Argentine women's writing during the late 1800s. It is my hope that other historians will build on this new history, using it as a basic overview text, but developing it in breadth and depth.

Chapter 1. Journals, Manifestos, Mentors, and a Best Seller

The first chapter of this history of the Ochenta's women writers reexamines a familiar topic, the publishing scene in Buenos Aires prior to the twentieth century, but this time from the perspective of women. It analyzes the mission statements that appeared in the first issues of several women's periodicals from 1830 to 1896, extracting from them the major issues and literary ideas that molded women's novels, poetry, and essays. Such an overview in a study of the male experience of the Ochenta would end with a discussion of *modernismo* and the circle of the Ateneo and Rubén Darío. The overview of the women's Ochenta, however, ends with an examination of the impact of the generation's bestseller, Emma de la Barra's *Stella*, which sums up the ideas about ideal womanhood found in women's periodicals during the previous seventy years.

Chapter 2. Speaking Up with Eyes Lowered

The codes of modesty and respectability that forbade Eduarda Mansilla from traveling alone as her brother did or from writing about childbirth also formed a fundamental narrative quandary: how could an author write with authority while also maintaining proper feminine modesty? After all, the essence of feminine modesty was believed to be silence, as this maxim from a reader for girls indicates:

> Un profundo silencio siempre ha sido
> De las mujeres el más bello adorno.[10]
>
> [A profound silence has always been
> Women's most beautiful adornment.]

Knowing that the reading public would judge them as women rather than as writers, many women authors felt obligated to incorporate at least some signs of conventional feminine modesty in their works. Such gestures could include writing under a male pseudonym, denying any real skill as an artist, or directing the work to an exclusively female audience. Agustina Andrade, Eduarda Mansilla de García, and Elvira Aldao de Díaz, for example, drew on these and other strategies—which I call the "rhetoric of femininity"—to create an acceptable feminine authorial self; although, as shall be seen, they also subtly undermined the rhetoric's modest appearance by drawing attention to its falseness. Josefina Pelliza de Sagasta, on the other hand, genuinely strove to write like the ideal domestic angel, yet in a curious twist of fate, she ended up defending women's right to write in a newspaper debate with a male writer. After the debate, Pelliza abandoned the conventions of authorial modesty and began to write with anger, defiance, and despair.

Chapter 3. Women in the Era of "Progress, Glory, and Electricity"

To advance their cause of reform, women appealed to the most cherished belief of the Generation of 1880: that they were living in an age of material and moral progress. Basing their arguments on a Darwinian model of social evolution, they demanded more education, training in income-earning skills, and the same legal and economic rights for married women that single women and widows enjoyed. Women's concept of their historical evolution is examined in the novels based on the colonial era's Lucía Miranda legend and in the futuristic short story "El ramito de romero" [The Sprig of Rosemary] by Eduarda Mansilla de García. But how far should these rights go? Just as disagreement in the United States during the 1900s turned on the word *feminism*, discord in the 1800s centered on the word *emancipation*. To many, it implied women's participation in political affairs—even the right to vote— while to others it meant the right to pursue their individual destiny, whatever that might be. Some writers feared that an emancipated woman would be unfeminine and an unfit mother and wife, but others saw no conflict between womanliness and emancipation. These argu- ments are followed in the debate carried out in the pages of *La Ondina del Plata* by María Eugenia Echenique and Josefina Pelliza de Sagasta.

Chapter 4. The Cliché of Love: Desires, Exasperations, and Better Things to Do

Women's writing has often been stereotyped as being little more than idealized love stories that end happily in a kiss. But for these women writers, love is rarely simple, and if the ending is happy, it is a hard-won triumph. Women's love stories are replete with fears: threatened incest in Pelliza's *Margarita*, fiery death in the Lucía Miranda novels, and near-fatal starvation in Larrosa's *Los esposos*. Language itself is an enemy in many of the works, particularly the "He and She" works by Silvia Fernández and Lola Larrosa. One poet consistently avoids the issue of love: Ida Edelvira Rodríguez. She writes about starry nights, the opera, politics—anything but love. Elvira Aldao also avoids the cliché of love by writing her childhood memoirs.

Chapter 5. Readers Then and Now

The conclusion of this history focuses on responses by readers of the writers' work during three historical moments: the critical reception by the writers' contemporaries, Ricardo Rojas and his role in marginaliz- ing women from the canon in the 1920s, and the rediscovery of the Ochenta's texts by today's readers. The formation of the canon is one of the more controversial subjects in North American literary criticism today, and it is no less complex a subject in Argentina. In the case of these women writers, their historical fate rested almost entirely in the hands of one man, Ricardo Rojas, the first professor of Argentine literature at the University of Buenos Aires. Germán Arciniegas has said, without much exaggeration, "No es posible acercarse a ningún problema en la historia intelectual de la Argentina sin familiarizarse primero con la obra de don Ricardo Rojas"[11] [It is not possible to address a problem in the intellectual history of Argentina without first familiarizing oneself with the work of the honorable Ricardo Rojas]. Indeed, Rojas' double-edged rhetoric of inclusion and exclusion is key to understanding these women's erasure from public memory.

The twentieth-century reader accustomed to thinking of nineteenth-century women's works as sentimental romances or idealized stories of domesticity will find examples of those types discussed here. However, there are surprises, too. The texts challenge assumptions that "respectable" women writers did not engage in political writing or social criticism. They also contradict the stereotype of women intellectuals being humorless, puritanical, or dowdy. These writers were rational, passionate, argumentative, contradictory, funny, inquisitive, ironic, angry, dreamy, and ambivalent. In other words, they were lively human beings whose works deserve to be dusted off and read again.

Please note: all translations are mine. Spelling in the text has been changed to conform with modern standards. For example, *secso* is written *sexo*, and *muger* is written *mujer*. However, the original spelling is preserved in the bibliography. The original, often quirky, punctuation of the Spanish quotation is repeated in the English translation, in order to convey the flavor of the writer's style.

Endnotes

[1] María Emilia Passicot, "Social," *El Búcaro Americano* (15 February 1896): 45-46.

[2] However, references will be made to many more, including Juana Manuela Gorriti, Margarita Rufina Ochagavia, Clorinda Matto de Turner, and Edelina Soto y Calvo.

[3] Edwin Ardener, "Belief and the Problem of Women" and "The 'Problem' Revisited," *Perceiving Women*, Shirley Ardener, ed. (New York: John Wiley & Sons, 1975), 23.

[4] Janet Todd, *Feminist Literary History* (New York: Routledge, 1988), 136.

[5] Mercedes Pujato Crespo, "Historia de las revistas femeninas y mujeres intelectuales que les dieron vida," *Primer Congreso Patriótico de Señoras en América del Sud* (Buenos Aires: Imprenta Europea, 1910), 157-79; and Adelia Di Carlo, "El periodismo femenino literario en la República Argentina, hasta el año 1907," *Caras y Caretas* 1762 (1932): n.p.

[6] Clorinda Matto de Turner, "Las obreras del pensamiento," *El Búcaro Americano* (1 February 1896): 5-14; reprinted in *Boreales, miniaturas y porcelanas* (Buenos Aires: Juan A. Alsina, 1902), 245-66.

[7] Lisa Tuttle, *Encyclopedia of Feminism* (New York: Facts on File, 1986). For further discussion, see Elaine Showalter, "Introduction: The Rise of Gender," *Speaking of Gender*, Elaine Showalter, ed. (New York: Routledge, 1989), 1-13.

[8] Seminar on Feminism and Culture in Latin America, *Women, Culture, and Politics in Latin America* (Berkeley: University of California Press, 1990), 2.

[9] Another ideology entirely was expressed in publications such as the anarchist magazine *La Voz de la Mujer* (1896–1901). See Maxine Molyneux, "No God, No Boss, No Husband: Anarchist Feminism in Nineteenth-Century Argentina," *Latin American Perspectives* 13 (1986): 119-45; and Dora Barrancos, *Anarquismo, educación y costumbres en la Argentina de principios de siglo* (Buenos Aires: Contrapunto, 1990).

[10] José Bernardo Suárez, *El tesoro de las niñas: coleccion de articulos estractados i traducidos de los mejores autores, i publicada para servir de texto de lectura en los colejios y escuelas* (Buenos Aires: Pablo E. Coni, 1868), 18. I am grateful to Lily Sosa de Newton for pointing out this text.

[11] Germán Arciniegas, "Don Ricardo Rojas," *El Mundo* (10 June 1956): 24.

Cecilia Grierson
6 PESOS
R. ARGENTINA

1

Journals, Manifestos, Mentors, and a Best Seller, 1830–1905

W omen's literary culture in nineteenth-century Argentina was forged in the crucible of journalism. In periodicals edited by and for women, writers could debate ideas, learn about others' works, and find a sympathetic source of publication. At a time when women had little or no public voice, these ladies' journals were virtually the only forum for their concerns. Periodicals with such genteel titles as *El Album de Hogar* [Home Album], *La Camelia* [The Camellia], and *El Búcaro Americano* [The American Flower Vase] included sentimental poems, household hints, fashion news, and gossip columns—the sort of writing that the term "ladies' magazine" automatically conjures up. Between these stereotypical items, however, appear articles that reveal how misleading the stereotype can be.[1] *La Camelia*, for example, published excruciatingly sentimental stories alongside essays that demanded increased rights for women. Similarly, *El Búcaro Americano* included dress patterns and reports on society parties, but it also showcased women writers from all over Latin America and was one of the first periodicals in Argentina to use the newly coined term *feminism*. Through their journalism, women began to form a sense of community based on more than common obligations of domesticity. This remarkable publishing evolution began in 1830, when the first newspaper written by women appeared, and culminated in 1905, when the best seller *Stella* burst on the scene to sum up the ideas found in seventy-five years of women's journalism. It is a history of high hopes, frustrations, unconventional personalities, crusading zeal, and an abiding will to write.

La Aljaba, the First Periodical Written by Women

The struggle by women to edit their own periodicals and to gain acceptance as writers began in 1830 when two newspapers for women appeared in Buenos Aires. *La Argentina* had its debut in October. It purported women's authorship, but it actually was written by Manuel Yrigoyen, a man.[2] *La Argentina* seems to have been designed to preempt the competing newspaper, *La Aljaba*, which came out in November and also was advertised as written by women. The editor of *La Aljaba*, Petrona Rosende de Sierra (1787–1863),[3] was definitely female, and she wrote vigorously in defense of her sex in the pages of her newspaper. The word *aljaba* refers both to a quiver for arrows and a flower, the fuchsia. The symbolic connection of the quiver and the fuchsia with female sexual organs is more evident to today's readers than it was in those pre-Freudian days of 1830, but *La Aljaba*'s readers would indeed have recognized Diana the Huntress, usually portrayed carrying a quiver on her shoulder, as an image of female power. The title's double meaning conveys both determination—the editor speaks of her arrows "empapadas en el melifluo licor de la verdad"[4] [dipped in the honeyed liquor of truth]—and femininity, which conventionally was described in floral metaphors. This double voice is characteristic of *La Aljaba*. Its masthead slogan, for example, was "Nos libraremos de las injusticias de los demás hombres, solamente cuando no existamos entre ellos" [We will be free of the injustices of other men only when we cease to live among them], a motto which can be read as an indictment of men in general or as resignation to an imperfect world. The prospectus advertising the forthcoming publication of the paper emphasized the inoffensiveness of its content:

> ¡Porción hermosa de la sociedad!! . . . Contad por vuestro este periódico. . . . Siendo vuestra, nada os dirá que ofenda vuestra delicadeza: ella se desviará del campo de Marte; no pisará los umbrales do moran las opiniones encontradas. . . . Sus trabajos no llevan más objeto que formar hijas obedientes, madres respetables y dignas esposas; y por estos medios contribuirá a que más y más resalten los dones con que la naturaleza os ha distingido tan pródigamente. Variedades instructivas, anécdotas selectas, pasajes históricos, y la poesía (que tan apreciada es para las americanas), también se mezclarán para vuestra recreación.[5]

[Beautiful half of society!! (...) Consider this your newspaper (...). Being yours, it will say nothing to offend your delicacy: it will avoid the field of Mars; it will notcross the thresholds where opposing opinions abide (...). Its works have no objective beyond forming obedient daughters, respectable mothers, and worthy wives; and thus it will help make conspicuous the gifts which Nature has so generously bestowed on you. Instructive news, select anecdotes, historical passages, and poetry (so appreciated by American women) will also be mixed in for your recreation.]

Indeed, articles on religion and morality, and patriotic or moralizing poems appear in almost every issue. *La Aljaba* comes out in favor of believing in God, and in a series of articles, Rosende proposes that women's true happiness lies in carrying out their domestic duties.[6] These articles and poems are written in a calm tone that could hardly offend anyone; their sentiments are utterly conventional.

But in spite of the prospectus' promise not to tread where "opposing opinions abide," the majority of *La Aljaba*'s articles do enter into controversy by seeking improved education for women. The inoffensive rhetoric of other topics is dropped when Rosende attacks the male oppressors who deny education to women:

ellos las prohibían hasta saber conocer las letras del *alfabeto*: decían con la elocuencia de sus más fuertes razones, que las mujeres que sabían leer y escribir *eran las que se perdían, &c. &c.* . . . ¿Puede un hombre manifestar de un mejor modo su estupidez? . . . ¡Casi parece imposible que un racional se exprese tan toscamente!!! Atribuir a los conocimientos la perdición de las jóvenes, es el delirio mayor de un cerebro descompuesto; creer que, por no saber leer y escribir, las ponen al abrigo de toda corrupción, es el mayor absurdo.[7]

[they prohibited them from even learning the letters of the *alphabet*: they said, with the eloquence of their strongest reasoning, that the women who knew how to read and write *were those who fall into perdition, etc. etc.* (...) How could a man better demonstrate his stupidity? (...) It almost seems impossible that a rational man would express himself so crudely!!! To attribute the perdition of young women to their education is the greatest delirium of an unbalanced mind; to believe that, by not knowing how to read or write, women will be sheltered from all corruption, is the greatest absurdity.]

Rosende connects the false rationality of men who deny women an education with the false protection of illiteracy for women. Literacy, then, is related to true rationality and morality. She also responds to the traditional justification for denying women an education, that of Eve's disobedience in the Garden of Eden. Rosende quotes a passage from a male-edited newspaper in which God tells Adam that Eve is "privada de razón" [bereft of reason] and "incompleta y en nada semejante al hombre" [incomplete and in no way similar to a man]; thus she "no debe hacer más representación en el mundo que saber obedecer y callar" [should not present herself in this world as knowing more than how to obey and be quiet].[8] In *La Aljaba*, however, Rosende places the interpretive emphasis on Eve's equal creation with Adam rather than on Eve's fall, saying that women were also created in God's image, with the same intelligence and the same prohibitions: "¿No habrán visto en las palabras de Dios la igualdad, la equidad, y la justicia, cuando dirige su voz a los dos seres que hizo a su imagen . . . ?"[9] [Haven't men seen in the words of God the equality, the equity, and the justice, when he directs his voice to the two beings that he made in his image (...) ?]

Despite its endorsements of traditional roles for women, *La Aljaba* does crusade for the defense of women, using both its poetry and its prose for this serious purpose. However, 1830 was a dangerous time to protest: Juan Manuel Rosas had just been elected governor of Buenos Aires, and he was no admirer of either rights or education for women. *La Aljaba* was shut down after just three months of publication, and Petrona Rosende returned to Uruguay where she lived out her life.

La Camelia and Patriotic Self-Sacrifice

Twenty-two years later, Rosas fled Argentina after his defeat at the battle of Caseros. In the ensuing national euphoria, many new periodicals appeared.[10] Among them was another women's newspaper, *La Camelia* [The Camellia], which first appeared on April 11, 1852. The editors elected to remain anonymous for reasons of modesty,[11] but it may be assumed that they were also wary of public reaction. Like *La Aljaba*, with which it shared a femininely floral title, *La Camelia* employed a double rhetoric of sweet femininity and determined crusading, as can be seen in its masthead mottos. Above the logo of blind Justice is "¡Viva la confederación argentina!" [Long live the Argentine confederation!] in the space reserved during the Rosas years for slogans urging the death of his opponents. Arching over the image of Justice is the motto "Libertad! No licencia; Igualdad entre ambos sexos" [Liberty! Not license; Equality between both sexes], while a smaller banner flanking her reads "Siendo flor/se puede vivir sin olor./Siendo mujer/no se puede vivir sin amor" [Being a flower/it can live without a scent./Being a woman/she cannot live without love]. This ornate typography reflects the newspaper's three-point program: celebrating the fall of Rosas, interpreting the era's liberty to include justice for women, and defending the traditional roles of wife and mother.

La Camelia repeatedly urges men to extend to women the liberty they have won for themselves: "entramos en una era de Libertad y no hay derecho alguno que nos excluya de ella"[12] [we are entering a new era of Liberty and they have no right whatsoever to exclude us from it]. This claim is justified by pointing out that women, too, suffered under the dictatorship:

> Nosotras como los hombres, hemos participado de las persecuciones de la fe política, en esa época funesta de luto y de sangre: nosotras al lado de nuestros padres, de nuestros esposos, de nuestros hermanos, de nuestros hijos; hemos corrido a mendigar la hospitalidad del suelo extranjero: a nosotras también, la mano criminal del asesino, se ha dirigido muchas veces, acometiendo nuestra existencia, violando nuestro honor, y vejando nuestra delicadeza; nosotras en fin, hemos contribuido a la alta empresa de libertad, y de derrocar ese poder absoluto y bárbaro, que por veinte años, ha hecho gemir a los pueblos Argentinos.[13]

> [We, like the men, were included in the persecutions for our political faith in that fatal time of mourning and blood; we, at the side of our fathers, our husbands, our brothers, our sons, fled to beg the hospitality of foreign soil; many times the criminal hand of the assassin was lifted against us too, attacking our existence, violating our honor, and offending our delicacy; in short, we contributed to the lofty cause of liberty and the overthrow of that absolute and barbarous power that, for twenty years, made the Argentine people weep.]

In this passage, the editors carefully define women in terms of their relationships with men rather than as autonomous individuals, thus underlining their adherence to proper, traditional womanhood. In the same breath, the reference to "violating our honor" reminds men that women suffered a crime particular to their sex—that is, rape—and that their victimization "contributed to the lofty cause of liberty." By emphasizing women's powerlessness and suffering—the image of *mater dolorosa*—the editors of La Camelia strengthen their demand to be rewarded.[14]

This supreme sacrifice by women has gone unavenged and unnoticed by men, charge the editors. The same men who ignore the value of women's modesty deny women an education beyond sewing and playing the piano:

> Dotadas nosotras como los hombres, con las mismas facultades que la naturaleza les ha concedido, con las mismas obligaciones para con la sociedad, con el mismo fin de civilizar y engrandecer los pueblos y el Universo todo; ¿por qué pues, se niega el cultivo, a una mitad de los seres de la tierra?[15]

[Like men, we are endowed with the same faculties that Nature has given them, with the same obligations to society, with the same goal of civilizing and expanding nations and the whole Universe; why, then, is training denied to half the beings on earth?]

Once again, the editors of *La Camelia* are careful to specify that they do not make demands for women's personal self-fulfillment, a goal that could offend both men and traditional women. Instead, they desire education in order to be better mothers, wives, and citizens:

> No se crea que al pedir un nuevo orden de enseñanza, nos animan aspiraciones indebidas a nuestro sexo . . . no señores, tratamos solamente de llenar el vacío, que el orden social nos prescribe, y que la misma naturaleza nos impone; *cuidar de la educación de nuestros hijos, defender sus derechos, y dar ciudadanos útiles a la Patria.*[16]
>
> [Don't think that by asking for a new system of education, we are motivated by aspirations that are improper for our sex (...) certainly not, we are only trying to carry out the duties that the social order prescribes for us and that Nature itself requires; *to look after the education of our children, defend their rights, and give useful citizens to the nation.*]

In this and similar passages, *La Camelia*'s writers take advantage of the double meaning of educación in Spanish, which means both education in the formal instructional sense and the upbringing of children. Theirs is a discourse of "powerful motherhood" that makes demands for the good of their children; they ask nothing for themselves except respect.[17] Still, the newspaper's shield of womanly propriety and patriotic self-sacrifice did not protect it from attacks. *La Camelia* closed after just two months, the victim of harassment of the female editors by the satirical magazine *El Padre Castañeta.*[18]

El Album de Señoritas: Literature and Politics

Two years later, the visionary educational reformer Juana Manso (1819–75) founded *El Album de Señoritas* (1854), which is even more explicit than *La Camelia* in its advocacy of women's education. Foregoing fancy masthead slogans, Manso comes right to the point in the statement of purpose included in the first issue:

> Todos mis esfuerzos serán consagrados a la ilustración de mis compatriotas, y tenderán a un único propósito—emanciparlas de las preocupaciones torpes y añejas que les prohibían hasta hoy hacer uso de su inteligencia, enajenando su libertad y hasta su conciencia, a autoridades arbitrarias, en oposición a la naturaleza misma de las cosas . . . he de probar que la inteligencia de la mujer, lejos de ser un absurdo, o un defecto, un crimen, o un desatino, es su mejor adorno, es la verdadera fuente de la virtud y de la felicidad doméstica. . . . Y no se crea que *la*

familia no es de un gran peso en la balanza de los pueblos, ni que la desmoralización y el atraso parcial de los individuos no influye en bien o en mal de la sociedad colectiva.[19]

[All my efforts will be consecrated to the education of my compatriots, and will tend toward one sole purpose—to emancipate women from the stupid and antiquated worries that prohibit them today from making use of their intelligence, alienating them from liberty and even their consciences in favor of arbitrary authorities, in opposition to the true nature of things (...) I intend to prove that women's intelligence, far from being absurd, or a defect, a crime, or folly, is her finest adornment, it is the true source of virtue and domestic happiness. (...) And don't think that *the family* is not of great weight in the balance of nations, nor that the demoralization and unjust backwardness of its individuals does not influence collective society for good or bad.]

Manso displays in this passage the articulate political thinking that got her into so much trouble during her lifetime. She claims that lack of education has perverted women from their natural liberty and morality, that a woman's true worth is based on her intelligence rather than on her physical beauty, and that the oppression of women within the structure of the family is harmful to the nation's well being. These were—and are—radical ideas. The first point, concerning women's natural freedom and morality, was not widely held, even in that age of Romanticism and revolutionary ideals. Certainly Jean Jacques Rousseau would have disagreed with Manso, though Mary Wollstonecraft would have cheered her on. More important, Manso's belief is contrary to traditional Catholic doctrine about Eve's original sin, the disobedient bite of the apple that tainted women's souls for eternity and doomed them to bear children in pain. The second point, Manso's questioning of the cult of womanly beauty, was not common evenamong women, since physical beauty was virtually the only means for women to gain fame and influence. The third point, about the parallel between familial and national oppression, was in direct opposition to the public rhetoric of male politicians who were promoting the patriarchal family as the model for national reconstruction.[20] Moreover, most Argentine women urged only reform of the family; they did not question its fundamental structure. Manso, who was reviled for being Protestant and unattractive, was indeed a lonely voice in Argentine society. It is significant that her journal, unlike *La Aljaba* and *La Camelia*, had no other writers except "Señorita Anarda," who wrote two columns on fashion before disappearing from its pages, and the Count of Castelneau, whose travel memoirs were excerpted. Though she solicited contributions from her readers, she evidently did not receive a response. Manso wrote all the other articles alone.

EL Album de Señoritas was the first women's periodical to integrate political issues with literary selections. *La Aljaba* and *La Camelia* had included poems and stories, but they affirmed ideas of traditional femininity and avoided the more inflammatory issues of social equity and education. The first issue of *El Album de Señoritas*, however, contains the beginning installment of Manso's novel, *La familia del comendador*, which illustrates in literary terms the newspaper's stated mission. The plot revolves around the romantic tribulations of the brother and three children of the Comendador das Neves in Brazil. All eventually find happiness in marriage, but not before Manso uses their obstacles to discuss a variety of social ills. In particular, she attacks slavery (outlawed in Buenos Aires only in 1861), the Catholic Church, and forcibly arranged marriages. It is, as Lea Fletcher has pointed out, a domestic novel that draws parallels between injustices in the home and those in society at large.[21] In the first chapter, a key scene sets up the relationship between society and the family when Manso contrasts life in England with that in Brazil:

> Nada tan opuesto en fisonomía y costumbres como la modesta y pobre casa del Dr. Smith y el lujoso ingenio de Macacú.
>
> Allá la práctica simple de la virtud, de la caridad, del amor a sus semejantes.
>
> Aquí la ausencia absoluta de la caridad, incompatible con la esclavitud, la ausencia de la virtud que no transige con la inmoralidad de instituciones viciosas. La crueldad y la opresión en vez del amor a sus semejantes.[22]
>
> [Nothing more opposite in appearance and customs than the modest and poor house of Dr. Smith and the luxurious sugar plantation of Macacú.
>
> There the simple practice of virtue, charity, and love for one another.
>
> Here the absolute absence of charity, which is incompatible with slavery, the absence of virtue, which cannot coexist with the immorality of depraved institutions. Cruelty and oppression instead of love for one another.]

Like many anti-slavery novels, Manso focuses on the whites who own slaves, revealing how the institution of slavery corrupts and oppresses them as well. For instance, the matriarch of the das Neves family is so accustomed to whipping her slaves that when her son Juan angers her, she has him whipped, too.

Neither the novel nor *EL Album de Señoritas* was accepted by the reading public. Other books by Manso, particularly her sentimental novel *Los misterios del Plata* and her textbook *Compendio de la historia*, were successful and went through several editions. *La familia del Comendador* exists only in its 1854 edition. *El Album de Señoritas* attracted admiring comments in the press and at least some distinguished readers such as Mariquita Sánchez,[23] but it did not gain enough readership to justify its expenses, which were paid out of the editor's own pocket. It survived just six weeks (January 1–February 17, 1854).

The 1870s and New Opportunities

Given this discouraging beginning, it is remarkable that women remained dedicated to journalism and even aspired to create literary works. Nonetheless, in the ten years following the fall of Rosas, Juana Manso published her novel, *La familia del comendador* (1854), Margarita Rufina Ochagavia another, *Un ángel o un demonio oel valor de un juramiento* (1857), and Rosa Guerra and Eduarda Mansilla both wrote novels called *Lucía Miranda* (1860). Manso, Guerra, Mansilla, and other women also were writing steadily for general-interest newspapers and periodicals such as *La Tribuna*. By the 1870s, Argentine society had progressed enough that *La Ondina del Plata*, a magazine edited by a man but featuring women's writing, could prosper for four years (1875–79). Other publications of this key decade were hospitable to women's writing as well, most notably the national newspaper *La Nación*, founded by Bartolomé Mitre in 1870, and the popular magazine *El Album del Hogar* (1878–84), edited by Gervasio Méndez.

This change in opportunities for women writers was just one manifestation of a profound social revolution that paralleled the Argentine population boom: between 1870 and 1910, the inhabitants of Buenos Aires soared from 180,000 to 1,300,000.[24] This growth created a demand for more newspapers and magazines, which poured forth in astonishing numbers and variety. And, while the elite continued to dominate the production and content of many journals, other classes were hardly silent. As the culture moved away from the anti-education Rosas years, the working classes became increasingly literate. In 1857, when Domingo F. Sarmiento began his literacy campaigns, only about 8,000 children were enrolled in the public schools, but by the end of the century more than ninety percent of Argentines were literate,[25] a skill they did not hesitate to use in writing everything from poetry to anarchist manifestos.

The rapid rise in literacy was complemented by a widespread determination to imitate European culture and to downplay Argentina's Hispanic heritage; both as a reaction to the Rosas years and in recognition of the flowering of the arts in Europe, French culture in particular reached cult status. By way of this love for all things French, Argentine readers discovered the French women writers who had influenced nineteenth-century literature throughout Europe. Germaine de Staël's *Corrine ou l'Italie* (1807), for example, was widely read and admired in Argentina during the 1870s. Similarly, the novels of George Sand (1804–76) were read by those who considered themselves sophisticated enough to tolerate her scandalous life. In short, being a woman writer carried a certain Gallic *cachet* among Argentina's elite—within reason, of course. It was important to deny that one wrote for any reason other than amusement, as Emma de la Barra protested in an interview when she said, "Yo no he pensado nunca en escribir regularmente, por un deber . . . llamémosle profesional, si ustedes quieren, sino por una satisfacción íntima, mía . . . ."[26] [I have never intended to write regularly, out of (...) shall we say, professional obligation, but only for my own, intimate satisfaction]. In light of De la Barra's prodigious journalistic output, this statement is not credible. It nevertheless preserves the convention that occasional writing, particularly the sort of poetry that could be published in a women's magazine or friend's album, was a suitable pastime for a woman of good family.[27] As long as it was presented as a hobby rather than as a profession or passion, versifying was considered a genteel accomplishment, rather like needle-work or playing the piano.

Juana Manuela Gorriti's *La Alborada del Plata*: The Galvanism of Literature

While an expanding literary market and the example of foreign writers were important factors in the increase of women's literature in Argentina, the arrival in Buenos Aires of two remarkable women, Juana Manuela Gorriti (1816–92) and Clorinda Matto de Turner (1852–1909), made an even greater impact. Gorriti arrived from Peru in 1875. She was of impeccable Argentine lineage and had even married a president of Bolivia. These credentials helped to insulate her from criticism about her illegitimate children and her habit of dressing in men's clothing á la George Sand. She had previously lived in Lima, where her literary salons were famous. Her *La quena* (1845) was one of Latin America's earliest novels.[28]

Gorriti did not try to hide the fact that she was a professional who wrote for money. Her distinguished lineage did not include wealth, and unlike others, such as Eduarda Mansilla, Gorriti lived by the earnings of her pen. Writing was more than work, however. Her memoirs reveal her joy in writing, an emotion she calls the "galvanism of literature." Writing was her tonic for the weaknesses of a sixty-year-old body and the accumulated sorrows of a difficult life, as this diary passage from March 11, 1876, attests:

> Me levanto a las seis de la mañana, tan enferma, que me es preciso hacer un esfuerzo para dejar la cama, porque cuerpo y espíritu están mortalmente abatidos. Mas a medida que me engolfo en el trabajo, la vida vuelve, y me siento fuerte para pensar, sufrir, luchar y vivir . . . torrentes de vida se agitan en torno mío, y agitan la mía con el poderoso galvanismo de la literatura.[29]

> [I get up at six in the morning, so sick that I have to make an effort to get out of bed, because my body and mind are mortally dejected. But as soon as I become immersed in my work, life returns, and I feel strong enough to think, suffer, fight, and live (...) torrents of life pulse within me, and energize me with the powerful galvanism of literature.]

Such dedication reveals that her writing was no mere hobby or genteel accomplishment. It is significant that Gorriti chose to pose for her portrait seated at her desk, pen in hand—an unusual pose for both women and men at that time.

Not only was Gorriti a model of female professionalism, she was also a generous mentor to other women writers, giving personal encouragement, arranging publication opportunities, and making introductions. That Gorriti enjoyed encouraging young writers can be seen in her response to a poem dedicated to her: "Grato es a los trabajadores del espíritu que hemos hecho nuestra jornada y estamos al borde del sepulcro, dejar tales recuerdos en los genios jóvenes que han de sucedernos"[30] [It is pleasing to us workers of the spirit who have finished our journey and are on the edge of the sepulchre, to leave such memories in the young talents who will succeed us]. Her actions bore out her words. For example, Gorriti helped Lola Larrosa resuscitate *La Alborada del Plata* in 1880 when Larrosa was just twenty-three years old. Indeed, since Gorriti was out of the country at the time and involved in other projects, it is likely that she lent her name to the magazine solely to help out Larrosa. Perhaps most touchingly, Gorriti tried to organize a memorial album after the poet Josefina Pelliza's death, but the beauty and charm that had brought Pelliza such admiration in life were soon forgotten and the album was never published, a failure that Gorriti still lamented four years later in *Lo íntimo* (100-101).

In keeping with her desire to expand women's publishing opportunities, Gorriti founded *La Alborada del Plata* [Dawn of the River Plata] in 1877. Unlike its predecessors, *La Alborada* faced competition with other periodicals that also promoted women's writing, principally *La*

Ondina del Plata. Therefore, it had to define itself in terms of difference rather than uniqueness, which it did by emphasizing its pan-American content:

> Así, *La Alborada del Plata* será un periódico internacional destinado a enlazar nuestra literatura a la de las otras repúblicas americanas, y a propagar sus rápidos progresos. . . . Verdadero repertorio de ciencia, literatura y poesía de América, nada contendrá que no sea original y relativo; limitándose a trasmitir noticias bibliográficas de las obras notables editadas en Europa, y la revista de sus acontecimientos de importancia trascendental.[31]

> [Thus, *La Alborada del Plata* will be an international periodical destined to join our literature to that of the other American republics and to publicize their rapid progress. (...) A genuine repertory of American science, literature and poetry, it will contain nothing that is not original and relevant, limiting itself to reporting bibliographic news of the notable works published in Europe and reviewing the events of transcendental importance.]

Gorriti, with her continent-wide contacts, was unusually well qualified to carry out this plan. There was little doubt that she had the prestige among Argentines to accomplish it: the first issue carries congratulatory letters from such notables as Bartolomé Mitre, Domingo Sarmiento, Santiago Estrada, and Nicolás Avellaneda.

La Alborada's co-editor, Josefina Pelliza de Sagasta, envisioned the magazine as a voice for women: "Adelante pues, comience la obra de la regeneración intelectual de la mujer argentina . . ."[32] [Onward then, let the work of the intellectual regeneration of Argentine women begin]. But in fact, more than half the articles and poems are written by men, and the essays' topics—episodes from the War of Independence, a philological study of the Aimará language, impressions of travel, etc. —reveal that the intended audience includes both men and women. Gorriti was no Petrona Rosende: there is no angry rhetoric in *La Alborada*, no impassioned defenses of women. Even the literary selections are inoffensive love stories in the style of late Romanticism.[33] There are surprising silences and missed opportunities to defend women and their accomplishments; one such case is an article on the nature of genius, in which twenty-four men—but no women—serve as examples.[34]

Yet *La Alborada* does show concern for the education of women, expressed in terms of the new catch phrase of the day, *human progress*:

> [La mujer] es un elemento radical del verdadero progreso; y éste es más sólido, positivo y permanente cuando más se eduque e ilustre las condiciones intelectuales y morales de la mujer, a fin de que pueda

desempeñar en la sociedad su parte de labor fundamental en la grande obra del progreso humano.[35]

[Woman is an essential element in true progress, which is most solid, positive, and permanent when the intellectual and moral conditions of women are most educated and enlightened, so that she can carry out in society her part of fundamental labor in the great work of human progress.]

Like earlier female publications, *La Alborada* seeks education for women so that they can better raise their children. Unlike its forbearers, however, it employs the New Testament in its justification, thereby avoiding the pitfall of the Eden incident. In *La Alborada*'s version of history, when Christianity appeared, it singled out women:

la primera redimida fue la mujer: dignificada, ensalzada, divinizada, en suma, en la mano del inspirado y sabio fundador de la divina doctrina. . . . Y comprendiendo la misión de la mujer, su indispensable concurso y regeneradora influencia, la elevaron al puesto que le corresponde y desde entonces se trató de rehabilitarla con la educación moral y la instrucción intelectual, para que llevara, a la grande labor de la humanidad, la parte de obra que ella y solo ella debe trabajar, para que esta sea perfecta.[36]

[the first to be redeemed were women: dignified, exalted, deified, in essence, by the hand of the inspired and wise founder of the divine doctrine. (...) And understanding the mission of women, their indispensable help and regenerating influence, he elevated women to their appropriate place and from then on they have been rehabilitated by moral education and intellectual instruction so that they can carry out the great task of humanity, the work that women and only women can do, so that humanity can be perfected.]

Both the content and the style of this passage—the eccentric use of commas and the string of clauses with vague antecedents are unmistakable—indicate that Josefina Pelliza, not Juana Manuela Gorriti, wrote this article. However, since it appears unsigned in the place reserved for the editor's column, Gorriti must have agreed with its sentiment. In 1878, when Gorriti left *La Alborada* for reasons of health, she gave the editorship entirely to Pelliza.

While under Gorriti's leadership, *La Alborada* was less concerned with the theory of advocating women's writing than with its practice: it places women's writing side-by-side with men's with no apologies. It assumes that women will be interested in what interests men, and more radically, that men will want to read women's writing, too. The nationwide grief at Gorriti's death in 1892 is an indication of how Argentines had come to accept women writers after 1870; even the newspaper *La Prensa*, which typically did not cover women's activities or include their writing, wrote a lengthy and laudatory obituary in her honor and dedicated considerable space to her funeral, to which the Argentine government contributed a thousand pesos.[37]

El Búcaro Americano and International Emancipation

Gorriti's death did not leave Argentine women without a mentor for long. In 1895, Clorinda Matto de Turner, a Peruvian writer who had been a member of Gorriti's salons in Lima, came to Buenos Aires to escape the persecution her writing had inspired in Peru.[38] Matto de Turner was welcomed for her literary reputation and her antecedents among Peru's prominent families. Upon her arrival, she was invited to give a speech to the all-male Ateneo (the elite gentleman's club and literary salon), a sure sign that she was considered "one of us" by the Buenos Aires elite. If anything, Matto de Turner exceeded Gorriti in sponsoring women writers. Her extraordinary knowledge of women writers throughout Latin America was demonstrated in her talk before the Ateneo, which she published as a call to arms in the first issue of *El Búcaro Americano* [The American Flower Vase] (1896–1901, 1906–1908), the periodical she founded.[39] No Argentine woman reading *El Búcaro* could fail to see herself as part of an international movement: women everywhere were writing literature and urging expanded women's rights. The March 1, 1896 issue, for instance, includes a vignette of Carolina Lagos de Pellegrini, the president of the Damas de Beneficencia in Buenos Aires; an article by the Peruvian Mercedes Cabello de Carbonera that defends women's innate morality; a discussion of the ideas of Emilia Pardo Bazán, the Spanish novelist and essayist; the continuation of a history of Argentine women by José Juan Biedma; the announcement of a new book by Cecilia Grierson, the first Argentine female physician; and a play by the Chilean Casiana Flores. There is even a reminder that Alberto del Solar, who had just published his first novel, was the son of the writer Mercedes Marín del Solar. *El Búcaro* clearly believes that he inherited his talent from his mother since his father is not mentioned.

Like its predecessors, *El Búcaro Americano* combined the language of flowers with the cause of education in the statement of purpose published in the first issue. Now, however, education is presented as an element in a Darwinian sort of social evolution:

> Búcaro Americano, como su nombre lo deja comprender, recogerá toda la flora literaria exuberante hoy en América, para ofrecerla a los lectores. Pero, no es la literatura el único objetivo; hay algo más trascendental en el fondo de nuestros ideales: la educación de la mujer

en el rol que le depara el movimiento del progreso universal para que
pueda cumplir satisfactoriamente los deberes que esa misma corriente
evolutiva le señala.[40]

[*Búcaro Americano*, as its name implies, will gather all the abundant
literary flora in America today to offer to its readers. But literature is
not the only objective; there is something more transcendental in the
essence of our ideals: the education of women in the role that the
movement of universal progress bestows, so that they can satisfactorily
carry out the obligations that the same evolutionary current sets out for
them.]

Taking an approach similar to that of its forebear *La Camelia*, *El Búcaro*
presents women's education as perfectly proper and unobjectionable
—it even obeys the laws of Nature, the universal force that is above
petty social opposition. This evolutionary completion and perfection of
society allows equal and complementary roles for women and men.
However, universal progress does not eliminate traditional roles, and *El
Búcaro* emphatically affirms the nobility of being wife and mother.
Indeed, a biographical sketch of first lady Leonor de Tezanos Pinto de
Uriburu, the subject of the first cover engraving of *El Búcaro*, presents
her as a model precisely because she does not transgress the borders of
those roles:

> Apartada de la pretensión de inmiscuirse en los asuntos de la política
> y del Estado, si alguna vez inclinó la voluntad del esposo fue hacia lo
> noble y lo generoso; y si los salones más distinguidos de las hermosas
> argentinas, son el teatro donde brilla la dama bella y cumplida, el hogar
> es el templo azul donde actúa la matrona cuyas virtudes se reflejarán
> en su patria y fuera de ella.[41]

> [Far from aspiring to meddle in political and state matters, if she at
> some time influenced the will of her husband, it was toward what is
> noble and generous; and if the most distinguished salons of Argentine
> beauties are the theater where the lovely andaccomplished woman
> sparkles, the home is the enchanted shrine where abides the matron
> whose virtues are reflected in her country and abroad.]

Unlike Juana Manso's *El Album de Señoritas*, *El Búcaro* recognizes
beauty and charm as means for women to gain acclaim as individuals
in the public theater of the salons. But the private, domestic arena is
blessed by the religious term of *shrine*, for the collective well being of
the country depends on the virtue of women within the confines of their
homes and traditional roles. This passage reflects the conservative,
non-provocative stance that made *El Búcaro* the most successful and
longest lasting of the nineteenth-century women's periodicals in Argentina. Juana Manso had envisioned a new society based on different
values and institutions; but Clorinda Matto de Turner advocated moral

reform, not structural changes.[42] This non-threatening position coincided with the dominant opinion at the time, and *El Búcaro Americano* prospered from 1896 to 1901 and again from 1906 to 1908, when Matto's failing health prevented her from continuing it.

The Rejection of Modernismo

The network of support organized by Gorriti and Matto de Turner is particularly significant in light of women's exclusion from many of the other important literary circles in Buenos Aires. The most influential of these was the coterie of Rubén Darío (1867–1916), the Nicaraguan writer who arrived in Buenos Aires in 1893, bringing with him a growing fame as the head of the *modernismo* movement.[43] Like Matto de Turner, Darío knew no national boundaries in his love for literature, and he brought many international artists to the attention of Latin Americans for the first time. Also like Matto, Darío was an extraordinary mentor who nurtured a group of young writers in Buenos Aires. These disciples of Darío changed the course of Argentine literature and contributed to the flowering of Latin American literature in the first half of the twentieth century.

That is, Darío nurtured young *male* writers. In Buenos Aires, as far as I have been able to discover, there were no female practitioners of *modernismo*.[44] Women writers certainly knew about the movement since it was a regular topic in newspapers and magazines, and Darío's followers were skilled at gaining publicity for their personal antics as well. Many of his literary influences were equally well known to women; Eduarda Mansilla, for example, had published an interview with one of them, François Coppée, in 1885.[45] Moreover, Rubén Darío contributed articles to *El Búcaro Americano*,[46] as did other *modernistas* such as Julián del Casal and Leopoldo Lugones. Apparently, women's absence from *modernismo* was the result of neither ignorance nor accident; instead, the reasons for this exclusion have to do with social mores and literary goals. The social reasons are easy to identify, beginning with the location of the modernists' gatherings: they were held in the all-male Ateneo club and nightclubs where no respectable woman dared to go. Darío and his followers were widely known as the *decadents*, and that label was not just literary. In his memoirs, Darío says of his "bar-hopping" with literary friends, "se comprende que la sobriedad no era nuestra principal virtud"[47] [you understand that sobriety was not our principal virtue]. Photos of the nocturnal crowd at such haunts as Aue's Keller and the Café de los Inmortales show only male faces (except for the all-female dance band at Aue's Keller).[48] But the

Darío group also frequented far less respectable places in their search for "el peligroso encanto de los paraísos artificiales"[49] [the dangerous delight of artificial paradises]. While male writers could boast of their bohemian ways, women were still fighting the belief that any woman who wanted to write was somehow "loose" or brazen; to have consorted with decadents would have caused an utter scandal and sure expulsion from respectable literary publications.

Although the rules of female propriety were, no doubt, a major reason for women's avoidance of *modernismo*, there are other factors to consider as well. For example, few women of the time had the sort of education that would have allowed them to draw on classical and Renaissance models as the modernists did, nor did most women have access to libraries of substance. Even today, the public libraries in Buenos Aires suffer in comparison with private ones, and many of the best private ones, such as that of the Jockey Club, are difficult for women to gain access to. Moreover, the cult of beauty and art for art's sake that characterized *modernismo* must have seemed frivolous to women who were struggling to gain respect as serious intellectuals and who advocated projects of social reform. Darío's ethereal *princesas* were no crusaders for women's education, the right to work, or equal legal status. Indeed, *modernismo*'s repertoire of female images—asexual but well-dressed wraiths, *la belle dame sans merci*, and mute swans—had little to do with real women and everything to do with male mythology.

Stella: Women's Literature Has a Best Seller

Far from advocating art for art's sake, Argentine women had from the very beginning of the century linked their writing to the cause of women's rights. Later chapters will discuss in greater detail what "women's rights" meant in the context of the 1800s, but for the moment suffice it to say that literary women wanted to gain respect for womanliness as expressed in marriage and motherhood. As seen in this survey of their journals, they believed that the key to gaining respect was improved education (or indeed, any education at all). Therefore, it is not surprising that these women's literature was more concerned with instructing its audience than with entertaining it or encouraging its romantic fantasies. The writers never fail to idealize the good wife and mother, but urgent pleas for her education are close behind. Indeed, success in traditional roles becomes increasingly linked to a woman's access to education. From 1830 to 1896, the statements of purpose published in women's periodicals do not vary: women's literature should raise the status of women, especially in pursuing the right to education and intellectual work, while defending the nobility of the roles of wife and mother. This sort of fiction tends to have at its center a mother or maternal figure who defends her honor and motherly role while deploring women's lack of education and professional opportunities. Matrimonial love and honor take precedence over the single woman's quest for a mate, unless the single woman's quest is expressed in terms of a choice between a man who would be a faithful, responsible husband and one who would be weak and ineffectual. Such writing is self-consciously sentimental and high minded, in contrast with the crudeness of realism or naturalism.

Although this description fits almost every work written by the nine writers studied here, the book that most successfully employs it is Emma de la Barra's *Stella* (*una novela de costumbres argentinas*) [A Novel of Argentine Customs], published in 1905 under the name of César Duayen. *La Nación* dedicated a long and enthusiastic review to it, which accelerated the word-of-mouth recommendations.[50] Within days, the thousand copies of the first printing had sold out, and speculation about the author's identity had begun. The professor and literary critic Enrique Rivarola wrote an enthusiastic letter to *La Nación* a few days later in which he reveals his generation's prejudices about what an ideal author should be—a male politician of the elite class who writes as a hobby:

> No sé quién es el autor . . . pero es hombre de mucho mérito. Sus páginas revelan un carácter. Debe ser persona muy conocida y estimada en la sociedad porteña; tal vez algún político de vuelos, que descansa escribiendo, y que obtendría fácilmente muchos electores si el pueblo leyese *Stella*, y supiese calcular, por lo que un escritor produce, cuánto un hombre vale.[51]

> [I don't know who the author is . . . but he is a man of much merit. His pages reveal his character. He must be someone well known and esteemed in the society of Buenos Aires; perhaps a politician who in fleeting moments rests by writing, and who would easily receive many votes if the public read *Stella* and knew how to estimate, by what a writer produces, what the man is worth.]

Following this letter in the same issue, there was a letter from César Duayen himself, admitting that

> soy un neófito lleno de fe, de aliento y de inexperiencia, que se oculta detrás de un muro, que realmente lo esconde, porque ha sido levantado por una resolución sincera.

> [I am a neophyte filled with faith, hope, and inexperience, who hides behind a wall, which truly hides him, because it has been raised by a sincere resolution.]

The construction of this sentence allows its author to emphasize the masculine gender (*neófito* instead of *neófita*, and its pronoun *lo*) while implying that the wall hides the neophyte rather than the author. Note how the sense of the sentence would change if it read "which truly hides *me.*" This clever use of words helped stall the discovery of the true author, while simultaneously increasing public curiosity. Speculation began to rest on the journalist Julio Llanos, but on September 24, *La Nación* published a letter from Llanos denying authorship of *Stella*. Finally, on September 26, the author's true name was revealed:

> Muy poderosos eran sin duda los baluartes con que la delicada modestia de la autora había encerrado su secreto: pero el éxito resultó demasiado entusiasta para que se pudiera resistir su impulso. Y aún cuando el propósito de la reserva persistiera, los tanteos de la conjetura han dado por último con la verdad de las cosas, proclamando el nombre de la señora Emma Barra de la Barra junto a ese otro nombre de *Stella* ya prestigioso y tan notorio que desde ahora queda definitivamente incorporado a los anales de las letras argentinas.[52]

> [Without a doubt, very strong were the defenses with which the delicate modesty of the author had enclosed her secret: but the success became too enthusiastic for them to resist the pressure. And even when the purpose for the reserve persisted, the probings of conjecture at last discovered the truth of the matter, proclaiming the name of Mrs. Emma Barra de la Barra together with the name *Stella*, already so prestigious and notorious that from now on it definitely will remain incorporated into the annals of Argentine letters.]

The discovery of the author's true identity did nothing to stop the popularity of the novel among both male and female readers. By the end of November 1905, it was in its seventh printing; the ninth came out in December.[53] An employee at Möen's, the largest bookstore in Buenos Aires, was hired for the sole purpose of handling sales of *Stella*.[54] This unprecedented success led Casa Maucci to pay Barra an advance of 5,000 pesos for her next novel, publishing a first run of 6,000 copies.[55] A normal first run was 500 copies, and one of the highest-paid writers of the time, Florencio Sánchez, only received 2,000 pesos for *Barranca abajo*.[56] Translated into several languages, *Stella* had sold more than 300,000 copies by 1932[57] and continued to be printed in editions through the 1940s. In 1943, it was made into a film which still can be seen occasionally on late-night Argentine television.

The success of *Stella* merits footnotes in many literary histories. However, very few of those histories examine the content of the novel, and even fewer recognize it for what it was in the context of its day: the example of nineteenth-century Argentine women's literature par excellence. As other women had attempted before, De la Barra combined a sentimental plot with a critical examination of Argentine society, advocating women's right to education and work while reaffirming the importance of the maternal role and romantic love. The literary ideas spelled out in the pages of women's journals for the previous seventy years found their embodiment in *Stella*.[58]

The novel begins with the arrival of twenty-year-old Alejandra (Alex) and six-year-old Stella Fussller in Buenos Aires. Their mother, Ana María Maura Sagasta, had died after Stella's premature birth of complications that also crippled the little girl. When the novel opens, their father, the Norwegian explorer Gustavo Fussller, has lost his life on a polar expedition. Therefore, the two Norwegian orphans come to Argentina to live with their only remaining relatives, the Maura family. The Mauras are described as a family that once was part of the sturdy, hard-working country gentry, but who now suffer the corrupting effects of a fashionable life in Buenos Aires. The head of the family, Luis Maura, is a good man, as are three of his children: Emilio, Ana María, and Perla. By contrast, his wife, Carmen Quirós, is both frivolous and ignorant, and her influence extends over the other children: Carlos, Carmencita, Enrique, María Luisa, and Isabel. The family circle also includes Carmen's brother Máximo, who is described as a man suffering from *mal de siècle*; at forty, he is too rich, too educated, and too disillusioned. Athough he enjoys bringing gifts to the children, he is essentially indifferent to his family and humanity in general.

The two Norwegian orphans carry out different roles in the novel: Alex is the active focus, while Stella is its moral center. Each character in the novel is measured by his or her relationship with Stella: adopting a maternal or paternal stance toward her is evidence of a good heart. Máximo, for example, only appears to be hardhearted; his affection for Stella reveals his true nature as a man capable of love and noble actions. The plot complications, however, unfold according to the Mauras' acceptance and subsequent rejection of Alex. In contrast with the Maura women, Alex is educated, serious minded, and well traveled. Needing an outlet for her intellect, she offers to teach the various children in the family. Later she also does the bookkeeping for her uncle Luis, thus learning that his look of ill health comes from financial worry. The character of Alex is an inspiration: as she is single, the plot can revolve around her finding a suitable mate; as a substitute mother, she can uphold the ideal of motherhood; and as a teacher and a foreigner, she is in the position to make pointed remarks about the lack of education in Argentina, particularly among the men of the upper class. But if Argentine men appear uneducated to Alex, the women are even worse.

The description of the Maura family at the beginning of the novel is generally pitiless; that of the mother, Carmen Sagasta, is especially so:

> De inteligencia estrecha como su moral y su religión, de principios severos e intransigentes, de una virtud poco amable como su caridad, llena de prejuicios, sólo conocía un temor: los comentarios del mundo; una pasión: la maternal. Temor que era terror servil por el "qué dirán"; pasión absoluta, ciega, llena de debilidades y de transigencias por todo aquello que pasó por sus entrañas. . . . Su rigidez implacable en las prácticas religiosas, que no hubiera permitido faltar a misa a un agonizante, abstenerse del ayuno a un tísico, provocaba apenas una flaca observación de su parte . . . a los hijos que no pisaban una iglesia nunca.[59]

> [With an intelligence as narrow as her morality and her religion, holding severe and intransigent principles, with a virtue as unkind as her charity, full of prejudices, she knew only one fear: the comments of others; one passion: motherhood. A fear that was a servile terror of "what will people say?"; a passion that was absolute, blind, full of weaknesses and compromises for those to whom she gave birth. (...) Her implacable inflexibility in religious practices, which would not have allowed those on their deathbed to miss a mass or a consumptive to abstain from fasting, produced no more than a weak observance when it came to her children, who never set foot in a church.]

Carmen's ignorance is presented as a major cause of her pernicious mothering. Alex is ready to point out that by contrast Scandinavian women have the right to work in banks, offices, and hospitals (75), permitting them a more productive use of their time than the gossip that is the principal hobby of Carmen and her peers. The idea of working women amazes the Mauras, who think that it is unsuitable for even a man of their class to work (76-77). As the plot unfolds, there are opportunities to comment on other social ills in Argentina, such as the lack of serious literature (217), the impact of immigration (228), discrimination against the gauchos (213), and the fate of the abandoned lovers of upper-class men (264-68).

At Alex and Stella's arrival, the family is aflutter over three romances: Ana María, contrary to the wishes of her family, wants to marry a student who is from a good but poor family; Isabel is believed to be the intended of the wealthy and handsome Manuel Montero y Espinoso, though he has not formally proposed; and Enrique appears to be the favorite of the extremely wealthy Clara Montana. For a while, Alex lives quietly within the family, maintaining mourning for her father. But soon the family insists that she attend a dance where she charms the guests, especially the male ones, with her beauty, intelligence, and poise. Among the smitten is Manuel Montero y Espinosa, Isabel's intended.

To avoid an indiscretion by Montero, Alex enlists the wealthy Uncle Máximo to accompany her to dinner. By the time the night is over, all the Maura women, except Ana María, have become resentful of Alex.

Alex is again the unwilling star during an afternoon at the Hippodrome. Montero repeatedly turns his attentions to her rather than to Isabel, and although Alex always thwarts him, the attention does not go unobserved. The spiteful Maura women interpret Alex's coolness toward Montero as merely a strategem to catch him. They believe none of Alex's protests. Even Máximo begins to think that Alex is a schemer, and his friendly interest turns to cynicism. This suspicion is strengthened when one day he sees Alex entering the house of Samuel Montana, a rich banker who has paid considerable attention to Alex.

Unable to defend herself against the family's malice, Alex is miserable and would like to return to Norway. However, her responsibility to Stella, who is both happy and beloved in Argentina, prevents her departure. She suffers in silence, but is released when one of the children comes down with measles. To avoid contagion, the other children are sent under Alex's charge to El Ombú, the family's old-style *estancia*, or country house. Away from the inhospitable house in Buenos Aires, Alex gradually recovers her spirits and flourishes at schooling her own charges as well as the local children. Máximo, who is staying at his own nearby *estancia*, admires her way with the children and finds his friendship with Alex returning, although unsaid tensions sometimes make conversation awkward. Alex visits Máximo's *estancia*, which is a model of modernity and luxury, and impresses him with her innate good taste in art. He meanwhile pleases Alex by his affection for Stella. As their trust in each other grows, they confess their secrets and their fears. She reveals that she is completing her father's unfinished book, and he talks of his own father. Alex is deeply touched by Máximo's anguish over his father's death. As they bare their souls, they begin to fall in love. But this idyll is shattered by Stella's sudden death. Máximo is unable to bear the pain of losing the child who has awakened his capacity to love, and he flees on a journey to Chile, leaving Alex to grieve alone.

Four months later, Máximo returns to Buenos Aires. Alex summons him to her, and she tells him the secret she has guarded for so long: that his nephews Enrique and Carlos Maura have embezzled money from their father and put him dangerously in debt. Emilio and Alex have tried desperately to save the family's finances, to the extent that Alex even sells her Corot painting to Samuel Montana. Thus Máximo understands the true reason for her visit to Montana. Alex appeals to Máximo to complete the rescue, since Stella's death has released Alex to return to

Norway. Máximo, who now realizes how he has misjudged and failed Alex, is brokenhearted, but he agrees to save the Mauras and let her go. After Alex's departure for Norway Máximo falls into a depression. However, he is inspired by a visit to Stella's grave, and he decides to fulfill the potential that Stella and Alex saw in him. He becomes a political leader and philanthropist. Meanwhile he waits, knowing that Alex will return to collect Stella's remains to bury alongside her parents. Two years later, Alex returns to Buenos Aires and finds to her surprise that Máximo has built a home for disabled children in memory of Stella. At that moment, she realizes that she still loves Máximo. At last, she is free of the doubts that drove her away from him. From beyond the grave, Stella's influence has brought the lovers together.

The uproar that forced César Duayen to reveal her true name was an appropriate introduction to the novel itself that constantly plays on masks and unmasking. From the Mauras' apparent wealth to Carmen's public but unfelt charity, false poses and misdirected emotions cause all the trouble and pain for the novel's characters. Only Stella's pure soul and Alex's nobility of character can make things right. Their ability to unmask the truth derives from their feminine moral superiority nurtured by education; the innate goodness of women such as Carmen, however, is stunted by ignorance. In *Stella*, Emma de la Barra does not question the institutions of society, as Juana Manso did in *La familia del Comendador* and *El Album de Señoritas*. Instead, the novel adheres to the moral reformism of *La Camelia* and *El Búcaro Americano*, proposing that women's powers be fully developed so that they can exert their influence through their traditional roles. Apparently critical of Argentine society, in truth *Stella* affirms its traditional values.

Stella's intertwining of a sentimental plot with social criticism was recognized and applauded when the novel first appeared. The reviewer in *La Nación*, for example, noted that

> César Duayen conoce a fondo, y lo revela, la vieja tradición de la vida porteña, sus defectos y tolerancias, sus méritos y su ligerezas. . . . Toda [la] fuerza [de la novela] reposa en la pureza del sentimiento, en la elevación de las móviles, en el perfume delicado de idealismo que flota a través de todas sus páginas. . . . Se destaca sobre todo la ecuanimidad de espíritu y la suavidad de criterio con que mide los hombres y las cosas. . . . [Es] una obra de inteligencia y de sensibilidad que ni entre nosotros ni en ninguna parte podría pasar inadvertida.[60]

> [César Duayen knows in depth the old tradition of life in Buenos Aires, its defects and tolerances, its merits and its fickleness, and he shows it. (...) All the novel's force lies in its purity of sentiment, in the elevation of its parts, in the delicate perfume of idealism that floats throughout

all its pages. (...) Most outstanding is the equanimity of spirit and the gentleness of the criteria with which the author measures men and things. (...) It is a work of intelligence and sensibility that could not pass unnoticed among us or elsewhere.]

Clearly, Emma de la Barra knew her readers and how to move them. At a time when *modernista* novels were being published, often to the incomprehension of the reading public, *Stella* drew on the long-standing ideals of women's literature, finding a middle ground of sentiment and didacticism that was accepted wholesale by the readership, and created a sensation.

The journalistic tradition that made *Stella* possible played an important role in the development of women's literary voice. Codes of female modesty in the 1800s often prevented women from speaking freely in public. For example, when Juana Manso gave a series of lectures in 1866, she was shouted down, asafoetida was thrown on her dress, and even stones were thrown at her. Journalism, on the other hand, allowed women to express their ideas behind the safe barrier of the page. Within the protected arena of women's magazines, writers were able to articulate their own issues, and, in the process, gain the confidence to write literary works as well. The development of Argentine women's literature in the 1800s is intimately tied to the growth of their journalism. In the pages of their periodicals, women found a forum in which they could test their ideas, become aware that others shared their concerns, develop their writing skills, and gain pride in women's accomplishments.

Endnotes

[1] Nineteenth-century women's newspapers are exceedingly difficult to obtain; however, interested readers without access to the originals can now consult selected articles in the anthologies *La mujer y el espacio público: el periodismo femenino en la Argentina del siglo XIX*, Francine Masiello, comp. (Buenos Aires: Feminaria, 1994) and *La pluma y la aguja: las escritoras de la Generación del '80* (Buenos Aires: Feminaria, 1993). The 1875 and 1876 volumes of the important newspaper *La Ondina del Plata*, as well as other periodicals, have been microfilmed by the University of Texas at Austin.

[2] Néstor Tomás Auza, *Periodismo y feminismo en la Argentina, 1830–1930* (Buenos Aires: Emecé, 1988), 21-24.

[3] For biographical information, see the entry in *Diccionario de literatura uruguaya*, Alberto F. Oreggioni, ed. (Montevideo: Arca, 1987).

[4] "La Editora," *La Aljaba* (19 November 1830): 2.

[5] "Prospecto," *La Aljaba*, n.d.

[6] "Felicidad de las señoras," *La Aljaba* (19 November 1830): 3, and in subsequent issues.

[7] "Educación de las hijas," *La Aljaba* (23 November 1830): 1. The italics are those of Rosende Sierra. Both the affirmation of noble domesticity and the demand for improved education were typical of the concerns in women's periodicals in other Hispanic countries as well. See, for example, the overview of the Spanish women's press in Susan Kirkpatrick, *Las románticas* (Berkeley: University of California Press, 1989), 70-87.

[8] "A los que se oponen à la instruccion de las mugeres," *La Aljaba* (30 November 1830): 2.

[9] Ibid.

[10] For a well-documented survey of the newspapers and journals of this period, see Sara Jaroslavsky and Estela Maspero, "La cultura argentina en el decenio 1852–62," *Cursos y Conferencias* 31 (April–June 1947): 109–51. Also see Lily Sosa de Newton, "Incorporación de la mujer al periodismo en la Argentina," *Evaluación de la literatura femenina de Latinoamérica, siglo XX: II Simposio Internacional de Literatura*, Juana Alcira Arancibia, ed. (San José, Costa Rica: Instituto Literario y Cultural Hispánico, 1985), 263-70.

[11] Las Redactoras, *La Camelia* (11 April 1852): 1. Rosa Guerra is often suggested as one of the editors even though she and *La Camelia's* editors denied it in the issue of May 6. That the names of the editors were known to some of their women readers is suggested by the letter from "Eliza" on page four of the first issue. In the letter, she refuses to tell the names to an odious man who predicts that the journal will last no more than a month.

[12] "Las mugeres," *La Camelia* (11 April 1852): 2.

[13] Las Redactoras, *La Camelia* 1, 7 (25 April 1852): n.p.

[14] At times, *La Camelia*'s devotion to powerful weakness slips a bit, as when it points out that, since Eve was created last, she was more perfect than Adam, who was just a first effort (13 April 1852): 1.

[15] *La Camelia* (29 April 1852): 1.

[16] *La Camelia* (6 May 1852): 1.

[17] Elsa M. Chaney describes the uses and limitations of carrying motherhood into the political arena in her *Supermadre: Women in Politics in Latin America* (Austin: University of Texas Press, 1979).

[18] Auza, 169-73, 178-79. Auza interprets the barbs aimed at *La Camelia* from the periodical *El Padre Castañeta* as mere mischief on the part of its editors. Even if that is so, he underestimates the impact of such "playfulness" on women's effectiveness in a public role. By ignoring *La Camelia*'s words and attacking its editors instead, El Padre Castañeta weakened the respectability that provided women's only source of public authority at that time.

[19] Juana Paula Manso de Noronha, "La Redacción," *El Album de Señoritas* (1 January 1854): 1.

[20] For the best discussion of this topic, see Francine Masiello, *Between Civilization and Barbarism: Women, Nation, and Literary Culture in Modern Argentina* (Lincoln: University of Nebraska Press, 1992), 17-20.

[21] Lea Fletcher, "Juana Manso: una voz en el desierto," *Mujeres y cultura en la Argentina del siglo XIX* (Buenos Aires: Feminaria, 1994), 109.

[22] Juana Manso de Noronha, *La familia del Comendador* (Buenos Aires: J.A. Bernheim, 1854), 19.

[23] Jaroslavsky and Maspero, "La cultura argentina," 128-29; *Cartas de Mariquita Sánchez*, Clara Vilaseca, ed. (Buenos Aires: Peuser, 1952), 196-97.

[24] James R. Scobie, *Buenos Aires: Plaza to Suburb, 1870–1910* (New York: Oxford University Press, 1974), 11. For an overview of the changes in the city during this time, see his chapter on "Social Structure and Cultural Themes," 208-49.

[25] Adolfo Prieto, *El discurso criollista en la formación de la Argentina moderna* (Buenos Aires: Sudamericana, 1988), 27-28. Prieto's first chapter, "Configuración de los campos de lectura," is a good summary of the changing circumstances of literacy and publications in the nineteenth century. Literacy does not mean much more than that, however; most Argentine children at this time attended no more than two or three years of school.

[26] "Una novela y una vida," *Noticias Gráficas* (24 October 1932): 9. Consider also the uproar in Delfina Bunge's family when a magazine wanted to include her photograph next to her article. Evidently publishing was toler-

ated, but a photograph was too much. See Manuel Gálvez, *Amigos y maestros de mi juventud* (Buenos Aires: Hachette, 1961), 67-68.

[27] Men of the elite shared this disdain of professionalism. David Viñas calls them "gentlemen-writers" in his *Literatura argentina y realidad política: de Sarmiento a Cortázar* (Buenos Aires: Siglo Veinte, 1971).

[28] For more on Gorriti's life and work, see the article by Mary Berg in *Spanish American Women Writers: A Bio-Bibliographical Source Book*, Diane Marting, ed. (New York: Greenwood, 1990), 227-40. Also see Cristina Iglesia, ed. *El ajuar de la patria: ensayos críticos sobre Juana Manuela Gorriti* (Buenos Aires: Feminaria, 1993).

[29] Gorriti, *Lo íntimo*, 31.

[30] Ibid., 94.

[31] "Prospecto," *La Alborada del Plata* November 1877): 17.

[32] Ibid., 2.

[33] See Gorriti's horror at the naturalist novel, *Blanca Sol*, written by Mercedes Cabello de Carbonera (*Lo íntimo*, 103-105; 126-27). Her letter of reproof ended their long friendship.

[34] "¿Qué es el génio?" *La Alborada del Plata* (2 December 1877): 17.

[35] "Algo sobre la muger," *La Alborada del Plata* (9 December 1877): 25.

[36] Ibid.

[37] *La Prensa* (7 November 1892): 5; (8 November 1892): 5.

[38] See Mary Berg's biography and critical survey in *Spanish American Women Writers*, 303-15.

[39] Her speech, "Las obreras del pensamiento en la América del Sud," is also reprinted in *Boreales, miniaturas y porcelanas* (Buenos Aires: J.A. Alsina, 1902), 245-66.

[40] Clorinda Matto de Turner, "Bautismo," *El Búcaro Americano* (1 February 1896): 3.

[41] Ibid., 4.

[42] Cynthia Jeffress Little explores both the potential and the limitations of moral reform in her "Moral Reform and Feminism: A Case Study," *Journal of Interamerican Studies and World Affairs* (17 November 1975): 386-97, as does Elsa Chaney in *Supermadre*.

[43] In order to prevent confusion of this Latin American movement with Anglo-Irish Modernism, the term *modernismo* will be left in Spanish.

[44] Across the river in Montevideo, Delmira Agustini (1886–1914) was greatly influenced by *modernismo*, but her contact with Darío was through his books.

[45] See María Hortensia Lacau and Mabel Manacorda de Rosetti, "Antecedentes del modernismo en la literatura argentina," *Cursos y Conferencias* 31

(April–June 1947) 168-69; and Lea Fletcher, *Modernismo: sus cuentistas olvidados en la Argentina* (Buenos Aires: Ediciones del 80, 1986), 12-13.

[46] See pages 243, 323, 418, 445, 849, and so on in *El Búcaro Americano*.

[47] Rubén Darío, *Obras completas: Autobiografía* (Madrid: Mundo Latino, 1920) 15: 127.

[48] See Jorge B. Rivera, *Los bohemios* (Buenos Aires: Centro Editor de América Latina, 1971).

[49] Darío, 133.

[50] M. [Bartolomé Mitre], "Bibliografía: 'Stella,'" *La Nación* (15 September 1905): 5.

[51] E.E. Rivarola, *La Nación* (19 September 1905): 3.

[52] "Stella: Una Revelación del Exito," *La Nación* (26 September 1905): 8.

[53] *La Nación* (22 November 1905): 9; (18 December 1905): 8.

[54] Carmelo Bonet, "*Stella* y la sociedad porteña de principios de siglo," *Cursos y Conferencias* 44 (October–December 1953): 303.

[55] Lily Sosa de Newton, *Diccionario biográfico de la mujer argentina* (Buenos Aires: Plus Ultra, 1986).

[56] Rivera *Los bohemios*, 83.

[57] "Una novela y una vida," *Noticias gráficas* (24 October 1932): 9.

[58] Among the handful who have appropriately placed *Stella* in the context of women's periodicals is Marcela Nari, "Alejandra. Maternidad e independencia femenina," *Feminaria* 6, 10 (April 1993), Sec. 2: 7-9.

[59] César Duayen [Emma de la Barra], *Stella: una novela de costumbres argentinas* (Barcelona: Maucci, 1909), 58. Further page references will be noted in the text of the essay.

[60] *La Nación* (15 September 1905): 5.

2

Speaking up with
Lowered Eyes

The great task of the women writers of the 1800s was to invent a role for the professional woman writer that would balance the demands of feminine modesty in their lives and the need for discursive authority in their work. Discursive authority is, in Susan Sniader Lanser's words, "the intellectual credibility, ideological validity, and aesthetic value claimed by or conferred upon a work, author, narrator, character, or textual practice" or, more simply, the "quest to be heard, respected, and believed, a hope of influence."[1] Argentine society had no recognized appropriate role for women writers. This explains why, for example, Mariano Pelliza would praise Germaine de Staël by calling her a man: "no era escritorcilla sedentaria, sin erudición ni mundo, sin gusto ni talento: mujer por el sexo, fue hombre por el espíritu."[2] [she was not a sedentary female scribbler, without erudition or worldliness, without taste or talent: a woman in her sex, she was a man in her spirit]. His problematic praise reveals that Pelliza had difficulty imagining a writer who was both female and talented, although he had a clear enough image of ignorant, vulgar women writers. Pelliza's typifies the public attitudes that produced defensive and exaggerated claims of femininity by women writers (among them, his own sister Josefina Pelliza de Sagasta) who feared that their writing would masculinize them in the public's eyes.[3] The woman author's creation of an authoritative narrative voice was limited by her knowledge that she would be judged as a woman by the reading public, who failed to distinguish the identity of the woman writer from the narrator she created. A misjudgment in narrative voice could rebound in criticism of the author herself. This danger is evident in Elvira Aldao de Díaz's memoirs when she questioned her right to write about her own childhood: "Es arriesgado escribir impresiones de infancia y juventud—exponiéndose al público en bandeja—cuando no se tiene para ello representación especial, ni autoridad intelectual"[4] [It is risky to write impressions of childhood and youth—exposing oneself to the public on a silver platter—when one does not have a special expertise or intellectual authority for it]. But if Aldao herself did not commit her childhood memories to paper, who else would do it? Clearly, the alternative to creating authority for oneself was silence and oblivion.

The Club: Male Authorship Roles

While women were searching for appropriate representations of their writerly personae, male writers could choose from certain established images of the authorial self, such as the literary scientist (chosen by Eduardo L. Holmberg and Eduardo Wilde, for example), the worldly gentleman (such as Lucio Mansilla or Miguel Cané), or the Romantic hero (the favored pose of anti-Rosists such as José Mármol and *modernistas* such as Leopoldo Lugones). None of these roles was easily adaptable to a female representation of the self. For example, while women were welcome to applaud scientific advances from the sidelines, all but a privileged and embattled few were denied an education or a career in science-related fields. When Cecilia Grierson managed to become Argentina's first female physician in 1889, she became a hero to Argentine women. Yet Clorinda Matto de Turner reassured her readers in *El Búcaro Americano* that Grierson was properly feminine by noting that she was "cumplida e intachable en la vida social"[5] [accomplished and irreproachable in her social life]. This coded phrase is more semantically rich than it might appear at first glance: its unspoken referent was the cartoonish stereotype of women who broke professional barriers. Matto de Turner was actually saying that Grierson was not strident, dowdy, or disdainful of feminine manners. Evidently, even an intellectual such as Matto feared that becoming a scientist might masculinize a woman.

The worldly gentleman was just as distant a role for women as that of the scientist, since it was based on the Spanish tradition that the land-owning gentry should also be the country's military leaders, statesmen, and large-scale businessmen. Women could not serve in the military, vote, hold political or diplomatic posts, or, if they were married, control their own property or their own money. Elvira Aldao de Díaz was able to travel as freely and luxuriously as the arch-gentle-man Lucio Mansilla only because Aldao was a widow with no children and thus legally could manage her own finances. More typically, Eduarda Mansilla de García, Lucio's sister, traveled only when her diplomat husband received a new posting or when her grown sons could accompany her.[6] Moreover, the phrase "worldly gentlewoman" is an oxymoron; the bohemian overtones of a worldly gentleman's writing would have been scandalous in that of a a gentlewoman. What women could adopt from the gentleman writer was a taste for French luxuries such as clothes and perfumes, a preference for foreign literature, and a cavernous silence in their writings concerning the armies of servants necessary to a genteel way of life. In other words, women had to extract from the gentleman's role those attributes that would not transgress norms of feminine sexual propriety.

Least appropriate of all to women was the guise of the Romantic hero, as Susan Kirkpatrick points out:

> [The] forms in which Romantic writing characterized and libidinized the poetic subject strongly conflicted with the dominant feminine form of domestic womanhood. The Promethean rebel, fired by never-satis-fied desire, was almost a polar opposite of the selfless, compliant, passionless feminine ideal, while the Solitary's cultivation of his iso-lation and difference directly contradicted the domestic angel's com-mitment to familial interrelationship.[7]

While women could adopt certain Romantic characteristics, such as the validation of the personal and everyday language, their social and cultural identity was defined almost entirely through their relationships to others, which prevented them from fully adopting Romantic indi-vidualism. For women authors in Argentina, the conventions of Roman-ticism could become useful only by stripping them of their rationality, rebelliousness, and anti-domestic tendencies, while elaborating on their capacity to express emotion. When *La Ondina del Plata* intoned "como predomina en el hombre la inteligencia, predomina en la mujer el sentimiento"[8] [as intelligence predominates in men, sentiment pre-dominates in women], it was only repeating the concept of female nature held in Hispanic society since at least the Renaissance.[9] Thus, the emotionalism of Romanticism could be adopted by women without also acquiring its metaphysical or political rebelliousness. For women writers, Romantic rebellion boiled down to the decision to write at all.

The Angel in the House

As male authorship roles were unsuitable for women, so the established roles for women were equally antithetical to the literary female self.

The dominant social model for women during the 1800s was the "Angel in the House." This phrase is derived from a didactic poem published in 1858 by Coventry Patmore, an English clergyman, but the image itself has a long tradition in Hispanic culture.[10] Today's readers are likely to recognize the phrase from Virginia Woolf's wry essay, "Professions for Women," in which she explained that in order to become a writer she had to kill the Angel in the House by braining her with an inkpot.[11] Who and what was this obstructive Angel that could make even Woolf harbor murderous thoughts? Turning the pages of newspapers from the second half of the 1800s, seekers of the Angel find her everywhere: in poems dedicated to "my dear mother"; in articles on "lessons my mother taught me"; in stories in which a scoundrel was saved by a good woman; and in instructions on the proper deportment of women in public. One good source of definitions is *La Ondina del Plata*, the middle-class women's newspaper that most vocally supported female emancipation. That similar quotations could have been chosen from more conservative newspapers such as *La Alborada del Plata* or *El Album del Hogar* indicates the pervasiveness and acceptance of the ideal of the domestic angel.[12] A reading of *La Ondina*'s articles on women soon reveals that the domestic angel's leading characteristic was self-erasure, as Faustina Saez de Melgar pointed out in an article from 1875:

> El egoismo es cualidad del hombre; la abnegación lo es esencialmente de la mujer. . . . En todos los actos de la vida de la mujer, se ven rasgos de abnegación: ella no tiene nunca voluntad propia; de niña sacrifica sus gustos a las rarezas o a los caprichos de sus padres, de casada los sacrifica a su marido y al amor de sus hijos.[13]

> [Egotism is a trait of men; abnegation is the essence of women. (...) In all the acts of a woman's life, one sees traces of abnegation. She never has her own will: as a girl she sacrifices her desires to the whims or caprices of her parents, as a wife she sacrifices them to her husband or the love of her children.]

This self-erasure was often referred to as a sweet or willing servitude, as in the case of this description of motherhood: "Miradla en el hogar, su vida entera escalvizada a su marido e hijos, y dime si la buena madre no es la imagen de Dios sobre la tierra"[14] [See her in the home, her whole life enslaved to her husband and children, and tell me if the good mother is not the image of God on earth]. The terms used here—voluntary slavery, self-erasure, and motherhood as religious mission—were echoed in hundreds of similar writings, published equally in pro- and anti-emancipationist journals. The anti-emancipationist Lola Larrosa, who was well regarded in pro-emancipation circles as well, bluntly described the Angel as having no desires of her own: "los deberes de una buena casada se reducen a uno solo: *ser agradable a su marido*"[15] [the duties of a good wife are reduced to one only: *to be agreeable to her husband*]. The leading promoter of the domestic angel was the Spanish anti-emancipationist María del Pilar Sinués de Marco, who even founded a newspaper eponymously entitled *El Angel del Hogar*. Her books were widely circulated in Argentina, and excerpts were published seemingly everywhere. *La Ondina del Plata*, for instance, published one piece called "Las armas de la mujer" [Women's Weapons], in which Sinués summed up the female arsenal:

> La dulzura, la persuación, la belleza, el llanto: y cuando nada de esto baste, la paciencia: he aquí nuestros medios de conquista y nuestros recursos diplomáticos para alcanzar la felicidad en esta vida.[16]

> [Sweetness, persuasion, beauty, tears, and when none of these is sufficient, patience. Here we have our methods of conquest and diplomatic resources to achieve happiness in this life.]

Most of all, the domestic angel could not express anger or take action for her own sake:

> admiro más a la mártir de las oscuras penas del hogar doméstico que a las heroínas como Juan [sic] de Arco y la Monja Alférez . . . seamos dulces, aunque tengamos razón para estar resentidas, y mostremos *sentimiento*; pero *cólera*, jamás.[17]

> [I admire the female martyr to the obscure woes of the domestic home more than heroines such as John (sic) of Arc and Sister Alférez (...) let us be sweet-tempered, even when we have good reason to be resentful, and let us show *sentiment*, but never, ever *anger*.]

The silence and denial of self that Sinués and others proposed was expressed in many forms, both directly, in articles such as the ones mentioned above, and indirectly in symbolic language. Women's roles were so often expressed in terms of flowers, for example, that a writer had only to mention a flower and the readers would know what kind of woman was meant. For instance, a cliché of the 1800s compared the ideally modest woman to a violet, an unobtrusive flower often hidden under the leaves of larger, showier flowers. Similarly, as *El Album del Hogar* admonished, a woman-violet should be silent, self-effacing, and out of the public eye:

> Como la violeta, la mujer modesta, despide tan suave y delicado aroma, de tal manera embalsaman sus virtudes la atmósfera, que su presencia se adivina y su hermosura brilla tanto más cuanto mayor es la oscuridad del cuadro en el que voluntariamente se encierra.[18]

[Like the violet, the modest woman emits an aroma so soft and delicate that her virtues perfume the atmosphere; the darker the flowerbed where she voluntarily hides herself, the more her presence is felt and her beauty shines.]

In the year 1876 alone, *La Ondina del Plata* published five poems or articles wholly dedicated to comparing women to violets in these terms; moreover, that number does not include frequent passing references in articles on other topics. Such articles were written by both men and women—a reminder that the belief in female subordination by no means can be attributed exclusively to male writers. Few women questioned the ideal of the domestic angel or the woman-violet, though many sought to reform it through greater education. It is rare to find a criticism such as the one that appeared in a letter to *La Ondina del Plata* in 1876: "la mujer es una flor, un ángel, una hada, todo, menos un ser racional, un ser responsable de sus acciones! Cuánta adoración, pero en cambio cuan poco aprecio!"[19] [a woman is a flower, an angel, a fairy godmother, everything except a rational being, a being responsible for her actions! So much adoration, but so little respect]. However, this angry insight was published under the pseudonym of "A Subscriber." The fact that the writer would hesitate to sign her own name was a triumph for the Angel in the House.

The antipathy of the domestic angel and the woman-violet to a female writer is obvious. Hidden away in her house, entirely involved with domestic matters, and discouraged from expressing anything but happy thoughts that would please her husband, a genuine domestic angel could never hope to be a literary scientist, a worldy gentlewoman, a Romantic hero, or indeed much of anything beyond a columnist on household hints, published in a women's newspaper, of course. Nonetheless, many women writers tried to live up to the angel-violet ideal, including Lola Larrosa, who, in an article opposing female emancipation, suggested a way for the hidden woman to pursue an intellectual outlet: "Puede ser periodista, sin que por esto sea emancipada, y ni aún tenga que dar un paso fuera del círculo del hogar, ni desatender sus obligaciones de hija o de esposa ejemplar"[20] [She can be a journalist without having to be emancipated or even having to take a step outside the circle of the home or neglect her obligations as daughter or exemplary wife]. But Larrosa is not convincing. The very essay that counseled reticence for women was signed by a woman who lived by her writing and literary reputation; moreover, the essay appeared on the first page of a nationally circulated newspaper, *La Prensa*. Her written words broke her silence, and her published words placed her on public view; writing is, by its very nature, an immodest, unviolet-like act. Even the conservative Larrosa signed her own name, not a pseudonym, to her articles and novels.

Other than the domestic angel, nineteenth-century Argentine society presented few female roles. Women were gaining a claim to the role of children's educator, which indeed did not contradict the ideal of the home-bound woman, since the primary school was viewed as an extension of the home and the teacher as a kind of super-mother. As Luis Telmos Pintos said, "El hogar es la miniatura de la escuela"[21] [The home is the school in miniature]. However, the role of the elementary school teacher was virtually the only income-earning path available to educated middle-class or upper-class women. Even the genteel occupations of companion and governess, so beloved of English novelists, did not exist in the form of a job for Argentines. The companion role was fulfilled by relatives and friends of equal social status, and childcare was distinctly a servant's task. In elite families, governesses tended to be foreign, usually French or English.

With such a dearth of female professional social roles, the writers' task of inventing an appropriate authorial voice was far from easy or straightforward. These authors had to overcome more than just the disapproval of their society in general. More subtly, they had to overcome their own internalized socialization that writing was a masculine privilege and that a woman dared not abandon the trappings of the exemplary wife and mother. These attitudes produced disconcerting incongruities in the works of women writers. For instance, Eduarda Mansilla admired the women journalists of the United States, who were engaged in a profession she had struggled to achieve for herself.[22] However, in a telling lapse, she used masculine adjectives to describe them: *reporters femeninos* and *la mujer empleado*[23] rather than *reporters femeninas* and *la mujer empleada*. Equally revealing is the fact that, although Germaine de Staël's *Corinne* was mentioned often and always admiringly in the pages of women's magazines, none of the writers studied here created a fictional character who was a professional artist.

After all, Corinne might be a great artist, but she lost her man to her violet-like sister and died overwhelmed by unhappiness; that lesson was not lost on Argentine women. As Virginia Woolf knew from experience, the Angel of the House was hard to kill: "Her fictitious nature was of great assistance to her. It is far harder to kill a phantom than a reality. She was always creeping back when I thought I had despatched her."[24] Worst of all, once the Angel was dead, "what then remained? . . . Now that [the writer] had rid herself of falsehood, that young woman had only to be herself. Ah, but what is *herself*?"[25]

The Poet in the Gilded Cage: Agustina Andrade

The creation of a female authorial self was a real and difficult struggle for the women writers of the 1800s, who never entirely freed themselves from the iron grasp of the Angel of the House. Though probably the most-praised female poet of the 1870s, Agustina Andrade, for example, tried and failed to reconcile the conflicting claims of violet modesty and her poetic muse. Her poems were sought by the most important newspapers and magazines, and leading male poets lavished praise on her. In fact, her poems were so good that the audience at her public reading in 1875 concluded that her father must have written them.[26] In a similarly mixed message, the same magazine that featured an enthusiastic, three-page review of Andrade's book[27] also published an article that attributed the "degeneration" of Argentine literature to the growing number and influence of women writers.[28] Andrade's conflicting emotions about her success can be seen in her poem "Después del triunfo" [After the Triumph]:

> A eso llaman triunfar: palmas y gritos,
> Algunos ramos de venal laurel,
> Y después . . . el silencio y el olvido!
>
> ¿Y después? Oh! qué horrible es el después!
>
> Abrir el corazón, verter sin tasa
> El perfume y la miel;
> Arrostrar la mirada indiferente
> De las turbas sin fe!
> Todo eso para qué? Para que algunos,
> Con grosera avidez,
>
> Le claven los anteojos a la autora
> Y la aplaudan después!
>
> Si eso es triunfar, la gloria es el martirio,
> La gloria es la embriaguez!
>
> Vale más la sonrisa de mi madre
> Que el más rico laurel!

[This what they call a triumph: applause and shouts,/ a few branches of venal laurel,/ and afterward . . . silence and oblivion!/ And afterward? Oh! how horrible is the afterward!/ To open up your heart, pour out without limit/ its perfume and honey;/ to stand up to the indifferent gaze/ of the unbelieving mob!/ All this for what? So that some,/ with crude greediness,/ can fix their glasses on the woman author/ and applaud her afterward!/ If this is triumph, then glory is martyrdom,/ glory is rapture!/ My mother's smile is worth more/ than the richest laurel!]

There are two equal terrors in conflict here: the audience's prying eyes and its indifference. Clearly, Andrade desired applause because oblivion was "horrible." Yet she knew that the audience considered her more of a freak than a genuine poet. They were ready to consume her with "crude greediness," and then forget her. The religious vocabulary of the last lines indicates that Andrade was seeking salvation from her own desires. Fleeing both herself and her public, she rejected the pagan laurels of public notice, and turned to the private world of her mother, a semi-divine domestic angel.

In another poem, "El arpa muda" [The Mute Harp], Andrade chided a poet for not writing: since poetry is a gift from God, the poet did not have the right to suppress it. Andrade used the feminine word *ave*, a high-register word for *bird*, to represent the poet, thus allowing her to use female imagery throughout the poem:

> ¡Ah! Dios no quiere que calle el ave
> Que con sus himnos saluda al sol:
> Es el encanto de la arboleda,
> La mensajera del mismo Dios.[30]

[Ah! God does not want the bird to be silent/ who salutes the sun with hymns:/ she is the delight of the woods,/ the messenger of God himself.]

But in "¿Por qué estoy triste?" [Why Am I Sad?], Andrade compared herself to a wild bird that had lost its freedom. The age-old image of women as caged birds is particularly strong in Hispanic culture, where it is common for women to live literally behind bars of ornamental but unbendable wrought iron:

> Pero en la estrecha jaula calla y sufre
> En silencio obstinado,
> Como si nunca hubiera conocido
> El bello don del canto.[31]

[But in the narrow cage she suffers and is quiet/ in obstinate silence,/ as if she had never known/ the beautiful gift of song.]

The bird's "obstinate silence" is not merely capricious; since the songbird is caged *because* it can sing, silence is the bird's only means to protest imprisonment. To sing would be collusion with the jailor, but silence is also a kind of willed death, a denial of the songbird's very nature. It is painful to read Andrade's struggle to reconcile her poetic gift with the silence that her society expected of her. Ultimately, Andrade chose the obstinate silence of the caged bird, first in marriage, then in suicide.

Strategies of Wily Modesty

Andrade was not alone in having ambivalent feelings about her writing and her public reception. Doubts about female narrative authority and fear of public criticism for "unfeminine" behavior led women to adopt certain literary conventions in order to write in a woman's voice without alienating their audience.[32] In balancing the demands of modesty with the need for an authoritative voice, nineteenth-century women writers employed a variety of strategies that can collectively be called the rhetoric of feminine authority: a way of "speaking up with eyes lowered." However, these strategies could subtly subvert their own apparent modesty and quietly champion the legitimacy of women's voice, as Mary Poovey observes:

> the very act of a woman writing during a period in which self-assertion was considered "unladylike" exposes the contradictions inherent in propriety: just as the inhibitions visible in her writing constitute a record of her historical oppression, so the work itself proclaims her momentary, possibly unconscious, but effective defiance.[33]

Indeed, the authorial modesty of nineteenth-century women, though much in evidence, is often less credible than it appears at first glance. I prefer to think of it as wily modesty, a series of ruses that indirectly claim the authority to write that they appear to deny.

Eduarda Mansilla, for instance, chose to use a male pseudonym —Daniel, her son's name—when she published her first two novels, *Lucía* and *El médico de San Luis* (both 1860), though her later works carried her own name. Mansilla only hinted at the reasons for her youthful reticence in the note she added to the 1882 edition of *Lucía*, saying that "Los defectos, como las cualidades de esta novela, son inherentes a la juventud de su autor, Daniel entonces, hoy ya en plena posesión de su nombre verdadero"[34] [The defects, like the quality of this novel, are inherent in the youth of its author, Daniel then, today in full possession of her real name]. Since other women were writing under their own names at that time, it is interesting to speculate why Mansilla initially chose to mask hers. One possible explanation is that she feared the criticism that some women writers such as Juana Manso had endured. In that case, the choice of the Biblical name *Daniel*, of lion's den fame, has more than maternal significance. But Mansilla's pseudonym takes on a different meaning when it is remembered that most of her readers knew the true identity of *Daniel*. In the small literary circles of Buenos Aires, most pseudonyms were formalities, since the audience already knew who employed which false names or could discover the true identity easily enough: as noted in the previous chapter, the identity of the author of *Stella* was discovered in just a few weeks. Mansilla's brother Lucio wrote that *El médico de San Luis* was published "bajo el pseudónimo de Daniel por una persona a la cual me ligan los dulces lazos del amor fraternal"[35] [under the pseudonym of Daniel by a person connected to me by the sweet ties of brotherly love]—a sly aside that his readers knew how to interpret. An article published in 1875 called Mansilla's pseudonym an "open secret."[36] But if Eduarda Mansilla did not genuinely intend to hide her identity behind a male name, then why use one at all? I suggest that "Daniel" was a polite sham that communicated to her audience the appropriate feminine modesty expected from a woman of her class. While not fooled by the disguise, the audience nonetheless appreciated the importance of the gesture: Mansilla could project the *appearance* of genteel reticence while enjoying the *reality* of being known as a writer. In this way, she was able to pursue a literary career without directly challenging male control of literary production or the ideology of feminine modesty.

Unlike Eduarda Mansilla, however, most women writers of the 1800s did not choose to use male pseudonyms. Instead, they used their own names or a female pseudonym, which shifted the burden of modesty onto the narrative itself. The result was a curious discursive mixture of disclaimers and claims of authority that Alison Weber calls the "rhetoric of femininity." While studying the writings of Teresa of Avila, Weber was intrigued by Teresa's constant claims of unworthiness, claims far in excess of those by male writers:

> Did Teresa really believe that she was "the most wretched person on earth," or was she simply utilizing long-standing humility topics? Or was self-depreciation the only self-referential language available for women? . . . It seemed possible that Teresa's "rhetoric for women" was a "rhetoric of femininity," that is, a strategy which exploited certain stereotypes about women's character and language. Rather than "writing like a woman," perhaps Teresa wrote as she believed women were *perceived* to speak.[37]

Weber concludes that Teresa deliberately chose to use a feminine discourse employing specific techniques to disarm Inquisition officials who believed that women should not write about religious subjects:

> Teresa's style is seen as a pattern of linguistic choice motivated by deliberate strategies and constrained by social roles. I have found that by exploiting features from the low-register, private discourse of subordinate groups in general, and women in particular, she created a discourse that was at once public and private, didactic and affiliative, authoritative and familiar.[38]

Teresa's disarming strategies can be seen in the writings of many women of her day and since. For instance, they are fully evident in Sor Juana Inés de la Cruz's *Respuesta a Sor Filotea*, in which she defended her writing by claiming that it was God's gift, not her own, and thus could not be denied for earthly reasons.[39] These traditional ruses of female discourse were also employed by Argentine women authors of the 1800s. Typically, these ruses consisted of: disclaimers that belittled the author's writing as unskilled or of little interest; denial that her motive in writing was to seek fame or fortune; insistence that her muse forced her to write against her own desire for modest silence; addressing her work to friends and family rather than to a general—that is, male—audience; emphasis on her status as wife, mother, or other socially approved role for a respectable woman; claiming knowledge only of women's special tasks; and humor at her own expense. By manipulating some combination of these claims, women writers could highlight their adherence to traditional femininity and domesticate their voice in ways calculated to disarm their readers' resistance.

Writing to the Community of Domesticity: Elvira Aldao de Díaz

A full array of these conventional disclaimers appears in the memoirs of Elvira Aldao de Díaz, especially in her *Recuerdos de antaño* [Memories of Yesteryear] (1931). Aldao was adept at constructing sentences of obligatory modesty, inadequacy, and unimportance—which she then proceeded to contradict or undermine. Here, for example, is such a sentence from the opening pages of *Recuerdos de antaño*:

> Estas páginas son tan íntimas, tan familiares, y lo que es peor tan pocos interesantes, que sería imperdonable su publicación si no surgieran de ellas—en el concepto de la autora—algunas impresiones de interés general[40]

> [These pages are so intimate, so family-oriented, and what is worse, of little interest, that their publication would be unpardonable if there weren't among them—in the judgment of the author—some impressions of general interest.]

Aldao managed in one short sentence to belittle her memoirs as uninteresting and intimate, although she also pointed out that what happened in her family had general interest, since her family produced a host of important men worthy of inclusion in history books. This female Aldao, though, avoided treading on the heels of her male relatives (particularly her brother Martín, a noted novelist) by specifying that her audience was entirely female:

¿Me escuchará hasta el fin alguna contemporánea para revivar sus recuerdos de infancia y adolescencia? Y no digo contemporáneo, porque siendo diferente la infancia masculina de la femenina, los hombres no podrán leer las ingenuidades de una chica. . . . Son, pues, estas páginas tan femeninas, que son exclusivamente para mujeres. (362-63)

[Will some female contemporary listen to me to the end to revive her memories of childhood and adolescence? And I do not say male contemporary, because masculine childhood being different from the feminine, men will not be able to read the ingenuousness of a girl. ... These pages are, then, so feminine that they are exclusively for women.]

By identifying her audience as solely female, Aldao placed herself and her memoirs in a zone of safety and respectability. In addition, a female audience allowed her to concentrate on domestic life, about which she could speak with testimonial and experiential authority. She knew a world unfamiliar to men, and she displayed her knowledge before female readers who were able to judge her authority in these matters and appreciate the life she described.

In another ploy to identify her narration as respectable and modest, Aldao emphasized her status as an older woman (she was 73 years old when *Recuerdos de antaño* was published). She included, for instance, signs of faulty memory that could have been edited out: "Pero . . . me está pareciendo que esto pasaba en Rosario, no en Buenos Aires. Es claro—ahora lo recuerdo bien—,fue en Rosario" (36) [But . . . now it occurs to me that this happened in Rosario, not in Buenos Aires. That's right—now I remember—,it was in Rosario]. Such signs of age occur so frequently[41] that the reader builds an image of an old woman, telling (not writing) stories of her youth. Aldao's age provided a kind of safe authority, a kind that she shared with elderly male narrators; but it also deflected potential criticism within the system of gender rules, because she could no longer be accused of drawing attention to herself in sexual terms. A young female narrator was sexually marketable and thus received the full burden of social mores, while an older woman was assumed to be free of sexual motives (often a false assumption, but widespread nonetheless). In a society that defined women's role as child-bearer and child-protector, a woman past the age of seduction and childbearing became a social eunuch, not quite a man but no longer entirely a woman either. Thus, by combining signs of age with the appearance of orality, Aldao built an identity of safe authority and labeled her narrative as suitable reading for respectable ladies.

As in the case of Eduarda Mansilla's male pseudonym, however, these disclaimers do not necessarily reflect reality. Elvira Aldao might deny that her memories were interesting or important, but she wrote ten volumes of them, a number that brings into question how unimportant she really considered her life. In *Recuerdos dispersos* [Scattered Memories] (1933), for example, she said that "Sólo sé escribir—y no bien, y lo lamento—lo que veo y siento"[42] [I only know how to write—and not well and I regret it—what I see and feel]. Since she saw a great deal from her position in the wealthiest, most powerful circles in the country, her readers would know how to interpret this tidbit of obligatory modesty, especially since her most popular books, *Reminiscencias sobre Aristóbulo del Valle* [Reminiscence of Aristóbulo del Valle] and *Cartas íntimas de Lisandro de la Torre* [Personal Letters from Lisandro de la Torre], were precisely the ones that gave her readers insight into the back-room workings of government, politicians, and revolution. Indeed, in *Recuerdos de antaño*, alongside dollhouses and favorite dolls appeared references to the family's visitors, a virtual roll call of contemporary presidents, politicians, businessmen, and writers. Her pose as an elderly narrator was based on fact insofar as her age was concerned; but her sharp wit, clear prose, and lucid intelligence show no signs of anility. Her review of the novel *La gloria de don Ramiro* included in *Recuerdos dispersos* is a sweet hatchet job, and the final scene in the cemetery in *Reminiscencias sobre Aristóbulo del Valle* is a taut, moving description of her frantic search for Del Valle's tomb.

Unlike Eduarda Mansilla, who exercised her famous wit more often in person than on paper, Elvira Aldao knew how to use humor strategically at her own expense in her writing. Her wry wit is never too far from the scene, particularly when the situation might appear to overstep modesty to display her money and privilege. Fortunately, she had the grace not to deny that she was a wealthy woman of leisure; instead, she deflated her own pretensions through self-deprecating humor, especially evident in the passages describing spending a great deal of money and energy on clothes. Aldao's vanity of vanities was her hat, an object that took on sculptural, even monumental, dimensions at the turn of the century. The context of Aldao's hat humor was the snobbery of Parisian fashion, which she simultaneously promoted and mocked in *Recuerdos de antaño*, as when her ultrafashionable French *chapeau* caused laughter back home on Calle Florida:

> La burla que provocó en Buenos Aires, fue obra exclusiva del tiempo que tardan en nuestra Capital, en implantarse las modas francesas. Aunque se crea estar al día en esa grave cuestión, no se está. En cuanto llegan a París las argentinas, se evidencia ese retardo, sobre todo en los sombreros y especialmente en su colocación: siempre llegan a París con el sombrero mal puesto. (138)

[The mockery it provoked in Buenos Aires was the exclusive result of the delay in establishing French fashions in our Capital. Although they think they are up to date in this grave matter, they aren't. As soon as Argentine women arrive in Paris, that backwardness is evident, above all in their hats and especially in their placement; they always arrive in Paris with their hat placed wrong.]

The "grave matter" of extravagant hats even gave Aldao occasion to laugh at her age:

El modelo—como todos los modelos—acababa de llegar de París y bastándome esc salvoconducto le otorgué ciudadanía, sin detenerme a pensar que el modelo era del presente y yo ya pertenecía al pasado. (136)

[The style—like all styles—had just arrived from Paris and, satisfied with that safe conduct, I bestowed upon it citizenship, without stopping to think that the style belonged to the present and I belonged to the past.]

This gentle humor does not go so far as to "smash everything, to shatter the framework of institutions, to blow up the law, to break up the 'truth' with laughter,"[43] as Hélène Cixous hopes women writers will do. Instead, as Nancy Walker points out, domestic humor such as Aldao's fashion follies falls within acceptable boundaries of subordinate femininity:

[The] social sanctions against women's political humor, especially when that humor concerns women's own political agenda, have been far stronger than those governing the expression of humor about the domestic setting that has been considered women's "proper sphere." To write amusingly about cooking, cleaning, and children, and particularly to point to one's failures and frustrations in these areas, is to appear to occupy the subordinate role mandated by the dominant culture.[44]

That Aldao's wit did not revolutionize the situation of women does not lessen its interest for the reader, however, nor does it negate her narrative authority as fashion arbiter. On the contrary, Aldao employed hats as a common denominator to create a sense of solidarity among her female readers and to bridge the gap between her economic situation and theirs. Lacking a sense of political community and still in the process of forming an intellectual one, nineteenth-century Argentine women genuinely shared only the community of domesticity. One facet of such a community was fashion. Aldao's in-jokes about Parisian hats were possible only because she appealed to an in-group: her women readers. It is doubtful that male readers would be entertained by *hat* wit. However, even gentle domestic humor can covertly protest against the restrictions of women's obligations, as Zita Dresner explains,

The ability to recognize and laugh at the incongruities between the ideal "norm" and the realities of the average woman's life, as described in domestic humor, may be the first step a reader will take toward permitting herself, and others like her, some flexibility in deviating from the impossible cultural standard without guilt or shame.[45]

If Aldao's hats were not a call for revolution, they did take aim at the tyrannies of the ideal of female beauty and reminded her readers of their common situation as women. As such, her affectionate mockery of hats also mocked standards of modesty, since hats were a very visible sign of a woman's respectability.

Aldao was not the only writer to draw on domesticity for a language of female authority and community with her readers. Juana Manuela Gorriti, for instance, edited a recipe book, *Cocina ecléctica* [Eclectic Cuisine] (1877), although she pointedly stated in the introduction that she personally preferred reading to cooking.[46] Needlework provided women authors with an even richer imagery based on domestic culture. Edelina Soto y Calvo, for example, used knitting to represent remembrance in her poem "El tejido" [Knitting]:

> ¿Sonríes, tú, mirando
> Estos dedos torcidos
> Que vieja araña tejen
> La urdimbre de los hilos?
> Pues mucho más rieras
> Oh mi fraterno amigo
> si esta vieja cabeza
> Vieras con cual prodigio
> Teje y teje recuerdos
> Más blancos que estos hilos.[47]

[Do you smile looking at/ these twisted fingers/ that like an old spider knit/ the warp of yarns?/ Well, how much more you would laugh/ oh my fraternal friend/ if you could see with what prodigiousness/ this old head/ knits and knits memories/ whiter than these threads.]

Soto y Calvo knew that knitting was a female language that her male friend did not understand—he smiled patronizingly at her work—and she drew a parallel between his incomprehension of her handwork and of the thoughts in her head. The white threads were her yarn as well as her white hair; Soto y Calvo was eighty-five when this collection of poems was published. Just as the male observer underestimated the value of her knitting, he would be surprised by what this elderly woman was remembering. Silvia Fernández also employed the language of knitting to describe the process of writing poetry, when she could "entretejer un verso con un ensueño"[48] [knit together a verse with a dream]. Similarly, Eduarda Mansilla cited none other than George Sand when she recommended needlework for concentrating thoughts.[49] The language of needlework thus becomes a feminine code, an insider's communication based on a distinctly female culture, used to address other women and to exclude (to some extent, at least) male readers. There is no trespass of male territory in either language or audience. Soto y Calvo, Fernández, and Mansilla appealed to the community of domesticity among women, and thus were sure of their own voices and their readers' reception.

The Embattled Angel: Josefina Pelliza de Sagasta

Josefina Pelliza de Sagasta did not intend to trespass on male territory either. She was the most vocal proponent of the ideal of the domestic angel among the women writers studied here, and her early works showed a faithful effort to write with violet modesty. However, she eventually came to write more defiantly and angrily than any of her peers. This curious twist of fate reveals what passion and fury can be released when the Angel becomes embattled. At first, there was little hint of the opposition that would lead to Pelliza's defiance. She began writing while still in her teens, and her youthful poems, published in a variety of newspapers, were well received. Her first novel, *Margarita* (1875), was praised on the front page of *La Nación*:

> La interesante novela de la simpática e interesante escritora doña Josefina Pelliza de Sagasta, titulada *Margarita*, está haciendo furor entre el bello sexo. Sabemos que está por agotarse ya la primera edición de ese libro, que ha venido a poner el sello a la reputación literaria de que goza dicha escritora.[50]

> [The interesting novel by the charming and interesting writer Josefina Pelliza de Sagasta, entitled *Margarita*, is causing a furor among the fair sex. We know that the first edition of this book is about to sell out, which has confirmed the literary reputation that writer enjoys.]

While being called "charming" and "interesting" (a bland term in Spanish) rather than "talented" or "outstanding" may have been patronizing, it was still front-page recognition, and though the editor identified the novel's readership as female, there was at least one male reader—the editor himself. In fact, other men read *Margarita* too, as the glowing comments reprinted as the prologue to Pelliza's *Pasionarias* indicate. Pelliza herself regarded *Margarita* as a triumph of literary domesticity. In the novel's dedication, she reminded her cousin Florencia Pueyrredón that she began to write *Margarita* because Pueyrredón thought that Pelliza's pregnancy would end her writing career. Instead, Pelliza gave birth to both book and child:

te prometí que mi primera publicación, de cualquier género que fuere, te sería dedicada para que te convencieras de que una mujer, por más que sea madre y esposa, tiene tiempo, si sus ideas y su corazón la inclinan a ello, para escribir y hacer versos.[51]

[I promised that my first publication, of whatever genre it might be, would be dedicated to you in order to convince you that a woman, even though she is a mother and wife, has time, if her ideas and heart are so inclined, to write and make verses.]

Pelliza went on to plead indulgence for her "novelita" [little novel] that was "lleno de defectos" [full of defects].[52] The tone of this dedication was cordial and playful; her cousin's doubts were not seen as serious. Indeed, there was an air of triumph, a satisfied "I told you so," when Pelliza boasted that she could be a good mother and wife as well as a writer.

Two years later, in the preface to her collection of poetry, *Lirios silvestres* [Wild Irises], Pelliza again employed conventional phrases of humility, but this time there was a hint of critical opposition to her writing:

Amo tanto a mis pobres versos así en su rústica composición, que la corrección ajena me ha parecido un crímen, por eso lanzo al viento devorador de la crítica mis florecillas silvestres con todos sus defectos, con toda la pureza del pensamiento que se revela sin poderlo sujetar jamás a la forma perfecta que enseña el arte poética.[53]

[I so love my poor verses for their unpolished composition that correction by others seemed to me a crime, therefore I launch to the devouring wind of the critics my little wild flowers with all their defects, with all the purity of thought revealed in them, never being able to make it submit to the perfect form taught by poetic art.]

On the surface, this is indeed the rhetoric of femininity par excellence: the coy "poor verses," the feminine language of flowers, the repeated use of diminutives, and the claim that her poetic impulse was natural rather than an artifice. However, she protested too much: the preface is just three paragraphs long, but the other two paragraphs were just as emphatic as this one in the middle. It was common enough for women to present their poetry as the outpouring of sensibility rather than as deliberate craft, but Pelliza carried the cliché to an extreme.

The discordant note in this excessive femininity is the reference to the "devouring" critics, which makes us wonder what happened to the cordiality of *Margarita's* dedication. The pages of newspapers from 1875 to 1877 offer clues to Pelliza's defensiveness. For example, in May 1876, there was a brief notice in *La Nación* that she intended to publish a monthly magazine called *La Mujer*. Evidently this never came to pass.[54] Even more frustrating for her was the 1876 debate concerning women's emancipation carried on between Pelliza and María Eugenia Echenique in the pages of *La Ondina del Plata*. As the debate progressed, readers generally gave credit to Echenique for making a more convincing case, and Pelliza found her zealous opposition to emancipation out of step with the thinking of many young women. She co-edited *La Alborada del Plata* with Juana Manuela Gorriti, but the paper soon folded, the victim of inadequate funding and competition from the better-funded and more professionally written *La Ondina del Plata*. Although the years 1875 to 1877 were active ones for Pelliza, her outspoken opinions and thwarted projects brought her controversy and frustration.

Then, in the 24 November 1878 edition of *El Album del Hogar*, the writer Da Freito (pseudonym of Antonio Argerich [1855–1940]) published an article in which he took a world-weary pose as "the satiric writer." Everything—politics, literature, love—left him glum. Only the thought of women writers cheered him: "es cosa tan risible, que se derrumba por su propio peso sin necesidad de sátira: así cuando se sienta a la mesa a falta de otro plato, suele exclamar: ¡que me sirvan una literata!"[55] [they are so laughable that they collapse from their own weight with no need for satire: so when I sit at table with no other dish, I usually exclaim: serve me up a woman writer!]. Josefina Pelliza was not amused. In the next issue, she published her reply, "La mujer literata en la República Argentina" [Literary Women in the Argentine Republic], signing it with her modest but murderous pseudonym of Judith.[56] She framed her reply in terms of the nobility of women as superior creatures; it is a classic example of sentimental womanhood used to reprove vulgarity:

> ¿Por qué se le acusa, por qué se le burla a la mujer escritora? porqué se injuria la inteligencia, se ultraja el talento, se escarnece el alma de un ser superior y dotado de tan bellos y grandes sentimientos como los que abriga el corazón del hombre? Ah! es triste y profundamente desconsolador saber que en el alma y en el pensamiento de un hombre, se abriga la intención de la burla para un semejante a quien Dios le prodigió todo lo bello y sublime que guarda la Creación en sus obras más perfectas. . . . Nadie entonces tiene derecho para burlar a la mujer; nadie, señor Da Freito.[57]

> [Why do you accuse, why do you mock the woman writer? Why do you insult her intelligence, outrage her talent, ridicule the soul of a superior being endowed with sentiments as beautiful and grand as those harbored in the heart of man? Ah! it is sad and profoundly distressing to know that the soul and reason of a man could foster the intent to mock someone whom God gave all that is beautiful and sublime, all

that is reserved by Creation for its most perfect works. (...) Therefore no one has the right to make fun of women, no one, mister Da Freito.]

In her reply, Pelliza tried to maintain a lofty, pained-but-patient tone. However, when pointing out that literary women were still few in number, she could not resist a jab at the culinary theme of Da Freito's comment, which weirdly echoed the "devouring" critics mentioned the year before in *Lirios silvestres*. Now Pelliza too used the language of food to roast Da Freito:

> ¿Qué le arranca ese grito destemplado y sin eco, ese grito estúpido en que pide que le *sirvan una literata*, pues, ¿qué, son tan abundantes en este país? a fe mía que no lo sabía, y voy a decirle a Vd. mi error; creía que más abundantes eran los *pichones de literatos* que las mujeres de talento.[58]

> [What caused that rash, echoless cry, that stupid shout asking that *they serve him up a woman writer?* What? are they so abundant in this country? I swear I didn't know that, and I'll tell you my mistake; I thought that there were more *male literary pigeons* than women of talent.]

She rested her case, awaiting Da Freito's apology: "esperamos tranquilas su actitud—estamos seguras de vencerlo con la fuerza irresistible de la verdad y el respeto que la mujer inspira en general"[59] [we patiently await his response—we are sure to conquer him with the irresistible force of the truth and the respect that women inspire in general]. Thus Pelliza used the weapons of the Angel that María Sinués had advocated: sweetness, persuasion, beauty, tears, and most of all, patience.

No apology was forthcoming. Apparently, Da Freito had not read Sinués' article. Instead, his reply in the next week's issue used the evolutionary arguments then in vogue to prove that civilization and social order depended on the stability of the family, which meant women at home, fulfilling their biological destiny of childbearing and childraising. He did concede that mothers could read to improve their intellect, but then he exorted them "enseñe la virtud, no con la pluma, sino con su conducta en el hogar!"[60] [teach virtue, not with the pen, but with your conduct at home!]. Da Freito thus unknowingly touched a nerve with Pelliza, who had taken this same position on women confining themselves to the home in the Echenique debate. The difference was that she believed that an exemplary wife and mother could also be a writer, as indeed she thought she had proven with *Margarita*.

Pelliza's reply in the next issue was less patient and tolerant than her first one. She first addressed Da Freito's evolutionary history, emphasizing in her version of history how Christianity ennobled women. In this interpretation, civilization gave women a prominant role:

La civilización le señaló un puesto en el torneo del progreso y allí, de pie, con la frente alta, tras las paredes humildes del hogar o en el estruendo de los aplausos que los hombres sensatos le prodigan, ella se alza, sube como un astro y va a fijarse en su puesto, sin que el egoismo ni la mezquinidad alcancen a nublar su brillo.[61]

[Civilization designated her a place in the tournament of progress and there, on her feet, head held high, behind the walls of her humble home or in the tumult of applause that sensible men bestow on her, she rises up, she ascends like a star and goes to take her place, and no egotism or small-mindedness can manage to dull her brilliance.]

Since Da Freito obviously was not sensible but rather one of the egotistical and small-minded men trying to hold back women's progress, Pelliza carefully spelled out that writing was not incompatible with the domestic angel. She almost managed to restrain her impatience with her opponent:

Sea dicho una vez por todas: la mujer literata, cuando no olvida el zurcido, el aseo y dirección del hogar, el amor a la familia y ama más a esta que a sus papeles . . . cuando esa mujer después de ser esposa, madre y angel del hogar llega a ser escritora; yo digo y aseguro a Vd., señor *Da Freito*, que esa mujer es digna de aprecio, de profundo respecto y hasta de ayuda y simpatía.[62]

[Let it be said once and for all. The literary woman, when she does not neglect her mending, housecleaning, and management of the home, the love for her family and when she loves her family more than her pages (...) when that woman after being wife, mother, and angel in the house manages to be a writer; I tell you and assure you, mister *Da Freito*, that that woman is worthy of praise, of profound respect, and even help and sympathy.]

Unfortunately, in this plea for the writer who is also the Angel in the House, Pelliza called literature a glory while in another section she called glory a vanity. Da Freito was quick to use her words against her in his reply on December 22, with predictable effect. But then he ended the article with his own unfortunate phrases:

Da Freito, licenciado en veterinaria literaria, haciendo la autopsia del artículo de una anciana, vencióla con sus propios argumentos, sin necesidad de recurrir a su gran arsenal. . . .[63]

[*Da Freito*, doctor of literary veterinary medicine, performing an autopsy on the article of an old woman, conquered her with her own arguments, without needing to resort to his great arsenal.]

This bit of nastiness provoked Pelliza into a lofty response and her withdrawal from the debate, after repeating that she saw no conflict in a good mother also being a good writer. Then, in a clever move to shame her opponent, she signed her own name with her pseudonym in parentheses.[64] By signing her real name and placing it in a superior position to her nom de plume, Pelliza entered the male world—women readers already knew that she was the Judith of *La Ondina del Plata*, something Da Freito clearly did not know—and took a public stand in defense of women writers. Shedding the polite mask of a pseudonym, she defied Da Freito face to face.

Apparently Da Freito was disconcerted by discovering that his "old woman" was the famously beautiful and young Pelliza, who was indeed the exemplary mother and writer she championed. His tone was immediately conciliatory, and he specified that "con la señora de Sagasta nada tiene que hacer nuestra pluma, pero sí mucho con sus ideas, las que trataremos de refutar siempre que sea oportuno"[65] [our pen has nothing to do with Mrs. Sagasta but rather with her ideas, which we will try to refute at every opportunity]. He then briefly argued against the reasoning in her "last word," and ended the debate. He did not sign his real name.

But the debate was not really over. It had been followed by many readers, and references to it continued to appear in *El Album del Hogar* for months. In her gossip column, for example, "Tijerita" invented a conversation between two young women, using the same culinary language that had made Da Freito's original comment so insulting:

> —¿Quién es aquel jovencito, con aire de filósofo, que mira a todas las gentes que cruzan ante él con cierto aire de profundo desprecio? . . .
> —¡Cómo! ese es . . .
> —El mismo; odia tanto a las mujeres que se les come saladas, mucho más si esas mujeres son literatas.[66]

> ["Who is that young man, with the air of a philosopher, who looks at everyone who walks in front of him with a certain air of profound disdain? . . . "
> "It can't be! that's . . . "
> "The very one; he hates women so much that he eats them salted, all the better if the women are writers."]

Da Freito himself did not give up his ideas, repeating them at intervals over the following year in articles written with a defensive tone not present in his debate rhetoric.[67] The most enduring result of the debate was that it brought new pride in women writers. It began to dawn on the readers of *El Album de Hogar* that they were witnessing a new phenomenon: an entire generation of female writers rather than just a few isolated individuals. From this point onward, there was a distinct touch of pride in the women columnists' references to *literatas*.[68] The number of articles concerning the "woman problem" increased, and while most of them did not explicitly advocate emancipation, they did press for increased education and legal protections. Moreover, they all took women's right to a literary career as a given.

The debate with Da Frieto was less positive for Pelliza herself. Following so soon after the debate with Echenique, it left her disillusioned and defensive. Evidently, she honestly believed that she could convince opponents by means of the ideology of the domestic angel and that she could depend on the "respect that women inspire," as she wrote in her first reply to Da Freito. But, like many anti-emancipationist women, Pelliza had mistaken gallantry for respect. Da Freito left no doubt that he had no respect at all for women writers (nor much for women in general) and was not persuaded by avowals of exemplary housewifery. To anti-emancipationist men, it did not matter if women writers were domestic angels or slatternly shrews: the issue was that women were transgressing "male territory" by seeking an intellectual career. For example, in a devastating review of Pelliza's *Canto inmortal* [Immortal Song] (1881), Alberto Navarro Viola made clear that there would be no gestures of critical gallantry in his influential *Anuario bibliográfico* [Annual Bibliography]:

> Los que tienen la suerte de poder ser siempre benévolos y no se sublevan ante producciones de esta naturaleza, observan que el autor del *Canto* es una señora. Lo siento por ella: no debiera escribir.[69]
>
> [Those who have the good fortune to be always benevolent and who do not rebel at productions of this sort, observe that the author of *Canto* is a woman. I am sorry for her; she should not write.]

It must have been painful for Pelliza to be forced in so public a way to realize that her advocacy of the patriarchal ideal of femininity earned her little respect from the patriarchs themselves.

Understandably, the introductions to Pelliza's books published after the debate with Da Freito did not repeat the conventional feminine modesty of *Lirios silvestres*. The preface to *Pasionarias* [Passion Flowers] (1887), for example, consists of a collection of laudatory reviews of her work—all from prominent men. Of even greater significance, the introduction to *Conferencias: El libro de las madres* [Discussions: The Mothers' Book] (1885) is far different from the cordial dedication of the novel *Margarita*. In the ten years that separated the publication of the two books, the mild obstacles suggested by Pelliza's cousin had grown into full-fledged opposition from certain segments of society, although there had also been success and support from others. Both *Margarita* and *Conferencias* deal with troubled families, women's vulnerable legal position, and redemption through marital love. However, *Margarita* showed no signs of the bitterness and acrimony so often found in *Conferencias*. One indication of the heightened emotions of

Conferencias is that Pelliza entitled its introduction "Profesión de Fe"
[Confession of Faith] rather than the usual "To the Reader":

> He emprendido este libro bajo la mejor intención de buena fe,—no diré
> las frases con que la mayor parte de los autores comienzan el prefacio
> de sus libros:—"el consejo de los amigos ha influído para decidirme a
> dar a la luz pública estas páginas que, sin esa influencia afectuosa,
> estaban condenadas a vivir en el archivo privado, etc., etc." Yo, por el
> contrario, sin influencias, sin consejos, ni mucho menos amigos, doy
> mi libro a la publicidad.[70]

> [I have set about this book with the best intentions of good faith,—I
> will not say the phrases with which most authors begin the preface of
> their books:—"the urging of friends has influenced me to decide to
> bring these pages into the public spotlight, without this affectionate
> influence they would be condemned to live in my private papers, etc.,
> etc." On the contrary, I publish my book without influences, without
> urging, not to mention without friends.]

She said that "no he pensado en la ingratitud" (8) [I did not think about
ingratitude] when she wrote the book, but then she imagined exactly
such a situation:

> si mañana me gritaran al pasar, estas palabras, "tu libro no vale nada",
> yo me reiría y murmuraría estas dos sílabas, ¡tonto! y con la firmeza
> sublime de Galileo sonreiría murmurando, ¡tontos! ¡tontos! . . . No hay
> vanidad en este modo de decir, ni el átomo más leve, es pura convicción,
> por eso repito, que siempre oiga murmurar de mi libro, diré esto, "Y
> sin embargo creo que mi libro es bueno." (9)

> [if tomorrow people should shout these words at me as I pass, "your
> book is worthless," I would laugh to myself and whisper this syllable,
> "Fool!" and with the sublime resolve of Galileo I would whisper
> smilingly, "Fools! Fools!" . . . There is no vanity in this way of speaking,
> not the slightest atom of it, it is pure conviction, thus I repeat, that
> whenever I hear gossip about my book, I will say this: Nevertheless, I
> believe that my book is good.]

By choosing the cultural heretic Galileo as her hero, Pelliza dismissed
critics because she believed that she, like Galileo, would be vindicated
in time. In this preface, she abandoned the false modesty of the rhetoric
of femininity and now stated openly her belief in her work's value.
While there was still a large dose of defensiveness in this confidence,
it nonetheless marked a new stage in her writing: she allowed herself
to be angry and to write without the restraint of feminine modesty.

Without question, *Conferencias* is an extraordinary book. When
Pelliza wrote, not as a poet imitating the dominant Romanticism
controlled by men, but as a woman marginalized from intellectual
circles, she became a perceptive and daring social critic. While still

opposing women's emancipation, she now could employ her new angry voice to point out the reality of oppression hidden behind the façade of traditional motherhood. She openly advocated a law giving married women custody of their children, the right to enter into legal contracts, and a role in the control of the family's money and property, reforms that were not to be enacted until a hundred years later:

> Esta ley que quisiéramos ver efectiva para la mujer en vida del marido, está en vigencia tratándose de la soltera mayor de edad y de la viuda; ambas reintegradas en sus derechos las coloca la ley de nuestro Código en igual condición al hombre . . . la mujer esposa, la madre muchas veces en edad avanzada, es la única que está despojada de todo y en calidad de una servidora obligada a la maternidad, condenada en su santa resignación a dar la vida, ella la que padece, la que sufre y ama, sin un derecho, sin más prerrogativos que las del perro. (72)

> [This law that we would like to see effective for the women during their husbands' lifetime, is already in effect for single women of age and for widows; our law code places both of them, their rights restored, in equal condition with men . . . the wife, often a mother advanced in age, is the only one stripped of everything and in her capacity as servant compelled to maternity, condemned in her holy resignation to give life, she is the one who endures, who suffers and loves, without a single right, with no more prerogatives than a dog.]

There were no coy little flowers in this new voice, no woman-violet begging indulgence for her verses' unpolished form. Pelliza had learned from bitter experience that "la mujer argentina que escribe una carta —una página, un libro, en fin—tiene que ser antes que escritora, heróica!" (163) [the Argentine woman who writes a letter—a page, much less a book—must be more than a writer, she must be heroic!] In *Conferencias*, Josefina Pelliza wrote like a hero.

The Needle versus the Pen

The struggle for recognition of women's right to write was not only expressed in the floral symbols of violets and passionflowers, it was also carried out in terms of the needle and the pen. The image of the needle held a special power over nineteenth-century women because of its literalness: they spent hours every day involved in ornamenting, sewing, and mending clothing and linens. In contrast with the plain functionality of today's apparel, nineteenth-century clothing was complexly ornamented, many-layered, and grand in scope. Moreover, prior to the invention of the sewing machine, it was all sewn by hand.[71] Seaming, hemming, embroidery, knitting, lace-making, darning—sewing in all its myriad manifestations was far more than simple necessity;

it became a resonant symbol of traditional roles for women and the cult of ultradomesticity. As Rozsika Parker points out, needlework was thought to reveal "supposedly natural feminine characteristics: piety, feeling, taste, and domestic devotion."[72] For women across all classes, needlework was the physical expression of an ideology that prized female silence, passivity, and immobility. Like the violet, the picture of a woman seated in a chair, eyes lowered, and hands busy with a needle rather than a book was an ideological image that did not need explanation to a nineteenth-century audience.

As the century unfolded, the needle increasingly was placed in tense opposition with the pen, the symbol of education, intellectual fulfillment, and gainful employment. For example, an 1852 article advocating education for women concluded with "finalice entre nosotras ese fanatismo ridículo y perjudicial, de que no precisamos otros conocimientos que los de la aguja para ser felices"[73] [put an end to that ridiculous and harmful fanaticism among us, that we need no other knowledge but that of the needle to be happy]. Similarly, in an article from 1896 on women's role in the national destiny, the author pleaded, "Que haya no solo mujeres costureras y mujeres coquetas, que haya también mujeres pensadores y mujeres artistas"[74] [Let there be not just women seamstresses and women coquettes, but also women thinkers and women artists]. If the needle represented home-bound domesticity, the pen evoked an active role in society, intellectual pursuits rather than manual labor, and, perhaps most enticing of all, the possibility of genteel but paid employment. Writers particularly resented the loss of their time to needlework: it was representative of the standards of propriety that kept women occupied at ephemeral tasks with small recognition, while men had the leisure time to write. Moreover, women's craft with the needle was disposable, ultimately duplicated by machinery; art with the pen, however, could not be produced by mechanical invention. No wonder that Eduarda Mansilla admired the women journalists of the United States who earned their living by the pen and thus had freed themselves of "la cruel servidumbre de la aguja"[75] [the cruel servitude of the needle].

Silvia Fernández opposed the two symbols in her fable "La pluma y la aguja" [The Pen and the Needle]. In this poem, the needle taunts the pen, saying that it will never be welcome where women are busy using the needle. The pen then decides to leave the woman's house:

> Y desde entonces mostróse
> Con las agujas esquiva.
> Y como a la aguja, toda
> Mujer, bien o mal, maneja,

De ésta la pluma se aleja
Porque aquella la incomoda.
   ¿Fue de la aguja parlera
Discreto el juicio? ¡quién sabe!
Tal vez el hombre lo alabe,
La mujer lo vitupera.
   Que aguja y pluma, igualmente,
Sónle utensilios queridos:
Si uno sirve a sus vestidos,
El otro sirve a su mente.[76]

[And ever since has shown itself/ Disdainful toward needles./ And since every woman employs/ The needle, skillfully or not,/ The pen avoids them too/Because the needle annoys the pen./ Was the chattering needle/ Wise in judgment? who knows!/ Men may think so,/ But women deny it./ Because the needle and the pen/ Are tools they equally cherish:/ While one serves a woman's dress,/ The other serves her mind.]

This poem recognized that men encouraged the substitution of the needle for the pen: the domestic sphere had been rigidly divorced from the public one. For Fernández the division between public/pen/male and private/needle/female was unnatural: both the needle and the pen were equally useful though for different purposes. Fernández repeated this theme in "Zurciendo medias" [Darning Socks]:

Deja que zurza las medias,
   Musa mía,
Deja que tome sus puntos . . .
Cual un diablillo me asedias . . .
¡Venir a exponerme asuntos
de elevada poesía! . . .
Deja que zurza las medias,
   Musa mía.
Sin querer te presto oído,
   ¡Tentadora!
Que me hablas de hermosos temas
Mientras remato un zurcido.
¡Incitarme, seductora,
A escribir altos poemas
Cuando me ves, en la caña,
O el talón, o la plantilla
De una media, cual la araña
Laborando una telilla![77]

[Let me darn these socks,/ Muse of mine,/ Let me take these stitches/ Like a little devil you pester me/ Coming to show me themes/ Of high poetry!/ Let me just darn these socks,/ Muse of mine./ I can't help but

listen to you,/ Temptress!/ You speak to me of beautiful themes/ While
I cast off a row./ Inciting me, seductress/ To write high poetry/ When
you see me working the ankle,/ Turning the heel, or knitting the sole/
Of the sock, like a spider/ Spinning her web!]

Here the poet opposed two classical images of women: Polemnia, the
poetic muse, and Arachne, the spider-woman, refusing to recognize the
importance of both. Socks must be darned, but this domestic chore
could not command the intellectual joy that poetry evoked. The humorous tone of "Zurciendo medias" and the fable pattern of "La pluma y
la aguja" helped soften the seriousness of the central issue: the customs
of domesticity were unnaturally relegated to women's sphere, while
men unnaturally controlled the sphere of intellectual satisfactions,
especially that of writing.

Men were especially protective of their role as writers, because they
could earn money by it. Women wanted this avenue of employment,
too, which was much more desirable than the alternative: sewing. Silvia
Fernández, who was from a well-to-do family, did not face the compli-
cation of writing for money rather than for pleasure. She could afford
(literally) to adopt a wry point of view about darning socks; but for poor
women, there was nothing funny about sewing. In a society in which
women had little practical vocational training, sewing was one of their
few marketable skills. However, seamstresses made a miserable living,
selling at minimal rates the product of hours of concentration in
uncertain light and depending on the good will of patrons or sweatshop
brokers. Writing for newspapers and magazines, on the other hand,
offered both dignity and better pay.

Lola Larrosa de Ansaldo knew about both pay scales from personal
experience. She was a journalist, novelist, anti-emancipationist, and
fervent defender of the ideal of the domestic angel. She was equally
impassioned, however, about providing women with sufficient education to earn a living in case of loss of parents, widowhood, abandonment
by a husband, or the husband's incapacity. (Remaining single by choice
was not seriously considered by the women writers of the 1800s, with
the exception of María Echenique). Larrosa's passion on the subjects
of education and professional journalism was based on her own struggles to be a domestic angel while supporting a child and mentally ill
husband with the earnings from her writings. In her works, women who
do not have the education to earn a living by the pen have no other
recourse than to try to live by the needle. Larrosa's *Las obras de
misericordia* [Works of Mercy] (1882), for instance, is a series of
fourteen exemplary tales corresponding to the spiritual and corporal
works of mercy: counsel the wayward, forgive offenses, feed the

hungry, etc. Several of the stories feature virtuous women trapped in poverty due to the death of their husbands or parents. All of these good women turn to sewing as their only means of earning a living, wretched though it might be. In "Consolar al triste" [Comfort the Sorrowing], for example, the orphaned Margarita

> determinó buscar costuras, con cuyo producto podría subsistir muy escasamente y con menoscabo de su salud, porque la ingratitud del trabajo, haría sufrir su cuerpo y aniquilaría sus fuerzas, sin obtener a costa de fatigas y desvelos, más que una existencia amarga, sin distracciones, sin consuelo, y sin alivio.[78]

> [decided to look for sewing work, by which she could subsist very meagerly and to the detriment of her health, because the ingratitude of the work would make her body suffer and would destroy her strength, obtaining at the cost of fatigue and sleeplessness nothing more than a bitter existence, without joy, without comfort, and without relief.]

Larrosa's poor seamstresses are eventually rescued by rich benefactors as reward for their virtue and suffering. The novels never suggest that they could prosper by means of sewing. Larrosa may have been sentimental to a fault about domestic angels, but she had no illusions about seamstresses' earnings. Donna Guy, in her book *Sex and Danger in Buenos Aires*, confirms the ugly reality of this "genteel poverty" by documenting that seamstresses could not support their families on their wages and that many prostitutes in Buenos Aires were former seamstresses who turned to prostitution because the money was better.[79]

Larrosa made the point that an education would provide more opportunities than just sewing. Rosa, the widowed heroine of "Enseñar al que no sabe" [Instruct the Ignorant], was from a humble family and thus

> su educación había sido escasa y limitada. En la desgracia que la rodeaba solo el trabajo de la costura quedábale como único recurso. Asióse a este, como el náufrago a la tabla salvadora.[80]

> [her education had been scant and limited. In the misfortune that enveloped them, work as a seamstress became her only recourse. She grabbed it as a drowning man clings to a life preserver.]

Rosa's anguish was in knowing that her children would continue in her poverty, since the only local school was a private one. Its headmistress—apparently uninformed about the spiritual acts of mercy—refused to waive the fees for Rosa's children. The only woman in *Obras de misericordia* able to earn a satisfactory living for herself and for her widowed mother is Angelina, whose education allowed her to be a teacher. She is also the only one not in need of a benefactor, nor, interestingly enough, was there a love interest created for her. Angelina may have been Larrosa's ideal: a dutiful daughter making a decent living respectably with no need to depend on a man for rescue.

Larrosa struggled with the dilemma of being both a writer and a domestic angel, but she—like Josefina Pelliza and Agustina Andrade —found that the standards of womanly modesty could not be altered easily to fit the public pattern of a writer. In order to gain the right to write, she had to craft more than lace—she had to fashion her *self*. Stephen Greenblatt's descriptions of Renaissance self-fashioning can be made over somewhat to fit the women's desire for a writerly identity. Among the conditions of self-fashioning that he proposes are several that can be applied to the situation of nineteenth-century women authors. For example, they had no inherited title or identity that would automatically confer status. They showed submission to an authority outside the self. An alien, "threatening Other" defines them by contrast. Although the authority and the alien exist outside the self, they are "at the same time experienced as inward necessities." Language is the material used to construct the self; and, finally, "self-fashioning always involves some experience of threat, some effacement or undermining, some loss of self."[81] In the case of the Argentine women of the 1880s, their inherited gender identity was antithetical to the status they desired as writers. Their outside authority was the patriarchal culture that mandated their silence, and the threatening Other was a "masculinized," brash woman who became a target for patriarchal displeasure—George Sand, for instance, with her men's clothing, cigars, and unhidden lovers. Finally, in their narrative strategies of wily modesty, women writers often defended and collaborated with the very authority of modest silence that they struggled against. To Greenblatt's descriptions I would add the ideal Other, the created image of a model to which the writer can aspire. If George Sand can be seen as nineteenth-century Argentina's threatening Other, then Harriet Beecher Stowe can be its ideal Other. Stowe's impact as a writer was as great as Sand's, but she was also a high-profile domestic angel, the quintessential Angloamerican woman as fantasized by *argentinas* such as this one, writing in 1880:

> La medicina, la abogacía, las letras, la mecánica, la política todo es allí para la mujer. . . . La Norteamericana es la más sublime de las madres, la más grandiosa de las esposas. . . . Porque es un ser soberano que no ha abdicado su razón, mutilado su pensamiento, ni muerto su actividad.[82]

> [Medicine, law, letters, astronomy, politics, everything is there for women. (...) The Northamerican woman is the most sublime of mothers, the most grandiose of wives. (...) Because she is a sovereign being who has not abdicated her reason, mutilated her intelligence, nor killed her activity.]

This was the dream of the women of the 1880s: to be ideal wives and mothers without sacrificing their right to write. Trying to reconcile their dream with reality, their voice was often unsure, self-denying, cautious, and contradictory. But they did speak up, they did defend their right to a public voice, and thus they broke barriers for future generations of women writers.

Endnotes

1 Susan Sniader Lanser, *Fictions of Authority: Women Writers and Narrative Voice* (Ithaca: Cornell University Press, 1992), 6, 7.

2 M.A. Pelliza, *Críticas y bocetos históricos* (Buenos Aires: Imprenta del Mayo, 1879), 133.

3 Pelliza's belittling of women writers is all the more unnerving given that it was probably unconscious: after all, he was a pioneering historian of women's accomplishments in Argentina, a member of the editorial board of *La Alborada del Plata*, and a contributer to other women's periodicals.

4 Elvira Aldao de Díaz, *Recuerdos de antaño* (Buenos Aires: Jacobo Peuser, 1931), 363.

5 La Dirección, "Doctora Cecilia Grierson," *El Búcaro Americano* (1 June 1896): 126. This is the featured profile of the issue; Grierson's photo appears on its cover. Articles about Florence Nightingale, admired in Argentina, emphasized her femininity and interpreted her medical mission as motherly abnegation. See, for instance, Mercedes Cabello de Carbonera, "Miss Nightingale," *La Alborada del Plata* (10 February 1878): 94-95, 101-103.

6 Bonnie Frederick, "El viajero y la nómada: los recuerdos de viaje de Eduarda y Lucio Mansilla," *Mujeres y cultura en la Argentina del siglo XIX*, Lea Fletcher, comp. (Buenos Aires: Feminaria, 1994), 246-51.

7 Susan Kirkpatrick, *Las Románticas: Women Writers and Subjectivity in Spain, 1835-1850* (Berkeley: University of California Press, 1989), 23.

8 Luis Telmo Pintos, "El hombre y la mujer," *La Ondina del Plata* (14 March 1875): 61.

9 Gender concepts changed very little in Hispanic societies from the Renaissance to the mid-1800s; three centuries after it was written, the classic conduct book for women, *La perfecta casada* by Fray Luis de León (1583), was still read and quoted. Obviously, the unique Catholicism forged in Spain during the Reconquest has a large role in this static concept of gender. However, other factors should not be overlooked; particularly important are Spain's isolation from the rise of capitalism, Enlightenment ideas, and the early Industrial Revolution.

10 See Bridget Aldaraca's excellent discussion in "El ángel del hogar: The Cult of Domesticity in Nineteenth-Century Spain," *Theory and Practice of Feminist Literary Criticism*, Gabriela Mora and Karen S. Van Hooft, eds. (Ypsilanti: Bilingual Press, 1982), 62-87.

11 Virginia Woolf, "Professions for Women," *The Death of the Moth and Other Essays* (London: Hogarth, 1942, 1981), 151.

12 Throughout the following discussion, I will cite only works written by women themselves, by men identified with pro-women factions, or by male writers published in women's periodicals. While it is easy enough to find

opposition to female authorship from misogynists, it is, I believe, more significant and disturbing to detect it in the pro-women's camp and in the pages of publications directed at women.

[13] Faustina Saez de Melgar, "Estudios sociales sobre la mujer: la abnegación," *La Ondina del Plata* (7 November 1875): 471. Saez (Spain, 1834–95) founded and edited a newspaper called *La Violeta* (1862–66). Her sentimental novel, *La cruz del olivar* (1867), was parodied by Galdós in *La desheredada*.

[14] Sor Teresa de Jesús, "Educación del hogar," *La Ondina del Plata* (26 March 1876): 151.

[15] Lola Larrosa, "La mujer en el hogar," *La Ondina del Plata* (24 September 1876): 465.

[16] María del Pilar Sinués de Marco,"Las armas de la mujer," *La Ondina del Plata* (21 May 1876): 244. Sinués (1835–93) wrote nearly 100 novels, all advocating domesticity as women's *only* role. See the entry in Carolyn L. Galerstein, ed., *Women Writers of Spain: An Annotated Bio-Bibliographical Guide* (New York: Greenwood, 1986).

[17] Sinués, "Las armas," 242-43.

[18] M. Polo y Peyrolón, "La mujer y la flor," *El Album del Hogar* (13 July 1879): 12.

[19] Una Suscritora, "Educación de la mujer," *La Ondina del Plata* (12 March 1876): 124.

[20] Lola Larrosa, "La mision de la muger," *La Prensa* (21 October 1882): 1.

[21] Luis Telmo Pintos, "La mujer: habilitada para la enseñanza," *La Ondina del Plata* (1 August 1875): 301.

[22] See Domingo F. Sarmiento's reference to Mansilla's determination to be a journalist in a letter to his niece in April 1885 in vol. 46 of *Obras de D.F. Sarmiento* (Buenos Aires: Mariano Moreno, 1900), 276.

[23] Eduarda Mansilla de García, *Recuerdos de viaje* (Buenos Aires: Juan A. Alsina, 1882), 115.

[24] Woolf, "Professions," 151.

[25] Ibid.

[26] Miguel Cané, *Charlas literarias* (Buenos Aires: Sceaux, 1885), 51.

[27] Martín Coronado, "*Lágrimas:* Poesías de la señorita Agustina Andrade," *El Album del Hogar* (4 August 1878): 32-35.

[28] Oscar Weber, "Resultados inmediatos," *El Album del Hogar* (29 December 1878): 203.

[29] Agustina Andrade, *Lágrimas: ensayos poéticos* (Buenos Aires: La Tribuna, 1878), 44.

[30] Ibid., 49.

[31] Ibid., 21.

[32] Since I am studying texts in which the author is known to be female, I will omit one strategy, that of writing anonymously, though unfortunately, it is the ultimate in modest self-effacement.

[33] Mary Poovey, *The Proper Lady and the Woman Writer* (Chicago: University of Chicago Press, 1984), xv.

[34] Eduarda Mansilla de García, *Lucía Miranda: novela histórica* (Buenos Aires: Juan A. Alsina, 1882), 7.

[35] Lucio V. Mansilla, "Bibliografía y juicio crítico," *La Revista de Buenos Aires*, 2 (18 October 1864): 350. Mansilla signed this article "Ventura." His readers recognized the name he used to write literary criticism. In the same article, full of in-jokes, "Ventura" defends a work by Lucio Mansilla that had been criticized in a rival newspaper.

[36] "Eduarda Mansilla de García," *La Ondina del Plata* (9 May 1875): 158. Unfortunately, many pseudonyms that were open secrets in the 1800s have been forgotten with time, since few historians bothered to record them.

[37] Alison Weber, *Teresa of Avila and the Rhetoric of Femininity* (Princeton: Princeton University Press, 1990), 11.

[38] Ibid., 15.

[39] See the bilingual edition *A Woman of Genius: The Intellectual Autobiography of Sor Juana Inés de la Cruz*, Margaret Sayers Peden, trans. (Salisbury, Conn: Lime Rock Press, 1982).

[40] Elvira Aldao de Díaz, *Recuerdos de antaño* (Buenos Aires: Jacobo Peuser, 1931), 7. Further page references will be noted in the text of the essay.

[41] See ibid. pages 40, 57, 130, 186, 242, 302, etc.

[42] Elvira Aldao de Díaz, *Recuerdos dispersos* (Buenos Aires: Jacobo Peuser, 1933), 8.

[43] Hélène Cixous, "The Laugh of the Medusa," Keith and Paula Cohen, trans. *Signs* 1 (1976): 888. This essay is also widely reprinted in anthologies.

[44] Nancy Walker, "Toward Solidarity: Women's Humor and Group Identity," *Women's Comic Visions*, June Sochen, ed. (Detroit: Wayne State University Press, 1991) 59-60.

[45] Zita Z. Dresner, *"Domestic Comic Writers," Women's Comic Visions*, 99.

[46] See Nina M. Scott, "Juana Manuela Gorriti's *Cocina ecléctica*: Recipes as Feminine Discourse," *Hispania* 75 (May 1992): 310-14.

[47] Edelina Soto y Calvo, "El tejido," *Parque vetusto* (Buenos Aires: Juan Toia, 1929), 72.

[48] Silvia Fernández, "Mi rincón," *Antología de la poesía femenina argentina*, José Carlos Maubé and Adolfo Capdevielle, eds. (Buenos Aires: Ferrari, 1930), 215.

[49] Eduarda Mansilla de García, "Educación de la mujer," *La Nación* (18 July 1883): 1.

[50] "Conversación," *La Nación* (12 January 1876): 1.

[51] Josefina Pelliza de Sagasta, *Margarita* (Buenos Aires: El Orden, 1875), 6. Pelliza eventually had five children, who did not seem to slow down her writing output, probably because the Sagastas were wealthy enough to hire maids, cooks, and nannies.

[52] Ibid.

[53] Josefina Pelliza de Sagasta, "Al Lector," *Lirios silvestres: Album de poesías* (Buenos Aires: Imprenta del Porvenir, 1877), iii.

[54] Néstor Tomás Auza, *Periodismo y femenismo en la Argentina 1830–1930* (Buenos Aires: Emecé, 1988), 26.

[55] Da Freito, "Sin Nombre," *El Album del Hogar* (24 November 1878): 163.

[56] In the Apocryphal book carrying her name, Judith used her beauty and charm to first entice—without losing her chastity—then slay Holophernes, the Assyrian general sent to slaughter the Israelites. See in particular the song of triumph that Judith composes in Chapter 16. Wily modesty occurs frequently in the Bible; notable examples include Ruth and Esther.

[57] Judith, "La mujer literata en la República Argentina: Al señor Da Freito," *El Album del Hogar* (1 December 1878): 169.

[58] Ibid.

[59] Ibid.

[60] Da Freito, "La mujer en la naturaleza y la civilización," *El Album del Hogar* (8 December 1878): 178.

[61] Judith, "La mujer literata en la República Argentina," *El Album del Hogar* (15 December 1878): 185.

[62] Ibid.

[63] Da Freito, "Autopsia de un artículo," *El Album del Hogar* (22 December 1878): 194.

[64] Josefina Pelliza de Sagasta (Judith), "Ultima palabra," *El Album del Hogar* (29 December 1878): 202.

[65] Da Freito, "A la señora de Sagasta," *El Album de Hogar* (5 January 1879): 209.

[66] Tijerita, "Crónica de Palermo," *El Album del Hogar* (16 February 1879): 262.

[67] See his comments in "Escepticismo y fe," *El Album del Hogar* (19 October 1879): 125. Also see his testy reply to another gibe from Tijerita: "Párrafos de Da Freito a la comendadora Tijerita," *El Album del Hogar* (2 November 1879): 143-44.

[68] See for example, the note about Eduarda Mansilla in "Plumadas," *El Album*

del Hogar (22 June 1879): 407 and the listing of names in "Arco-Iris," *El Album del Hogar* (28 December 1879): 106.

[69] Alberto Navarro Viola, in vol. 3 of *Anuario bibliográfico de la República Argentina* (Buenos Aires: n.p., 1881), 376.

[70] Josefina Pelliza de Sagasta, *Conferencias: El libro de las madres* (Buenos Aires: Jeneral Lavalle, 1885), 7. Further page references noted in the text.

[71] To glimpse the impact of this statement, imagine making a skirt in the style of the 1850s. Start with the many yards of material needed to cover a hoop about 100 inches in diameter (typically, hoops ranged from about 90 to an astonishing 180 inches across). To hem the circumference of the skirt, the seamstress must sew by hand 314 inches, that is, almost 9 yards. Then, since simplicity was not a characteristic of the age, the dress might be ornamented with beading, embroidery, tucks, piping, lace, ribbons, and/or ruffles. The outside of the dress was not all; underneath it were petticoats, camisoles, corsets, and other mysterious undergarments, all with a little fancywork. Like clothing styles, interior decoration of the 1800s abhorred a plain surface. Tabletops, mantlepieces, chair backs, dressers, and shelves all had their crocheted doily, embroidered runner, or netted cover. Of course, once such items of clothing or linen were made, they had to be cleaned, ironed, and mended—again, by hand.

[72] Rozsika Parker, *The Subversive Stitch* (London: Women's Press, 1986), 164.

[73] "Las redactoras," *La Camelia* (6 Month of America [June] 1852): 45.

[74] Carlota Garrido de la Peña, "Tarea patriótica," *El Búcaro Americano* (1 April 1896): 100.

[75] Eduarda Mansilla de García, *Recuerdos de viaje* (Buenos Aires: Juan A. Alsina, 1882), 115.

[76] Silvia Fernández, "La pluma y la aguja," *Versos* (Luján: La Perla del Plata, 1913), 182-83.

[77] Silvia Fernández, "Zurciendo medias," *Antología de la poesía femenina argentina*, José Carlos Maubé and Adolfo Capdevielle, eds. (Buenos Aires: Ferrari, 1930), 214.

[78] Lola Larrosa, *Obras de misericordia* (Buenos Aires: Imprenta Oswald, 1882), 225.

[79] Donna Guy, *Sex and Danger in Buenos Aires* (Lincoln: University of Nebraska Press, 1991) 65, 70-73.

[80] *Obras de misericordia*, 12.

[81] Stephen Greenblatt, *Renaissance Self-Fashioning* (Chicago: University of Chicago Press, 1980), 9. My thanks to Jennifer Jenkins for bringing this source to my attention.

[82] Agar Willianson, "La emancipación de la mujer," *La Alborada Literaria del Plata* (18 Apr 1880): 115.

3

Women in the Era of "Progress, Glory, & Electricity"

Although they could never forget their lack of opportunities, legal rights, or social status, the women of the Generation of 1880 nonetheless were convinced that they were witnessing the birth of a marvelous new era: the age of progress. The impact of the idea of progress on Argentine women's thinking can hardly be overstated; in fact, it is difficult to find a contemporary article about women's issues that does *not* mention progress or evolution. Rarely has a society had such a clear awareness of living between the end of one era and the beginning of a new one, but a survey of Argentine writing from 1870–1914 reveals that the belief in a new age of progress was accepted across boundaries of class, gender, and ideology.[1] In 1897, Elia Martínez summed up the exuberance of the times by describing the 1800s as "el siglo de la libertad, del progreso, de la gloria, de la electricidad"[2] [the century of liberty, progress, glory, and electricity]. Whether in matters of electricity or liberty, Martínez and other women viewed their century as revolutionary as well as evolutionary. Progress, they believed, would cure the ills of the past: tyranny, ignorance, poverty, and, significantly, the oppression of women. Electric illumination became more than a technological feat: it was a metaphor for the arrival of spiritual light.

Everywhere in late nineteenth-century Argentina, especially in Buenos Aires, there was tangible evidence of progress: railroads, trams, a new port, and the telegraph. Public hygiene programs were freeing

Buenos Aires from the terror of yellow fever epidemics like the one in 1871 which killed 7,000 people. New amenities to daily life appeared, as well. For instance, there were national newspapers, indoor English-style bathrooms (previously, citizens of Buenos Aires had bathed in the river during good weather and not at all in bad), beautifully appointed restaurants, and imported French fashions and architecture.[3] However, to the Argentines of the late 1800s, these material signs of progress were mere manifestations of the even greater evolution in knowledge and morals that would lead to a regeneration of humanity itself. The rapid advances in the sciences that characterized the nineteenth century were not seen as isolated incidents of human inventiveness, but rather as evidence of an evolutionary framework such as the one proposed by Charles Darwin. The theory of evolution sketched a mental image of forward movement; this mental framework was linear, inevitable, and tending ever toward a shining future. If such a powerful force was molding physical nature, was it not also at work in human nature? Raymunda Torres y Quiroga thought so. She was an eloquent advocate of this belief, in which scientific and spiritual values are intertwined:

> El Progreso es la eterna ley de los pueblos y a él tiende sin cesar la humanidad. La civilización es la antorcha que ilumina al mundo: donde no penetran sus vivificadores rayos no existe más que la ignorancia y el embrutecimiento. . . . El siglo XIX sintetiza todo lo grande, resume en sí el saber, las ciencias de los siglos anteriores; ¡sintetiza el avance supremo de la inteligencia del hombre hacia lo divino, hacia lo supremo, hacia lo perfecto, hacia lo sublime![4]

> [Progress is the eternal law of nations, and all humanity reaches toward it without ceasing. Civilization is the torch that illuminates the world: where its life-giving rays do not penetrate, there exists nothing more than ignorance and degradation. (...) The nineteenth century synthesizes all that is great, it sums up all the knowledge and the science of the previous centuries; it synthesizes the supreme advance of man's intelligence toward the divine, toward the supreme, toward perfection, toward the sublime!]

Expressed in the image of light as enlightenment, the Romantic concepts of the sublime and human perfectability are here mixed with Positivist science and technology by means of Hegelian synthesis. The resulting ideas thrilled Quiroga y Torres and other women, who saw in them hope and optimism. Believers in progress could tolerate wrongs in the present, knowing that eventually and inevitably the future would make all wrongs right. The attraction of this world view for nineteenth-century women is obvious. No longer did they need to depend on the good will of men for reform of their roles; instead, they were confident that progress—which, being an historical force, could not be diverted —would make misogyny obsolete in the long run. Evolution toward human perfectibility could not turn and retreat into barbarism, that is, the oppression of women.

The optimism of inevitable progress was reinforced by North American women's advances, which were widely publicized in Argentina's press:

> Llegará, no hay que desesperar, el progreso civilizador a Sud América, haciéndose extensivo hasta el ser débil que todavía gime bajo injusta suerte; y tendremos el mismo derecho que nuestras compañeras del Norte, porque la corriente del progreso en el cauce de la luz va sin detenerse.[5]

> [There is no reason to despair, civilizing progress will arrive in South America, reaching the weak being who still sighs under her unjust fate; and we will have the same rights as our colleagues in the North, because the current of progress flows without stopping in the river of enlightenment.]

The image of progress as a river current—evoking a vivid feeling of rapid, unstoppable change—handily recognizes that Argentine women's present state is barbaric while simultaneously offering assurance that the situation is only temporary. Indeed, the women of the late 1800s were convinced that they would be lifted from backwardness toward a new state of civilization that, they believed, was already observable in France, England, and, most notably, in the United States. In those countries, women were gaining rights to education, gainful employment, and legal control of their own finances. The abundant feature articles in Argentine women's newspapers about contemporary women writers in other countries emphasized that their individual triumphs were triumphs for women everywhere and thus evidence of female progress. George Sand, for example, was described with typical effusiveness as a "gigante de la literatura, sol sin ocaso, monumento de la revolución social"[6] [giant of literature, sun that never sets, monument of the social revolution]. Writers such as Sand and Harriet Beecher Stowe were as inspirational for their earning potential as for their literary talents. The new occupations of nurses and teachers—Florence Nightingale and Clara Barton in particular, but also the New England schoolteachers brought to Argentina in the 1860s—fascinated Argentine women, who saw in them the professional applications of women's traditional nurturing roles.

To admire women's moral and material evolution in the United States was to reject Argentina's cultural roots in Spain, a heritage that seemed by comparison anti-scientific, superstitious, and misogynistic:

La América del Sur, descendiente de la raza española, la más ociosa, la más atrasada de todas, por ser allí donde se ha alimentado, crecido y vivido el catolicismo, el fanatismo y la superstición, no podía haber dado otra cosa que sus costumbres, fueros y preocupaciones sobre la Mujer.[7]

[South America, descendent of the Spanish race, the laziest, the most backward of all because there Catholicism, fanaticism, and superstition were nourished, raised, and lived, could not have inherited anything other than its customs, laws, and preoccupations concerning Woman.]

While this anti-Spanish, anti-Catholic diatribe is more vehement than most writers' opinions, it is representative of widespread questioning of the Hispanic tradition. English and North American accomplishments in the sciences, commerce, and literature were often pointed out in the Argentine press, and Protestant belief commonly was cited as a factor in Anglo material progress. The contrast between colonial powers seemed stark to Argentines: England left its American colony a heritage of self-sufficiency and prosperity, while Spain endowed its American colonies with internal dissension and a dependent economy. Women particularly focused on the roles of Anglo-American women, who enjoyed rights and freedoms unheard of in Spain. Catholic belief had the advantage of offering the semi-deity Mary as a female object of worship, and few *argentinas* were willing to give up the Marianic role of powerful, sanctified motherhood. However, other aspects of Protestant belief, such as its emphasis on individualism, seemed conducive to increased personal freedom to Argentine women. Moreover, Spanish values had come to be identified with the brutal dictator Rosas, who called himself "Restorer of the Laws"—Spanish law, that is, not the Enlightenment ideology of the War of Independence from Spain.[8] This preoccupation with the Anglo tradition signifies a radical critique of Argentine culture; its Spanish origins carry the fatal flaw of misogyny, and thus cannot be anything but "backward"—the ultimate insult in an age of progress.

Rejecting the nation's undeniably Hispanic past produced a dilemma for the writers of the Generation of 1880: how to eliminate the Spanish, Rosista elements of the past, while salvaging artifacts of progressive, European Liberalism? Women especially had difficulty with this strategy since evidence of Liberalism's benefits to women thus far was as scarce as in the Spanish tradition. Both traditions, as understood in Argentina, emphasized the necessity of keeping women in the home. The solution of women writers was to reinterpret evolutionary progress in terms of the polarity between Eve—symbolizing the Hispanic tradition of misogyny—and Mary, considered in light of Anglo-European models of ennobled, civic motherhood.

Barbarism's Mother-Slave versus Civilization's Lady Mother

An historical model of evolutionary progress implies movement from a state of past savagery, to a middle state of growing enlightenment (this stage is the "now" of evolutionary histories), to a future Golden Age of civilization. Dealing with women's remote past was relatively easy —most Argentines believed that one identifying characteristic of savagery was a family in which the mother did not have authority and thus could not practice the enlightened love of which she was uniquely capable. Lola Larrosa described this past state in an article that appeared on the front page of *La Prensa* in October of 1882:

> Entonces, la mujer, ese ángel custodio del hogar, no era reconocida como tal, sino que despreciada se le oprimía hasta el extremo de negarla los sagrados derechos que como madre tenía sobre sus hijos. . . . Bajo ese yugo, los sentimientos bellos y humanitarios de la mujer, habían llegado a degenerar de sus principios augustos, enmudeciendo su corazón y acallando la voz de su alma generosa. No existía la unión y el amor de la familia, por que había sido arrojada del seno de ella, el alma que le alentaba y daba vida.[9]

> [At that time, women, those angel keepers of the house, were not recognized as such, but instead scorned and oppressed to the extreme of denying them the sacred rights that as mothers they had over their children. (...) Under this yoke, the beautiful and humanitarian sentiments of women had degenerated from their august principles, numbing their hearts and silencing the voice of their generous souls. The unity and love of the family did not exist because it had been uprooted from their bosom, the soul that supported it and gave it life.]

The Marianic rhetoric of this quotation—women are "angel keepers of the house" with "sacred rights" over their children—casts this view of history in religious as well as temporal terms. The oppression of mothers, according to this viewpoint, is sinful, since it perverts their divinely created nature. Men are presented as the agents of this degradation of women because they were considered to have brutish sexual desires and to use force to keep women in submission, as Josefina Pelliza points out:

> El hombre primitivo, bajo el imperio de los sentidos, solo ve en ella, el *medio* de apagar sus instintos feroces. Es más salvaje que las fieras y hace de la mujer, la mitad bella y tímida de su propio ser, una injuria.[10]

[Primitive men, under the rule of their senses, only see in women the *means* to satisfy their ferocious instincts. They are more savage than wild animals and they insult women, the beautiful and timid half of their own being.]

Both Pelliza and Larrosa, the author of the previous quotation, express a dualistic concept of human nature, which, interestingly enough, was characteristic of conservative, anti-emancipationist writers. This view suggests that men are primarily physical and brutish in nature while women are spiritual and sentimental; thus, an ideal society would balance male and female forces in complementary—not equal—roles. Politics, for example, would be unsuitable for women because it was a male creation, far too grubby and brutal for women; on the other hand, childrearing was too noble an enterprise to be left in the hands of anyone but women. In the view of many women of the 1800s, the barbarism of the past came about because this complementary balance was disrupted, giving dominance to male forces. Thwarted in achieving her destiny as noble and respected nurturer, primitive woman became nothing more than a slavish childbearer, giving birth out of man's lust rather than any sentiment of love. Motherhood, which to nineteenth-century women was the triumph of feminine sentiment over masculine physicality, was degraded to little more than rape.

Most Argentines believed that women's salvation from this degraded state arrived in the form of Christianity, as Matilde Elena Wuili explains:

El paganismo degradó a la mujer; el Cristianismo debía rehabilitarla, colocarla en su verdadero puesto, darle un esposo—no un tirano—y constituirla en única y absoluta Señora del hogar.[11]

[Paganism degraded woman; Christianity properly rehabilitated her, placed her in her true role, gave her a husband—not a tyrant—and made her the sole and absolute ruling Lady of the house.]

The model for this Lady of the house was Mary, whose motherhood was powerful and divinely decreed. By giving birth to Jesus (neatly engendered through the spirit, not by ordinary sexual intercourse), Mary provided the savior for all humankind. Her reward for this crucial role was authority over the family and an egalitarian relationship with her husband. Mary's redemptive motherhood marks the end of the primitive era of Eve, whose motherhood signified sin and pain. Traditionally, Eve's fall provided patriarchal society with a justification for restricting women's freedom. Nineteenth-century ideas of progress, however, had the advantage of relegating Eve to the distant, primitive past, an era that the Generation of 1880 believed they had surpassed and abandoned. To women, Eve represented a primitive time when women's innate nobility was denied. This epoch, they believed, ended the day that Mary, the Lady Mother, gave birth. From that day onward, woman was restored to her true role: divine creator of life.

Once in her proper role, the Marianic lady mother organized the family in a way that permitted civilization to flourish:

> La cadena sagrada de la familia, destrozada por manos funestas, fue rehecha y la humanidad comenzó a elevarse sobre sus propios escombros. Y siguió avanzando la ola civilizadora, invadiéndolo todo, y las bárbaras costumbres de los remotos tiempos, iban desapareciendo ante los gigantescos esfuerzos de la nueva y venturosa época. . . . La mujer, vuelta al dominio del hogar, convirtió a este en un oásis de venturas y de delicias infinitas.[12]

> [The sacred ties of the family, destroyed by evil hands, were remade and humanity began to elevate itself above its own debris. And the civilizing wave kept advancing, invading everything, and the barbarous customs of remote times steadily disappeared in the face of the gigantic endeavors of the new and fortunate epoch. (...) Woman, restored to the dominion of the home, converted it into an oasis of infinite happiness and delight.]

During the time that women's complementary role had been overwhelmed by male forces, men had created a barbaric society, but the new civilization created by women through the "oasis" of their homes was one of "happiness and delight." This is a crucial point that both emancipationists and anti-emancipationists held in common: if women could not create homes modeled on that of the Lady Mother, then all society would suffer. Therefore, women must have adequate education to raise good child-citizens, they must have legal and economic rights to manage their household affairs independently, and they must receive proper respect in society for their nation-building role.

Throughout the nineteenth century in Argentina, there was widespread agreement that history had elevated the role of women from savagery to a noble, even divine place as the "angel in the house," the benevolent ruler of the family. Her role was critical in forming the Christian family, the building block of civilized society itself. Forces that thwarted her fulfillment of this destiny were, therefore, pagan, devolutionary, and destructive to society. Women authors, who considered themselves the inheritors of an ennobling and evolutionary history, frequently incorporated their awareness of being on an historical continuum into their writing. Like their male counterparts, women writers were fascinated by the concept of history and their own role in it; indeed, the nature of historical change itself became an obsession during the late 1800s in Argentina. Although they pinned their hopes on the future, the men and women of the Generation of 1880 examined their own and their country's past, searching for explanations for their current situation and evidence of the first signs of civilizing progress. They longed for more than a documentary past—they hoped to find a usable history.

A Foremother of Destiny: Lucía Miranda

Identifying anti-progressive forces in the present could be controversial, but by turning to the past, writers could take advantage of a group that both conservatives and liberals agreed was an obstacle to progress: the indigenous people. The campaigns of the 1880s effectively wiped out the native population of Argentina, allowing the writers of the time to feel that they were witnessing the end of a barbaric era. By linking the triumph of the European population to the progress of women, the authors reinforced both women's noble status and their importance in the national destiny. It is not surprising, therefore, that the second half of the 1800s saw a sudden proliferation of works dealing with the figure of Lucía Miranda.

The legend of Lucía Miranda was not new; it had been around since 1612, when it was published for the first time in the *La Argentina* by Ruy Díaz. He relates that in 1532 a Spanish woman, Lucía Miranda, comes to the New World with her husband, Sebastián Hurtado. Two Indian brothers, Mangoré and Siripo, see her and fall in love with her. Lucía, however, remains faithful to her husband. The Indians attack and overcome the Spanish garrison. Mangoré is killed in battle, Lucía and Sebastián are taken prisoner, and Siripo claims Lucía as his wife. Giving in to her pleas, he allows Sebastián to live, provided that he take an Indian wife. Lucía and Sebastián cannot hide their love for long, however, and they are denounced to Siripo. He orders a martyr's death for them both: Lucía to be burned to death and Sebastián shot with arrows. They both die calling on the mercy of God, and the story ends with the moral "es de creer que marido y mujer están gozando de su santa gloria"[13] [it is supposed that both husband and wife are enjoying their holy glory].

There is little reason to believe that the story of Lucía Miranda is factual. Efforts to find historical proof have failed,[14] and the story itself is suspiciously reminiscent of the saints' tales, which were so widely known on all levels of Hispanic society that they functioned as both secular and religious folklore. It cannot be accidental, for example, that Lucía is burnt after refusing sexual transgression, as was the saint of the same name. Similarly, the hero of the Miranda legend suffers the same fate as the Roman martyr St. Sebastian; gory statues of Sebastian are a common sight in Hispanic churches. Despite its fictional-folkloric nature, the story of Lucía Miranda so captured the attention of nineteenth-century writers that it repeatedly surfaced in popular works before disappearing again at the beginning of the twentieth century.[15] Three women writers explored the Miranda theme: Rosa Guerra in her novel *Lucía Miranda* (1860), Eduarda Mansilla de García in the novel *Lucía* (1860), and Celestina Funes in a long poem entitled *Lucía Miranda: episodio nacional* (1883). Guerra's version is the most sympathetic to the Indians, presenting Mangoré as a decent man misled by love. He is a noble, handsome man, and Lucía even feels tempted by him[16] and tells him as he dies that she would have married him if she had not already been married to Sebastián (62-63). Mansilla's version places Lucía in the context of a series of lovers whose happiness is tragically cut short; the episode in Argentina occupies only the final third of the novel. Mansilla, too, presents Mangoré (whom she calls Marangoré) as a noble savage whose good conduct toward the Spanish is corrupted by his desire for Lucía. Funes, on the other hand, portrays Mangoré as an unadulterated barbarian "extraño a la virtud"[17] [a stranger to virtue]. In all three versions, Lucía's death is a martyrdom, as inevitable as it is tragic.

What was it about the Lucía Miranda legend that captured the imagination of these writers? For one thing, it became popular simply because of lack of competition. Argentine history offers few woman-centered episodes suitable for literary exploitation, and if the episodes are further gleaned for those that feature a virtuous woman, then the number becomes small indeed. (Non-virtuous women seem to have led zestier lives and to have provided more fruitful material for storytelling). The need for female heroes can be seen in the many profiles of notable women of both past and present that became a staple of women's journalism after 1860. *El Album del Hogar*, for instance, ran a series called "Galería de mujeres célebres" [Gallery of Celebrated Women] in 1880. Mariano Pelliza, the brother of the writer Josefina Pelliza, was a prolific and pioneering writer of such sketches, several of which were collected and republished as early as 1879 in his *Críticas y bocetos históricos*.[18] Most of these profiles, though, were about foreign women or women who were noted for supporting their famous husbands. Among Argentine women, those who distinguished themselves during the War for Independence from Spain, would seem at first glance to be suitable subjects for historical novelization. There were drawbacks to such heroines, however. Some were still alive and thus not yet available for mythologizing. Many were from low socio-economic classes and from nonprestigious racial groups. Of greater importance, discussion of the Independence led naturally into the post-Independence Rosas era, which was and would be a bitter, disruptive topic for generations to come. Lucía Miranda, on the other hand, existed at a safe distance in the past, she was from the "correct" race and class, and she was virtuously married—altogether a safe, unproblematic hero.

Turning to the colonial past in search of foremothers drastically limited the choice of heroes. The European founding of Argentina was essentially a military enterprise; there were no female *conquistadoras* clad in armor and wielding swords. Indeed, few European women were involved in the Conquest at all. Unable to sacrifice a heroine on the field of battle, writers sacrificed her instead on the field of love, which was believed to be woman's sphere. Lucía, the civilized wife ennobled by Christianity, is prevented from establishing a family—and a colony—by barbaric forces. Thus, the conflict between Europeans and Americans was played out in sentimental terms rather than military ones, but the result was the same. The Indians were branded as savages incapable of respecting the nobility of white women, thus providing the justification for and necessity of genocide. Lucía sacrifices herself for marital fidelity, for "civilization" and "progress," as understood in the second half of the 1800s. The Indians, on the other hand, represent the pre-Christian barbarism that regarded women in purely sexual and procreative terms. Rosa Guerra treats this cultural disparity with Romantic fatalism in her version of the story. Eduarda Mansilla also focuses on fatalism, implying that Lucía's destiny is God's will. It is in the poem by Celestina Funes that the nationalistic overtones of the Miranda legend are most explicit; in this telling, the deaths of Lucía and Sebastián are "proof" that the Indians are not worthy of Christian civilization. In all three works, the authors present Lucía as an historical catalyst, since her Christian matrimonial love destabilizes relations between the Spanish and the Indians. Her death determines the national destiny; the Indians must disappear so that the Spanish can flourish.[19]

The Future: Civic Motherhood vs. Emancipation

While it was relatively easy to construct a model of the past that could be widely agreed on, the future was another matter. Many Argentines—mostly men, but many women too—believed that civic motherhood was women's true and *only* destiny. Thus, future evolutionary trends would be mere refinements of that already-existing state. This group saw some need for reforms such as wider access to basic education, giving legal custody of children to their mother rather than to their father, and opportunities for genteel employment among unmarried women. By genteel employment, they generally meant primary-school teaching. The new profession of nursing was still a bit dubious to be considered genteel, as it was thought to be too intimate and physical. Moreover, female employment was strictly for single or widowed women; married women's job was the family. To choose to marry served to significantly limit a woman's freedom; to choose not to marry placed her outside the social norm.

Not everyone saw women's evolutionary future in these terms, however. A growing number of women and some men believed that civic motherhood was flawed in its practice and that women's destiny could include more than just motherhood. Their beliefs came to be lumped under the word *emancipation*. Like the word *feminism* (which did not enter Argentine vocabulary until the 1890s), *emancipation* was sufficiently vague to include many programmatic issues and to incur many accusations and much opprobrium. Generally speaking, however, emancipation in the period 1870–1914 meant advocating these issues: changing married women's legal status from that of ward to adult, which would give married women the same right to manage their finances and to own property that single women and childless widows enjoyed; the right to pursue post-secondary education; and the right to earn a living by means of paid work both before and after marriage. Respectable emancipationist women did not mention the right to vote, in the early years at least, although there are hints that some secretly hoped for it. Until the turn of the century, suffrage remained a fringe issue suitable for radicals, the sort who might also advocate free love. Emancipation dove-tailed with other liberal causes of the time, such as secular education, civil marriage, and limited legal divorce. However, aspects of it were also in accord with anti-emancipationists who wished to bolster married women's status by giving them legal custody of their children. Both emancipationists and anti-emancipationists were concerned by increasingly visible prostitution, although they attributed it to different causes. The emancipationists usually traced its proliferation to women's economic distress, while anti-emancipationists typically considered it a moral failure.

Women's rights and women's emancipation were no minor issues in the second half of the 1800s. Newspapers and magazines frequently carried articles with titles like "The Emancipation of Women," "The Mission of Women," "Women's Education," and "Argentine Motherhood." The discussion was not entirely about women nor about the rights of individuals. At stake was the concept of national identity: many historians have pointed out that post-Independence political models in Latin America were simply the traditional, patriarchal family writ large.[20] To discuss changing the status of women was to propose fundamental alterations in society itself that potentially could unleash anarchy. It is no wonder that emancipationists were so cautious in their advocacy and anti-emancipationists so anxious in their opposition.

Among the many discussions of women's future was a debate in 1876 between two women writers, María Eugenia Echenique and Josefina Pelliza de Sagasta.[21] (Pelliza later engaged in the debate with Da Freito discussed in Chapter 2). It began with the publication of Echenique's essay "Pinceladas" [Brushstrokes] in the women's newspaper *La Ondina del Plata* on May 7, 1876. *La Ondina*, under the editorship of Luis Telmo Pintos, included literary works by the leading male and female writers of the day, but it also published, in almost every issue, discussions of women's roles in the new Argentina. Echenique had contributed several articles to the paper from her home in Córdoba. Some of her writings were literary in nature, but her growing reputation was based on her speculative essays, particularly the meditative series called *Cartas a Elena* [Letters to Elena], originally published in Córdoba in 1874 and reprinted by *La Ondina* in 1875. In *Cartas*, as in her other writings, Echenique shows herself to be a confirmed believer in an incipient Golden Age of progress, which she believed was attainable through a combination of scientific, economic, and social advances. In a telling phrase, she described the nineteenth century as the "siglo de las luces, de la libertad, de la emancipación de la mujer y de las grandes maravillas"[22] [century of enlightenment, liberty, the emancipation of women, and great marvels].[23] For Echenique, the emancipation of women seemed as astonishing as the century's scientific revolution; her view of the future included far-fetched wonders such as space travel[24] and women's financial self-sufficiency.[25]

This vision of a glorious future made Echenique strain against the material and intellectual restrictions on women of her time. In particular, she was deeply concerned with women's lack of economic autonomy, which she regarded as key to personal and social integrity. She was a pioneer advocate for women's role in the national economy, criticizing, for example, the government's policy of attracting male immigrant labor when native-born women were unemployed.[26] She was also suspicious of the sentimentalism that permeated women's existence, stating in "Pinceladas" that

> Nuestro corazón se rebela contra las ideas de espiritualidad, de sensibilidad, de poesía que cultivadas por la mujer han contribuido insensiblemente hasta el día, a su retraso en el camino del progreso y al mejoramiento de su condición.[27]

[Our heart rebels against the ideas of spirituality, sensibility, and poetry that, as cultivated by women, have callously contributed until now to women's delay on the road of progress and the improvement of their condition.]

After contrasting women's penchant for sentimentalism with men's striving for material wealth, Echenique then presents a manifesto of the duties that women writers owe to their female public. The manifesto is replete with the imagery of roads, paths, and currents that characterizes the rhetoric of progress:

Allanarle el camino de la civilización y de la cultura quitando los estorbos que se oponen al cumplimiento de los grandes pensamientos y de los deseos generosos que agitan el corazón de la mujer en el presente siglo, coadyuvando con nuestra pluma a la realización de sus más bellas esperanzas; enseñarla a sobreponerse a las preocupaciones que menoscaban sus derechos oponiéndose al torrente de las pasiones desarregladas que los destruyen; mostrarle la ruta que conduce a la felicidad en el cumplimiento de los deberes sacrosantos y el cultivo de las pasiones elevadas, infundiéndole el amor a las ciencias y a las artes, a la lectura y al trabajo; enseñarle, en fin, la manera de llenar sus necesidades físicas más habilmente según su rango en la sociedad.[28]

[To smooth the road of civilization and of culture, removing the barriers that oppose the achievement of the great thoughts and generous desires that stir women's hearts in the present century, contributing with our pen to the realization of their most beautiful hopes; to teach them to overcome the prejudices that diminish their rights, opposing the torrent of disorderly passions that destroy them; to show them the path that leads to happiness in the attainment of sacred duties and the cultivation of elevated passions, infusing in them love of the arts and sciences, of reading and working; in short, to teach them the way to care for their physical needs more skillfully according to their social standing.]

For Echenique, the proper elevated passions are "love of the arts and sciences, of reading and working," not Romantic sensibility, tears, and swoons. In this, as in her other essays, Echenique specifies that "this century" requires different behavior from women. Her program for the modern woman is infused with an urgent sense of historical change.

This essay caught the eye of Josefina Pelliza de Sagasta, a poet, novelist, and editor as well as a determined anti-emancipationist. She disagreed with Echenique's rejection of sentimentalism and advocacy of economic autonomy. In her reply to Echenique, Pelliza employed the imagery of sentimentalism common to late Romanticism in Latin America: women as flowers; men existing on a lower level, while women were on a superior one, seated on thrones, pedestals, and other objects signifying height; and weakness, even illness, as beauty. Her vision was ahistorical, with no mention of the word *century*, and static, with no images of motion such as roads or rivers. Moreover, while Echenique signed her own name, Pelliza used the pseudonym of Judith, the Biblical woman of seductive, deadly modesty. Pelliza rejected emancipation for its redefinition of women's strengths:

> La mujer enteramente libre, con tanta independencia como el hombre, perdería sus mayores encantos, y el prestigio poético de su debilidad; prestigio que forma el más bello atributo de su sexo—prestigio que más tarde cuando la mujer es madre la embellece doble y la coloca en el solio sagrado del hogar, que es donde mejor está colocada la mujer.[29]

> [Entirely free women, with as much independence as men, would lose their greatest charms and the poetic prestige of their weakness: the prestige that forms the most noble attribute of their sex, the prestige that later, when women are mothers, doubly beautifies them and places them on the sacred throne of the home, where women best belong.]

As for economic independence, Pelliza rejects that as well, saying that, just as women are born to love, men are born to protect and care for women; she compares woman to a vine that is supported by a trellis, that is, man.

Echenique's reply proclaims emancipation as the "consecuencia lógica de la altura de progreso a que ha llegado el mundo en el siglo XIX"[30] [logical consequence of the level of progress to which the world has arrived in the nineteenth century]. She also believes in an ideal, egalitarian love between men and women, but she brings up the case of the irresponsible husband who abandons his wife and children and gambles away the family's resources, leaving the children homeless and his wife vulnerable to vice as a means of support. Emancipation—that is, vocational education and the legal right to control her own earnings—would allow the wife to work to support her children honorably. As Echenique dryly points out, "Con el amor se puede enjugar las lágrimas y se endulzan las amarguras de la vida, pero no se puede satisfacer el hambre y ni cubrir la desnudez"[31] [Love can dry tears and sweeten the bitterness of life, but it cannot satisfy hunger nor cover nakedness].

Pelliza's reply brings up the vexed question of child care: if the mother is away working, who will take care of the children at home? Then she employs Echenique's economic analysis to criticize working women's household management:

> Se hace calculadora por economía, en tanto que en su casa se gasta doble;—todo es cubierto con dinero, hasta el alimento de sus hijos es comprado—¡¡Horror!![32]

[She becomes a calculator for business, in the meantime at home she spends double; everything is done with money, even the food for their children is bought—Horror!!]

For Pelliza, purchasing food in a restaurant and hiring someone to care for the household while the mother is away are not only expensive habits but also ones that deprive the family of the mother's special, divine influence. But Pelliza soon drops the practical arguments and returns to the spiritual ones, which she believes are more important. She is an extremist in maternity's defense; for example, she believes that any woman who prefers study to motherhood is unnatural and should be kept away from the company of other women. Too much education, in her opinion, makes women unfit for their divine mission as mothers and wives.

Both writers regard the question of women's rights as a patriotic, nationalistic issue. Echenique borrows Pelliza's phrase "women's mission" to state her view that the mission is more than motherhood per se:

Yo renunciaría y renegaría de mi sexo si la misión de la mujer se redujese solo a la procreación, sí, renunciaría; pero la misión de la mujer en el mundo, es mucho más grandiosa y sublime, es más que la del bruto, es la de enseñar al género humano, y para *enseñar* es preciso *saber*.[33]

[I would renounce and disown my sex if the mission of women were reduced only to procreation, yes, I would renounce it; but the mission of women in the world is much more grandiose and sublime, it is more than the beasts', it is the one of teaching humankind, and in order to *teach* it is necessary to *know*.]

Here Echenique is drawing on the widely held belief that women were innately superior in morality and spiritual sensitivity, and she projects from it the need for civic motherhood, that is, an educated mother who passes on her enlightened values and knowledge to her children, thus improving the national character. Pelliza shares Echenique's belief that superior motherhood is a patriotic matter as well as a personal one: "a pesar de ser abolicionista de la emancipación quiero a la mujer fuerte y atrevida en sus empresas admisibles, en sus arranques de heroismo, capaz de ser esposa, de ser madre, y de ser patriota"[34] [in spite of being anti-emancipationist, I want women to be strong and daring in their admissible ventures, in their outbursts of heroism, in their capacity to be wife, mother, and patriot]. However, she is fearful of the consequences of too much education; she especially opposes education in the sciences, which Echenique passionately advocates, because of scientific conflict with religion. For Pelliza, undoubting female religious faith is essential to the national well-being:

> en lugar de pensar con Vd. que las ciencias sostienen y cimentan los principios, alejándonos de los sofismas engañosos, creo por el contrario que ellas nos acercan aún más a las dudas infinitas, nos hacen vacilar y si algo bueno encuentro a esos profundos estudios para que en ellos se interese la mujer sudamericana es solamente, que las ideas se despiertan, vacilan las viejas creencias, y cae derribado el ídolo del fanatismo religioso; la fe! quizá vacila también—las ciencias por cualquiera faz que se profundicen minan las creencias e introducen la duda.[35]

> [instead of thinking as you do that the sciences sustain and uphold principles, keeping us from deceitful sophisms, I believe to the contrary that they bring us more to infinite doubts, they make us vacillate, and if I find something good in those deep studies that a South American woman should interest herself in, it is only that ideas awaken, shake old beliefs, and fell the idol of religious fanaticism. Faith perhaps wavers as well! The sciences, under whatever mask, dig deep to undermine beliefs and introduce doubt.]

It is unusual for Pelliza to use the phrase "a South American woman" rather than "an Argentine woman" or simply "a woman"; the unspoken opposite is "North American woman" and the Anglo, Protestant cultural tradition that Pelliza considered alien to Argentina. While Echenique praises the freedoms granted to North American women, Pelliza regards North American women as cold and ridiculous and then quotes the Spanish writer, María del Pilar Sinués de Marco, to support her position.

This point may seem minor to North American readers, but it was not to Echenique. In general, she had kept her participation in the debate on a lofty, theoretical tone, avoiding *ad feminum* remarks and unlady-like sarcasms. Pelliza's remarks, however, sparked an angry response that invoked the martyrdom of those who opposed the anti-Enlightenment, pro-Hispanic dictator Juan Manuel Rosas:

> Es preciso no conocer la historia de nuestro país, o haber olvidado la sangre de la gente ilustrada que a torrentes han derramado en nuestro bello suelo los vandálicos cuadillos hijos de la *ignorancia* que, teniendo su cuna en la naturaleza bruta, han carecido de una madre instruida en *las ciencias sociales* que les hiciesen comprender las teorías de Rivadavia y las grandes aspiraciones de aquellos a quienes degollaban como a corderos, para oponerse al cultivo de las ciencias en la mujer.[36]

> [To oppose the cultivation of the sciences by women, it is necessary not to know the history of our country—or to have forgotten the blood of enlightened people spilled in torrents on our beautiful soil by barbaric tyrants, sons of *ignorance* who, having their cradle in brute

nature, lacked a mother educated in the *social sciences* that would make them understand the theories of Rivadavia which were the great aspirations of those who were slaughtered like lambs.]

To imply a comparison of Pelliza with the much-reviled mother of Rosas was a nasty cut, especially since Pelliza's family had opposed Rosas. Pelliza herself was born under a wagon during her parents' move to Entrerrios to distance themselves from the dictator. Now the debate had been stripped bare. The declarations of respect and friendship may have been genuine, but Echenique and Pelliza held utterly different views of women's future and consequently of the future of Argentina.

In truth, the two writers did not share enough philosophical premises to communicate well with each other, and although the debate continued from May through October of 1876, they always spoke at cross purposes. Echenique's view of historical evolution, which led her to believe in the need for women's economic independence as a guard against abuse, made little sense to Pelliza, who believed in an unchanging, ahistorical femininity that would command men's fidelity and protection. Echenique was a fervent believer in the sciences as the ultimate proof of religion and a source of power for women. Pelliza, on the other hand, was disturbed by scientific challenges to Christian belief and traditional nationalism. Echenique believed that the egalitarian love component of emancipation would strengthen the family; whereas Pelliza believed that it would destroy the family altogether. They agreed on few issues aside from woman's innate superiority and her importance in raising good citizens.

The debate had a rather poignant postscript. Echenique became ill soon after its end and died in early 1878 at the age of twenty-seven. Pelliza wrote a tender and generous obituary in her honor. By 1885, when she published her book *Conferencias*, Pelliza had come to share Echenique's evolutionary concept of women's history and had adopted many of her economic ideas. Pelliza, too, died young at age forty; she saw her own death in a dream and wrote a poem about it a few days before she succumbed to kidney failure.

Eduarda Mansilla's Dream of the Future

The debate between Echenique and Pelliza is just part of the background of speculation about women's future that forms the context for works such as Eduarda Mansilla's short story "El ramito de romero" [The Sprig of Rosemary] (1883). Like Echenique, Mansilla foresaw future advances for women and was impatient with those who tried to deny an intellectual life to women. But, like Pelliza, she feared many of the changes she foresaw, and "El ramito" reflects her ambivalence.

The story's main character is Raimundo, a medical student. As the tale opens, he is a stereotypical Positivist and utilitarian who views women as barely human:

> Ya conoces tú mi opinión sobre la mujer, o sea el elemento femenino en la creación; contribuir al desarrollo vital y nada más; lo contrario no es sino sentimentalismo enfermizo que pasará.[37]
>
> [You already know my opinion of women, that is, the feminine element in creation; they contribute to life's continuation and nothing more; contrary opinions are nothing more than morbid sentimentalism that will pass away.]

Strolling to the medical school, Raimundo's thoughts on the triumph of materialism over the soul are interrupted by the memory of his encounter with his cousin Luisa. Raimundo is fond of Luisa, although he thinks she is ridiculous and particularly comic when she is serious or admonishing. He likes her best when she is deferent: "nada hay que me encante como esa timidez respetuosa de la mujer, en presencia del hombre, homenaje tácito del débil ante el fuerte." (64) [nothing so charms me like that respectful timidity in a woman in the presence of a man, tacit homage of the weak before the strong]. When they meet, Luisa insists on giving Raimundo a sprig of rosemary—symbol of remembrance—which he sticks in his jacket pocket.

Once at the medical school, Raimundo is intrigued, then obsessed, by the cadaver of a beautiful woman. He lifts her arm to kiss it, and the dead woman embraces him and whispers enticements to join her in the realm of the dead. He must leave behind his soul, which she knows he is not especially interested in, and, by the way, he does not need that sprig of rosemary either. But Raimundo refuses to give it up, even though its presence prevents his soul from leaving him altogether and thus clouds his vision of the other world. In spite of his refusal to give up the rosemary, Raimundo's cadaverous temptress shows him the souls of deceased loved ones as well as those of famous men such as Aristotle. Then she shows him the history of existence, a vision that needs to be quoted at length in order to grasp its complexity:

> [V]eíase allí . . . el camino de la humanidad, en espirales ascendentes, obedeciendo a leyes tan inmutables, como lo son las de atracción y gravitación en el mundo físico, retrocediendo en apariencia durante siglos, pero avanzando siempre. Vi la ley del progreso humano, reducida a ecuación algebráica, vi el surco que dejaron tras de sí los pueblos esclavos, desde el origen del mundo conocido, marchando cual rebaño de ovejas al matadero sin murmurar ni esperar. Vi el despotismo,

triunfante un día, convertirse luego bajo otra forma, en otro despotismo. Vi las santas aspiraciones de los creyentes, naufragar en mares de sangre y lágrimas, vi aparecer la era de la fraternidad, esa igualdad combatidas, sofocadas por aquellos mismos a quienes incumbía la misión de redimir. Vi a los enviados de paz y humildad, pactar con los soberbios poderosos, para oprimir al desvalido y quitarle hasta la esperanza, invocando una doctrina santa. Vi la incredulidad y el ateismo triunfantes olvidarlo todo, para no acariciar otra idea, otra esperanza, que el amor al dinero; vi la destrucción de la familia, tal cual hoy la conocemos; vi surgir nuevas leyes, nuevos derechos, y como el tiempo no existía para mí, vi la llegada triunfante de la humanidad a una zona luminosa y armónica, y la visión cambió. (75-76)

[I saw there (...) the path of humanity in ascending spirals, obeying laws as immutable as are magnetism and gravity in the physical world, apparently regressing during some centuries but always advancing. I saw the law of human progress reduced to an algebraic equation, I saw the furrow left behind by enslaved peoples from the beginning of the known world, marching like a flock of sheep to the slaughter house without protest or hope. I saw despotism, once triumphant, change later into another despotism in another form. I saw the holy aspirations of believers shipwreck in seas of blood and tears, I saw appear the era of fraternity and equality, embattled, suffocated by precisely those whose mission should have been redemption. I saw the envoys of peace and humility make pacts with the arrogant powers in order to oppress the helpless and take from them even their hope, invoking a holy doctrine. I saw triumphant skepticism and atheism forget everything so as to embrace no other idea, no other hope, than the love of money; I saw the destruction of the family as we know it; I saw new laws, new rights, and since time did not exist for me, I saw the triumphant arrival of humanity at a shining and harmonious region, and then the vision changed.]

Until the last lines, this vision seems like a description of history as understood by the Generation of 1880. That is, it includes a barbaric past, crushed efforts to throw off enslavement, the dominance of materialism and male forces, and finally, the triumph of humanity. The ambiguity of the last lines results from not knowing where Mansilla is inserting the present, that is, 1883. Did she view her era as the triumph of skepticism, atheism, and materialism? If so, she also was predicting the destruction of the traditional family, a bold prophecy indeed for the niece of the ultra-conservative Rosas. In any case, the shining future seemed very far away for Mansilla, since Raimundo requires the suspension of time and the loss of his soul to see it at all. The very distance of the future harmony casts a pessimistic pall over the prospects of the present and near future. Mansilla, like most of the women writers of the 1800s, was a member of the privileged classes. She was a beneficiary of the traditional, patriarchal way of life, yet she personally knew its limitations and exclusions for women. In Raimundo's dream, Mansilla is able to describe the past's abuses, but her fears about the inevitable future are evident in her inability to describe the Golden Age beyond a mere two adjectives: shining and harmonious. Women's future, for Mansilla, was glorious but troublingly unknown.

When Raimundo finally awakens from his vision, he realizes that it was a delirium induced by illness. He credits Luisa, who nursed him through the illness, for the talisman of rosemary that saved his life, and he claims to be a new man who recognizes the superhuman strength of good women who nurture their loved ones. As proof of his new attitude toward women, he marries Luisa in a happy, non-Positivist ending. All the men at the wedding wear rosemary in their lapels.

In one sense, "El ramito de romero" is a conventional story of the 1880s in Argentina, with the stock figure of the medical man who gets his "comeuppance" by being forced to admit the supremacy of the soul over the material world.[38] Eduardo Wilde's works, for example, often deal with this idea. It is also typical in that a woman's love conquers all. For Mansilla as for Echenique and Pelliza, women's innate superiority was unquestionably greater than men's physical strength or intellectual education. She would have understood what the feminist Elia Martínez meant by advocating intellectual and economic equity for women but refusing suffrage because women's scope of action should be "más amplia y más grande"[39] [wider and greater]. Yet if women's supreme virtue of moral superiority was already a fact in 1883, where was the "law of human progress" taking women? Echenique could envision travelling to other planets; Mansilla could only see a harmonious light.

World War I and the Failure of Progress

The arrival of World War I effectively ended the belief in inevitable progress. The cynical reasons for declaring war and the horrifying numbers of men slain for no appreciable gain or loss of territory led to a world-wide questioning of nineteenth-century optimism. Was progress nothing more than a series of innovations in the technology of slaughter?

Argentines, though not directly involved in the fighting, took a personal interest in the war. The ruling class had imitated France and England, from importing French architects to design the new center of Buenos Aires, to having tea at four o'clock, to adopting French as a first language (for example, the founder of *Sur* magazine, Victoria Ocampo, had to struggle to express herself in Spanish when she began to write professionally). Wealthy Argentines often lived in Paris for years at a time, and made a point of reading Parisian journals when at home in Buenos Aires. Working-class Argentines, on the other hand, felt intimate ties to Italy and Russia; the workers' revolts and anarchist terrorism there attracted considerable sympathy in Argentina.

The nineteenth-century women writers who were still living in the war years—that is, Elvira Aldao, Emma de la Barra, and Silvia Fernández—turned to military themes in their writings. Barra worked as a popular journalist in Europe reporting to Argentines the news of the war, diplomatic maneuvers, and homefront privations. Aldao also spent most of the war in Europe, an experience that inspired her first efforts at publication. Fernández kept up with the news from her home near Buenos Aires, where she nonetheless recognized the apocalyptic nature of the war. By 1915, she was already writing poems imploring the Virgin Mary and Jesus to bring peace. Putting her trust in women's superiority, Fernández asks Mary to use her maternal powers to save her "children":

> ¡Oh, María! ruega, ruega, ¿cómo no has de ser oída?
> ¡Salva a Europa con tus ruegos de ese horrible cautiverio!
> No demores, que mañana la hallarías convertida,
> No ya en campo de batalla, sino en mudo cementerio![40]

> [Oh, Mary! pray, pray, how could you not be heard?/ Save Europe with your prayers from that horrible captivity!/ Don't wait or tomorrow you will find it changed/ From battlefield into silent cemetery!]

But the end of the war was brought about by exhaustion rather than by women's intervention. The innate spiritual superiority of women, even that of Mary herself, could not prevent war's horrors.

The intellectual revolt that followed the war served to discredit faith in inevitable progress. Technological innovations, such as the electric illumination that had captured the imagination of the women writers of the 1800s, became ordinary, but also tainted by military applications. Twentieth-century writers could no longer call their era—without irony —the "century of liberty, progress, glory, and electricity," as Elia Martínez had said of the nineteenth century. Yet, writers such as Martínez were able to accomplish a great deal through their evolutionary view of history: a powerful defense of motherhood, the linking of women's status with national progress, the insertion of women's issues into intellectual debates, and insistence on greater legal and economic rights. The 1900s brought new rhetorical systems and different views of history, but the 1800s contributed a historical legacy in which women took great steps toward progress.

Endnotes

[1] Hugo Biagini is the principal historian of the idea of progress in Argentina. See, for example, his "El progresismo argentino del Ochenta," *Inter-American Review of Bibliography* 28 (1978): 373-84; and *Cómo fue la generación del 80* (Buenos Aires: Plus Ultra, 1980). Also see Marcelo Montserrat's "La mentalidad evolucionista: una ideología del progreso," *La Argentina del Ochenta al Centenario*, Gustavo Ferrari and Ezequiel Gallo, eds. (Buenos Aires: Sudamericana, 1980), 785-818. Progressism outside Argentina is studied in, for example, W. Warren Wagar, *Good Tidings: The Belief in Progress from Darwin to Marcuse* (Bloomington: Indiana University Press, 1972) and R. Nisbet, *History of the Idea of Progress* (New York: Basic Books, 1980).

[2] Elia M. Martínez, "Reminiscencias patrióticas," *El Búcaro Americano* (15 May 1897): 217.

[3] For further discussion of material progress during this period, see James R. Scobie, *Buenos Aires: Plaza to Suburb, 1870–1910* (New York: Oxford University Press, 1974).

[4] Raymunda Torres y Quiroga, "Progreso," *La Ondina del Plata* (15 October 1876): 497-98. Also see her "La mujer y la sociedad," *La Ondina del Plata* (26 March 1876): 147-49, especially the opening section in which she calls progress "a second Nature."

[5] Eva Angelina [Zoila Aurora Cáceres], "La emancipación de la mujer," *El Búcaro Americano* (1 June 1896): 130.

[6] Zoraida [Eufrasia Cabral], "Jorge Sand," *La Alborada del Plata* (1 March 1878): 117.

[7] Agar Willianson, "La emancipación de la mujer," *La Alborada del Plata* (25 April 1880): 115.

[8] David William Foster, *The Argentine Generation of 1880: Ideology and Cultural Texts* (Columbia: University of Missouri Press, 1990), 2-4, 7-8, 68-84.

[9] Lola Larrosa de Ansaldo, "La mision de la muger," *La Prensa* (21 October 1882): 1.

[10] Josefina Pelliza de Sagasta, *Conferencias: El libro de las madres* (Buenos Aires: Jeneral Lavalle, 1885), 15. See Da Freito's version of this same evolutionary state in his debate with Pelliza: "La mujer en la naturaleza y la civilización," *El Album del Hogar* (8 December 1878): 177-78.

[11] Matilde Elena Wuili, "La gran causa del bello sexo: educación de la mujer," *El Album del Hogar* (23 March 1879): 301. Josefina Pelliza, ever the unconventional, did point out, though, that "Si bien es cierto que el cristianismo salva a la mujer, también es cierto que la deja igualmente sujeta a la voluntad del marido" [While it is true that Christianity saves women, it is

also true that it leaves them equally subject to the will of their husbands]. *Conferencias*, 29.

[12] Lola Larrosa, "La misión de la muger," 1.

[13] Ruy Díaz de Guzmán, *La Argentina* (Buenos Aires: Espasa-Calpe, 1945), 61.

[14] Martiniano Leguizamón, "La leyenda de Lucía de Miranda," *Revista de la Universidad de Córdoba* 6 (1919): 3-11. Concha Meléndez reviews his arguments in her "La leyenda de Lucía de Miranda en la novela," *La novela indianista en Hispanoamérica* in *Obras completas*, 2 vols. (San Juan, Puerto Rico: Instituto de Cultura Puertorriqueña, 1970) 1: 169-77.

[15] For discussion of the various authors who have explored the Miranda legend, see Myron L. Lichtblau, "El tema de Lucía Miranda en la novela argentina," *Armas y Letras* 2 (January/March 1959): 23-31; and Concha Meléndez, "La leyenda de Lucía de Miranda en la novela."

[16] Rosa Guerra, *Lucía Miranda* (Buenos Aires: EUDEBA, 1956), 42.

[17] Celestina Funes, *Lucía Miranda: episodio nacional* (Rosario: Imprenta El Mensajero, 1883), 14.

[18] Mariano Pelliza, *Críticas y bocetos históricos* (Buenos Aires: Imprenta del Mayo, 1879). This collection includes articles on Harriet Beecher Stowe, Juana Manso, and Juana Manuela Gorriti, as well as a series on women in the Argentine War of Independence. Pelliza was a serious historian whose works on women represent a pioneering attempt at writing women's history. His comments may seem patronizing to today's readers, but, for his own time, they were quite enlightened.

[19] For further discussion of the linking of women's sexual danger with calls for genocide of the Indians, see Bonnie Frederick, "Reading the Warning: The Reader and the Image of the Captive Woman," *Chasqui* (18 November 1989): 3-11. For a complementary reading of the Lucía Miranda story that emphasizes its linguistic aspects, see Francine Masiello, *Between Civilization & Barbarism* (Lincoln: University of Nebraska, 1992), 36-43.

[20] Francine Masiello offers a useful summary and analysis of this model in her *Between Civilization & Barbarism*, 17-20.

[21] For the text of this debate, translated into English, see The Palouse Translation Project, "The Emancipation of Women: Argentina 1876," *Journal of Women's History* 7 (Fall 1995): 102–26.

[22] María Eugenia Echenique, "Carta IX (en una quebrada)," *La Ondina del Plata* (14 November 1875): 487.

[23] "Las luces" in Spanish means both "enlightenment" and literally "lights." This was a common nineteenth-century pun that reveals that gas and electrical lights were interpreted as more than material advances.

[24] Echenique, "Carta VII (en la cima de una colina)," *La Ondina del Plata* (31 October 1875): 463.

[25] Echenique "Carta IX," 487.

[26] Echenique, "Necesidades de la mujer argentina," *La Ondina del Plata* (16 January 1876): 26.

[27] Echenique, "Pinceladas," *La Ondina del Plata* (7 May 1876): 217.

[28] Ibid., 218.

[29] Judith [Josefina Pelliza de Sagasta], "La mujer," *La Ondina del Plata* (4 June 1876): 267.

[30] Echenique, "La emancipación de la mujer," *La Ondina del Plata* (2 July 1876): 319.

[31] Ibid.

[32] Judith, "Emancipación de la mujer," *La Ondina del Plata* (23 July 1876): 351.

[33] Echenique, "La emancipación de la mujer," *La Ondina del Plata* (13 August 1876): 387.

[34] Josefina Pelliza de Sagasta, "La emancipación de la mujer," *La Ondina del Plata* (10 September 1876): 436.

[35] Ibid.

[36] Echenique, "La emancipación de la mujer," *La Ondina del Plata* (8 October 1876): 482.

[37] Eduarda Mansilla de García, "El ramito de romero," *Creaciones* (Buenos Aires: Juan A. Alsina, 1883), 64. Further references to this story are included in the text.

[38] For further discussion of the ambiguity of the scientist in Ochenta literature, see Bonnie Frederick, "A State of Conviction, A State of Feeling: Scientific and Literary Discourses in the Works of Three Argentine Writers, 1879–1908," *Latin American Literary Review* 9 (July–December 1991): 48-61.

[39] Elia M. Martínez, "Evolución femenina," *El Búcaro Americano* (15 February 1897): 170.

[40] Silvia Fernández, "En el mes de María de 1916," *Versos* (Buenos Aires: Bayardo, 1922), 26.

4

The Cliche of Love: Desires, Exasperations, and Better Things to Do

A cliché of nineteenth-century literature is that women wrote love stories with happy endings, while men wrote unhappy ones. The cliché is often inaccurate, but it does point out two important truths: that both men and women usually chose the love plot over other narrative possibilities, and that they used it for different purposes. Argentine women of the 1800s believed that their sex was "born to love," and thus it is not surprising that nearly all of them wrote about romance. Yet women's happy endings do not necessarily mean that they wrote happy stories. Love may have been women's highest calling, but it also led them into a world of threatening men, sexual and economic vulnerability, and few recourses for resistance. Without education, legal rights, or economic autonomy, a woman in love was a woman in danger.

As Rachel Blau DuPlessis observes, "the romance plot is a trope for the sex-gender system as a whole,"[1] and that is certainly true for nineteenth-century Argentine society and literature. Just as Argentine society offered few roles for women besides those of wife and mother, so too its literature turned out variations on the romance plot in the absence of other imaginative possibilities. The precise nature of the sex-gender system is reflected in the recurring marriage plot: the heroine's energies are focused on selection of the appropriate marital mate; she must overcome a series of obstacles that lead not to self-realization, but to marriage and child-bearing; and thus she fulfills her biological role in the perpetuation of traditional society. A variation on this idea is the post-marriage plot: the heroine must defend her happy marriage from destructive seductions (by a man bent on adultery or by the hedonism of high society). If successful, she is rewarded by having children. Yet another variation on the married heroine is the widow's plot: after the death of her beloved husband, the widow must struggle to maintain her respectability against cruel odds. If she is successful, she is rewarded by having her children well cared for. In all these versions, the female main character is defined by her relationship with men and children. Her own development is of interest only insofar as it facilitates her participation in the socially desirable unit of father-mother-child.

As Doris Sommer aptly points out, the romance plot is not just about love:

> Romantic novels go hand in hand with patriotic history in Latin America. The books fueled a desire for domestic happiness that runs over into dreams of national prosperity; and nation-building projects invested private passions with public purpose.[2]

As the heroines of women's fiction in nineteenth-century Argentina struggle to obtain and protect their marriages, they also reveal the disquiet that women had about their national as well as personal roles. The patriarchal family was the most common metaphor for the state in Argentina during the 1800s: the father represented the leadership of the nation, the children represented its future, and the mother was the link who both produced the children and passed along the father's values to them. Wedding "private passions" to "public purpose" can clearly be seen in virtually all the works women wrote. Yet, the patriarchy typically projected from male writers' love plots is routinely critiqued in women's plots; indeed, the most common villain is a father figure.

The Marriage Plot in *Margarita* and *Stella*

In novels such as *Margarita* and *Stella*, the marriage plot is in full view. Each chapter brings a new obstacle to the modest maiden and her noble admirer, yet eventually good love (self-sacrificing, companionate, respectable) triumphs over parallel possibilities of bad love (narcissistic, unequal, violent, illicit). Beneath the soap opera machinery of the plot lies the insistence that women have the right to exercise their will, retain their dignity, and enter into marriage on their own terms.

Josefina Pelliza de Sagasta's *Margarita* (1875) was popular enough that the first edition sold out immediately, and it is not hard to see why.

Free from any post-Freudian self-consciousness, Pelliza wrote a sensationalist plot that has everything: threatened incest, a lover's midnight visits, kidnapping, murder, and more. Margarita, the beautiful heroine, lives in her own garden-tower dwelling, which she has decorated with refined luxury paid for by her loathsome father, Luis. She has always felt that Luis could not be her true father, and one night, she overhears a conversation confirming her intuition. Luis tells her that she will be his lover, but Margarita, appalled at the quasi-incest, remains true to her own choice, Plácido, the dashing lover who visits her at midnight in her tower. To Plácido, Margarita offers up no "resistencia ridícula"[3] [ridiculous resistance], and soon she is pregnant. Plácido must leave for Santiago to attend his dying father; Margarita refuses to marry him and accompany him until she knows her true name. She believes that a religious marriage is an "estúpida forma social" (47) [stupid social formula], not good enough for their divine love. As tokens of their affection, Margarita gives Plácido a ring, and he puts a golden chain, with a pendant portrait of himself, around her neck.

After Plácido leaves, Margarita gives birth to a child, whom she also names Plácido. Spurned and angry, Luis threatens her again, and she leaves, renting a small house and earning her living as an embroiderer. Luis hires Jacobo to kidnap the child and kill him, but Jacobo takes pity and gives the baby to his wife instead. Margarita, in despair, temporarily loses her sanity. When she recovers, she becomes a sister of charity, adopting the name Providencia for her nursing duties. Meanwhile, Plácido returns; Luis has been intercepting his letters, and sends assassins to kill Plácido. The intended victim, however, shoots Luis before being stabbed himself by the thugs. At the hospital, Margarita and Plácido are reunited. One of the patients is a servant of Margarita's true parents, Augusto and Andrea, and he reunites her with them. Meanwhile, Augusto and Andrea have adopted Margarita's lost son. Luis finally dies, revealing that he had sought revenge on Margarita's grandfather, who had been the lover of Luis' wife. Andrea was the child of their adultery. At last, Margarita and Plácido are married, not by a priest, but by Augusto, Margarita's true father.

The curious aspects of *Margarita* are its willful, sexy heroine and its disdain for institutional religion. The unembarrassed sexual aspects of the novel are highly unusual, although not unexpected by those who know Pelliza's passionate defense of motherhood in her many journalistic essays. Margarita is described as "ardent" on several occasions, while her best friend, Teresa, is said to be destined to love "sin deseo, sin ardor, con un amor purísimo, enteramente espiritual" (74) [without desire, without ardor, with the purest love, entirely spiritual]. Not surprisingly, Teresa and her husband never have children. In her news-paper essays, Pelliza had virulently attacked nuns and feminists because they did not pursue motherhood as a primary destiny.[4] She herself was pregnant when she wrote *Margarita*. Margarita's passion is approved in the novel, because it leads to motherhood, which is portrayed as a higher calling than mere obedience to religious strictures. Religious rites are presented as nothing more than submission to human rules, not divine ones. Margarita argues that God has already joined her with Plácido, and that a wedding ceremony is to satisfy an "irrisoria imposi-ción de los hombres" (47) [absurd man-made burden]. Throughout the novel, Margarita is an active character, neither passive nor pliable. By the end, she has achieved her goals on her own terms: marriage and motherhood, unsanctioned by male-created institutions. She defies the patriarchy repeatedly, from rejecting her "father" to ignoring the very male Church. Her triumphs are matriarchal: earning a living by embroi-dery and raising a child without male interference. The child, who shares his father's name, seems to be a satisfactory substitute for him as well. Plácido, the father, is a minor character in the novel; his appearance at the beginning and the end form a frame for the real action that centers entirely on Margarita.

Just as Margarita must find her own way in the absence of a good, true father and the presence of a bad, false one, Alejandra, the main character of Emma de la Barra's novel *Stella* (1906), must establish a life for herself after the death of her enlightened father. She moves in with her uncle's family, who provide the surrogate patriarchy. But just as Margarita's false father perverts his role, Alejandra's uncle fails to carry it out, due to his weak character. Máximo, Alejandra's love interest, has also abdicated his patriarchal role. Only Alejandra's re-demptive love can effect his restoration to his proper status as husband to Alejandra and politician to the nation:

> Su país es joven, rico, inteligente, pero marcha como una grandiosa nave que navegara en alta mar sin jefes y sin guías. Sea una de ellos, Máximo. . . . Ese gesto de desdén que veo imprimirse en su cara, debe desaparecer, sí, desaparecer ante todo. . . . ¿No sabe, viejo tío—agregó despojándose un momento de su gravedad y sonriéndole mimosa, —que me he propuesto derrotar su pesimismo? Mi corazón tenaz tiene su táctica y tiene su estrategia.[5]

> ["Your country is young, rich, intelligent, but it moves like a great ship that navigates in high seas without leaders and without guides. Be one of them, Máximo. (...) That expression of disdain that I see stamped on your face, should vanish, yes, vanish first of all. (...) Don't you know, dear uncle," she added, relinquishing for a moment her gravity and

smiling at him indulgently, "that I have decided to defeat your pessimism? My tenacious heart has its tactics and it has its strategy."]

On hearing Alejandra's flirtatious exhortation, Máximo "sintió un sacudimiento en el corazón" (223) [felt a tug at his heart] and begins to feel love rather than friendship for Alejandra. Until he gains the will to "father" the nation, Máximo is equally unable to be father to the children he and Alejandra are destined to have.

Stella neatly fits Sommer's paradigm of linking romance with nation-building. However, it also echoes women writers' concerns about the failures of patriarchy that leave women vulnerable to poverty, improper sex, and childlessness. Both Margarita and Alejandra are forced to be strong, active characters because their lovers are not.

Lola Larrosa's Novels of Poverty and Romance

Few writers in nineteenth-century Argentina explored the connections between women and poverty the way Lola Larrosa did, although even she shied away from the implications of her own works. Larrosa was a staunch advocate of the patriarchal family; she firmly believed that the husband should earn the living for the family, and that the wife should remain at home, caring for the children. Therefore, it is sadly ironic that she was forced to work to support her young son and mentally ill husband. The failure of her husband to fulfill his role is reflected in the absent, weak, or dead father figures in her writings. The paternal failures leave the female characters vulnerable, especially to the threat of poverty. Unlike Pelliza's and Barra's heroines, Larrosa's are unable to fend for themselves due to their lack of education and marketable skills.

Liceta, the lead character in Larrosa's *Los esposos* [Husband and Wife] (1895), lives with her husband Henry Silver near the mill where he works. The owner of the mill, Manuel Nélter, is a don juan who casts his eye on Liceta; she tries to avoid him and to keep her husband from knowing about Manuel's pursuit. Carlos and Blanca, friends of Henry and Liceta, live nearby. Blanca was raised by her uncle after her mother's death, thus she was deprived of the womanly kind of upbringing. Worse, her uncle allowed her to read romantic novels. The narrator disapproves of the sentimental portrayal of marriage in such novels, in which the spousal relationship is more important than that of parent and child:

> En el matrimonio deben desaparecer las seductoras nimiedades y futilezas del amor, para dar paso a las serias dedicaciones de la vida de la familia. Pero no por eso desaparece el cariño. Por el contrario, éste se ahonda más y más, echando raíces profundas, que la mutua estima-

ción se encarga de cultivar, formando así el árbol de la existencia, que da por frutos los hijos, que son la savia de la vida de los padres.[6]

[In marriage, the seductive trifles and futilities of love should disappear, to give way to the serious devotions of the family. But this doesn't mean that affection disappears. On the contrary, it becomes deeper and deeper, sending out deep roots, that mutual esteem is responsible for cultivating, thus forming the tree of existence, that bears the fruit of children, who are the sap for the life of the parents.]

This agricultural/genealogical metaphor fails to convince Blanca, who is bored with marriage and has become involved with the playboy Jorge Vallier. Liceta implores her to break up with Jorge and be happy with Carlos. Blanca, however, leaves Carlos, who dies of sorrow.

One afternoon, as Liceta embroiders by the window, Manuel makes his play. First, he flatters, then he reminds Liceta of the benefits of his patronage, then he accuses Henry of being unfaithful—but Liceta stands fast. The vengeful Manuel fires Henry, saying that he has had some business setbacks, but if a certain pending negotiation comes through, then Henry can not only have a job again, he can be a manager. Manuel tells Henry to be sure that Liceta knows this news. Liceta understands what the negotiation is, but she still does not tell Henry. He cannot find work, and finally decides to return to his native Spain, where he has friends who can help. But first, a letter arrives offering Henry a job in the city. He leaves immediately, Liceta will follow later. Henry does not return, however, and Manuel tells Liceta that Henry is dead. After a month, Manuel comes to visit and gives Liceta a drugged glass of wine. Before he can carry out his nefarious plan, none other than Henry shows up at the door. He has escaped Manuel's imprisonment and now knows his employer's true nature.

He and Liceta go to Spain; misfortune follows them. Henry's friends were not able to help after all, and now the couple lives penniless in a garret. This situation gives the author the chance to praise housework as a way to stave off the indignity of poverty (148). Liceta is pregnant and so weak that she cannot sew for hire. Still, she goes out to look for sewing commissions. At the feet of Manuel Nélter, she falls in a faint. He has followed her to Spain, and now is able to threaten her by saying that she will lose her baby from hunger. Liceta flees; the effort worsens her already desperate condition. She gives birth to triplets (one of whom dies), and the anguished Henry cries for help. The nursing sister caring for a patient downstairs comes to his aid; she is Blanca, the faithless wife now repentant and in a religious order. Manuel, who has followed Liceta to her garret, flees in horror at the birth scene. In the street, he is hit by a carriage, and dies. Before he breathes his last, though, he leaves all his money to Liceta. The novel ends with Liceta and Henry back home with their two surviving children, happy and well-to-do at last.

As in most of Larrosa's works, the main character of *Los esposos* is a woman betrayed by the patriarchy who must fend off poverty by sewing, her only skill. In stable economic circumstances, sewing is a woman's proof of virtue, but in poverty, it is a symbol of helplessness, of not having the skills to be self-sufficient. The novel's father figure, Manuel, perverts his role into a threatening sexual one; on the other hand, the husband, Henry, is powerless to change the couple's circumstances. Only childbirth, the maternal power, can finally send Manuel away for good. In an intriguing parallel, the third triplet dies, as does Manuel, leaving the proper assortment of twos: two parents and two children. Blanca, however, is punished for her infidelity by having to enter an order and remain childless for life.

In Larrosa's novel, *¡Hija mía!* [My Daughter!] (1888), the men are also absent, helpless or evil, and the vulnerable women are in danger. The motherless Enriqueta is given by her father, José Montero, to the widow doña Marcela to be raised along with Marcela's daughters, Berta and Matilde. The girls share a governess, Margarita, a young woman with a melancholy air. Berta is resentful of Margarita's preference for Enriqueta, but Matilde is not. Matilde tells Margarita that a young man, Alberto, is courting Enriqueta. However, Renato, a hardened don juan who is courting Berta, is also trying his luck with Enriqueta.

When Matilde tells Margarita that Montero, Enriqueta's father, is coming for a visit, Margarita almost faints. Alberto's petition for Enriqueta's hand cannot be granted by Marcela, so she has asked the girl's father to meet Alberto. Montero refuses to allow the marriage, saying that he has already promised Enriqueta to a rich friend. Meanwhile, Renato and Berta plot to dishonor Enriqueta. Thinking that she is going to visit Margarita's friends, Enriqueta is taken instead by Berta to a house where Renato is waiting for her. Fighting him off, Enriqueta first pleads to God for help, then calls on her mother in heaven. This time there is an answer, as Margarita and Matilde burst in and save her. Temporarily thwarted, Renato makes a deal with Montero that Renato will marry Enriqueta. She tells her father about the attempted rape, but he does not change his mind.

Montero goes to Margarita's friend, Soledad, to borrow money to pay off his gambling debts. When she refuses to loan it to him, he becomes enraged and stabs her. Margarita arrives in time to witness the murder. Montero recognizes Margarita as the wife he abandoned on the fatal night when he stole his own baby daughter after killing his brother. Margarita makes Montero sign a confession to Soledad's death and promise to support Enriqueta in her marriage to Alberto. He then flees, but not before grabbing some of Soledad's money.

The joy of Enriqueta and Alberto at being allowed to marry is interrupted by the news that Margarita has been arrested for Soledad's murder. Margarita confesses her innocence to a priest, but maintains her silence in front of the judge so that she can sacrifice herself for Enriqueta's happiness. Montero falls ill, begs Enriqueta's pardon from his deathbed, tells her that Margarita is her real mother, and confesses his murder of Soledad. Margarita is saved; she becomes famous for being an "abnegada madre" [self-sacrificing mother] (323) without having to die after all. Berta, who has run away with Renato but is soon abandoned by him, is reduced to a life on the streets. Enriqueta and Alberto live happily ever after.

Just as the boss/father in the workplace "family" in *Los esposos* fails in his role, Montero in *¡Hija mía!* distorts his responsibilities as father, husband, and brother. He gives his daughter to someone else to raise and participates in her life only when he sees an opportunity to sell her to a rich husband. He abandons his wife, simultaneously depriving her of her raison d'être: her child. Montero even kills his own brother, in a Cain and Abel drama. This mockery of family roles is echoed in the evil "sister" Berta, who is punished for her role in setting up the rape of Enriqueta by childlessness and a life as a prostitute. Margarita, on the other hand, is both surrogate and real mother to Enriqueta, and as such comes to her aid when God does not. As in *Los esposos*, the good husband figure, Alberto, is little more than a cipher, present because convention demands that there be a good lover parallel to the bad lover Renato.

Larrosa's most important novel, *El lujo* [Luxury], was published in 1889; it was the first of the genre of "stock market novels" that dealt with the frenetic speculation that brought on the market collapse of 1890. Unlike other authors who deal with the same theme, Larrosa does not blame foreigners or Jews for the collapse.[7] Instead, she uses the tale of the prodigal son (in this case, the prodigal daughter) as a microcosm of Argentina's own prodigal ways. The novel opens with the news that Rosalía and Catalina, sisters who live with their widowed mother in the country, are about to marry the brothers Bernardo and Antolín. Catalina is thrilled, but Rosalía is not. She loves Bernardo, but she also dreams of living fashionably in the city, an idea she picked up from reading romantic novels. Catalina gets up with the dawn, wears an ankle-length black apron over a simple work dress, and goes about her chores with a song on her lips. Rosalía gets up reluctantly, wears a ruffled dress with overskirts, and her lace-trimmed aprons barely cover half her skirt. The farm chores do not inspire her to song. It is not long before the narration again refers to the larger implications of clothing and needlework: "Rosalía soñaba con algo mejor que levantarse con la luz del alba, preparar la comida, arreglar la casa, cuidar de la huerta y del corral, y luego hacer encaje"[8] [Rosalía dreamed of something better than getting up at dawn, preparing meals, cleaning house, taking care of the garden and the barnyard, and then making lace]. Making lace is the sustenance of the family, although it is a poor living: "hacían primorosísimos encajes, que luego vendían a una mujer, que comerciaba en este ramo, revendiendo con ganancia cierta en la ciudad, lo que en el pueblo adquiría por poco" (18) [they made exquisite lace that they then sold to a woman who did business in this product, reselling for quite a profit in the city what she acquired cheaply in the village].

Rosalía's mother had hoped that marriage to Bernardo, who works in his father's mill, would cure her daughter of romantic daydreams. But after five months of marriage, Rosalía is still yearning for novelistic fantasies. She only perks up when she is given an elegant satin dress by the Monviel sisters, rich visitors from Buenos Aires. Rosalía is enchanted by their fine clothes, jewels, and talk of entertainments in the capital; her sister Catalina is suspicious of them for the same reasons. Rosalía tries to convince her husband to move to Buenos Aires, but he refuses to leave his job in the country. When the Monviels invite Rosalía to visit with them in the city for twenty days, Bernardo reluctantly gives his permission. After six weeks in Buenos Aires, the prodigal writes letters home describing her glittering life. She cannot bring herself yet to expose a fashionable low décolletage on her borrowed ballgowns—a *lace* scarf fills in handily. She also rejects the approaches of a young man. Nevertheless, she shows no intention of returning home. Indeed, she is cultivating a government official who could give Bernardo a job in the city.

One day, Rosalía reads a letter that the Monviels toss aside; it is an appeal from a woman named María for sponsorship of her French translation. Rosalía is touched and goes to visit María and her invalid mother, whom she finds living in misery in a slum. María does not earn much from her sewing and her translations, just as Rosalía's family did not prosper from making lace.

Catalina writes to Rosalía with the news that she is pregnant and that Bernardo is ailing. At first Rosalía feels guilty, but as time goes by, she writes home less and less, and stops visiting María. Finally, however, she overhears the servants gossiping about the Monviels: they have lost land that they had mortgaged, the moneylender is pressuring them for repayment, and they are in debt to all their merchants. Rosalía realizes that there have been fewer new dresses and parties, and the best pieces of furniture are missing. As the Monviels fall in society, so does Rosalía; her former friends snub her, and finally the Monviels eject her from their house. Rosalía seeks help from the government official, which he is happy to give provided that she become his mistress. Ashamed to go home, ashamed to renew friendship with María, Rosalía is forced to find lodging in a slum and earn a living by the needle, sewing piecework for a sweatshop broker. The Monviels, hoping to benefit from Rosalía's earnings as someone's mistress, have been disappointed. They spread rumors about her until her boss fires her, saying that he only gives work to respectable women. Now Rosalía is truly desperate: "¡Ay! miseria horrible, sin pan y sin luz! Hambre, tinieblas y soledad, desesperación y lágrimas!" (239) [Oh, horrible poverty, without bread and without light! Hunger, gloom and loneliness, desperation and tears!].

But there is a benefactor for Rosalía, just as there is in all of Larrosa's novels: a rich lady dedicated to charity gives Rosalía money to return home. There she finds her family by the bedside of Bernardo, who is on the verge of death. The prodigal flings herself into his arms, begging forgiveness and vowing never to leave him again. The novel ends with a letter from Rosalía to María in which Rosalía explains that she has changed her ways. Now she even enjoys domestic chores. With her new knowledge of hardship, she makes sacrifices so that she can be charitable to the poor. The reformed Rosalía has discovered new economic laws, the first identifying true wealth with family love: "¡Felices las que solo viven para el hogar y sus honestos goces, y no ambicionan otras riquezas que el amor acendrado de sus esposos y de sus hijos!" (287) [Happy are those women who live only for their home and its honest pleasures, and who have ambitions for no other riches than the pure love of their husband and children!]. In the second, Rosalía appropriates economic language to express the Biblical idea of casting bread upon the waters: "él que reparte su pan con el pobre, duplica su capital" (284) [he who shares bread with the poor, doubles his capital].

In *El lujo*, as in Larrosa's other novels, the main character cannot extricate herself from her own predicament; she must be rescued by the gift of a rich benefactor or by the death of a rich predator. Her society is all askew: her father is absent and her husband is weak (he literally cannot live without her), while the nation-father has created an economic system that undermines the traditional family. Womanly skills, such as sewing, are inadequate in this new capitalist, speculative economy. The happy ending, in which Rosalía embraces the way of life she once rejected, would be more convincing if Larrosa had not previously painted such a grim picture of its economic realities. Lace may have covered Rosalía's chest with womanly modesty, but it could not pay the bills.

¡Hija mía! and *Los esposos* are the most conventional of Larrosa's novels. Their structures, characters, and themes follow the established pattern of nineteenth-century sensational romances, complete with perverse family and imperiled heroine. But in *El lujo*, Larrosa dared to rewrite the prodigal son story in terms of the prodigal daughter. She was defeated, however, by the need to have a married protagonist who avoided being prodigal. Her heroine's one transgression is a prolonged visit with family friends in the city, which hardly qualifies her as a prodigal, although it was enough to chasten her with childlessness at the end of the novel. What if Rosalía had committed a few serious sins, such as an illicit love affair or becoming a prostitute instead of a seamstress? What if she had embezzled some of the Monviels' money? Would her family have welcomed her and her husband forgiven her? Even Larrosa would have been unable to make that ending happy.

Rachel Blau DuPlessis asks: "What stories can be told? How can plots be resolved? What is judged narratable by both literary and social conventions?"[9] Larrosa would have answered that happy-ending love stories can be told by women, political ones or unhappy ones cannot. The plot *must* be resolved by the death of the bad man, the sudden enrichment of the virtuous heroine, and the reward of the heroine with a good husband and children. Clearly, Larrosa had an intuition that the marriage plot was confining for a creative writer, but she did not have the vision to scrap it altogether nor to make it pleasant and fully developed like Barra did in *Stella*. Instead, Larrosa's *El lujo* is a failure, intriguing for what it attempts rather than for what it achieves. To give her credit, the author chose an unconventional plot for a woman's novel—the prodigal son is so *masculine*, like Huckleberry Finn or Don Quijote—and included rare scenes of female poverty. Unfortunately, grafting the prodigal son plot onto the marriage plot is an awkward and unfruitful hybrid. Genuine scenes of economic crisis simply do not fit into the conventional marriage plot; similarly, the prodigal son plot loses its impact when the heroine is not a sinner. The patched-together plots end up being ineffective. Larrosa, like Josefina Pelliza, was conservative in her ideas opposing women's emancipation. As a consequence, she was left with little choice but the marriage plot, since it was the convention that most conveyed her philosophy of marriage and motherhood as women's only roles. That Larrosa tried and failed to make the plot carry more than its usual love scenes is both a tribute to her as a writer and a recognition of the limitations of women's literary choices in the 1800s. These limitations still shadow women's writing today, as writers continue to seek possibilities beyond the marriage plot.

Eduarda Mansilla and Elvira Aldao: Ironic Love

Eduarda Mansilla de García also wrote romantic novels, but it is her short stories that best display her talents and her jaundiced view of society. She was a pioneer among Argentine women in exploring the genre, which she knew in its North American and European forms. Mansilla published two collections of short stories, *Cuentos* [Stories] (1880) and *Creaciones* [Creations] (1883), and a long story separately, *Un amor* [One Love] (1885). *Cuentos* is a collection of children's stories, but *Creaciones* and *Un amor* are adults' stories that often view love with less than an idealizing eye.

The title of *Un amor* is more than it seems: not *a* love, but *one* love. The main character of the story is a spoiled young beauty, Silvia Rojas, who falls in love with a handsome North American, Eduardo Sandford, whom she meets at the opera one night. But on later occasions, Sandford acts as if he has never met Silvia or her family. The puzzle is solved when it is revealed that Eduardo has an identical twin, Leopoldo. Silvia, who thought that her love would help her recognize Eduardo, discovers to her dismay that she cannot tell the twins apart. They both love her, she loves both of them (or at least, she loves them both as if they were one). Unable to choose, she rejects them both, and lives unmarried but dressed in black for the rest of her days. What unnerves Silvia is that she cannot depend on love for the essential knowledge that would allow her to distinguish the brothers; it is an unusual case of love being blind. Silvia's concept of love is shown to be naive and even foolish, and the idea that there can be only one true love is punctured.

Equally naive is the protagonist of "Sombras" [Shadows] in *Creaciones*. Malvina is madly in love with her new husband, Julian. One night, he goes out alone to the Geographic Institute, an all-male society, where he is to be named secretary. Malvina begs him not to leave her alone, and at first, Julian tries to console her, but he eventually becomes annoyed by her clinging and leaves. In his absence, Malvina tries to occupy herself with sewing, with an article on music in a magazine, with rearranging furniture—she can't concentrate. She worries that she is ugly, that Julian is seeing his former girlfriend. Spending most nights away from home, Julian does begin seeing his former flame. One night, Malvina becomes feverish and the doctor, whom she has seen in her dreams, prescribes rest, a sedative, and that Julian not go out dancing so often. The story ends obliquely, with a blue light coming out of the darkness, but it is not another of Malvina's dreams. Two little hands caress her and a voice says "I am little Julian."

> ¿Qué ha pasado? . . . Nada y todo: el tiempo ha marchado; y ese amigo fiel de los que sufren, ha consumado su obra. ¡El misterio de los misterios! La vida por la vida. . . . Nubes sonrosadas![10]

> [What has happened? . . . Nothing and everything: time has gone by; and that faithful friend of those who suffer has completed his work. Mystery of mysteries! Life for life. . . . Clouds turned pink!]

Evidently, the arrival of little Julian satisfactorily replaces the husband Julian, and Malvina's dark clouds turn pink.

This story is hardly a picture of the romantic marriage as it appears at the beginning; the husband who continues his social life as if he were single is presented as a common occurrence and something that Malvina simply has to accept. (In case she missed that lesson, Julian's mother and sister spitefully remind her of it). Only by diverting her attention from her husband and refocusing it on her child can Malvina find happiness. In "Sombras" and other stories by Mansilla, the parameters of the typical love story plot are clearly visible, yet Mansilla pushes against them. Without quite breaking the plot's conventions altogether, she distorts them enough to make them incongruous. While Larrosa exposes the limitations of the marriage plot by taking it seriously, Mansilla reveals its fragility by making it ironic.

An even colder, more calculating look at love is in Elvira Aldao de Díaz' *Mientras ruge el huracán* [While the Hurricane Rages] (1922). The hurricane of the title is World War I, and while the war rages in France, Aldao resides at the Hotel Flora in Rome. The war enters the world of the hotel in the form of news items, soldiers on leave, and women making bandages as they gossip. Worst of all, it causes food shortages that greatly annoy the residents of the hotel. Although Aldao presents herself as a passionate supporter of the Allies, her real passion is observing the other guests, whom she often describes as if they were actors in her own private movie. Without the slightest embarrassment, she relates how she and her buddies, who call themselves the "Entente Sudamericana," position their chairs for the best view. The military language is both self-deprecatory and malicious:

> Al siguiente día la nueva "Entente" ocupó el sitio estratégico: sentados los cuatro en los amplios sillones rojos del hall formamos una trinchera inexpugnable. Teníamos las espaldas bien guardadas por una estantería para revistas y periódicos, apoyada contra la rejilla del calorífero. . . . No pudiendo nadie pasar detrás de nosotros, la abigarrada concurrencia desfilaba a nuestro frente, obligada a recibir sin defensa el fuego de nuestras ametralladoras.[11]

[On the following day, the new "Entente" occupied the strategic site: seated on the ample red armchairs of the hall, the four of us formed an impregnable trench. We had our backs well guarded by shelves for magazines and newspapers, reinforced by the grille of the heater. . . . Since no one could pass behind us, the colorful crowd paraded before our front, forced to receive, defenseless, the fire from our machine guns.]

From this vantage point, Aldao describes the many varieties of flirtation that occupy the hotel residents. Each protagonist receives a nickname: *La Rubia* [Blondie], *Pimpollín* [Cherub], *Ratón* [Mouse], etc. The use of these names makes Aldao's reporting style grotesque and cold-blooded:

> Visiblemente el Ojo blanco empezó a perseguir a la Negra—se lo hice notar a ella misma, discretamente, y medio confusa, me dijo que ese "professore" buscaba con preferencia la sociedad de las "jeunes filles," e hizo un gesto de fastidio. También era visible que la Gigatona había notado la persecución de su marido a la Negra, porque cuando aparecía el Ojo blanco tras de la Negra, infaliblemente tras de aquél aparecía la Gigatona—grave y serena. Esta situación duró algún tiempo hasta que la Negra le dio un corte definitivo, por lo que me dejó entender.[12]
>
> [White Eye visibly began to pursue Blackie—I discreetly pointed it out to her myself—and somewhat embarrassed, she told me that the "professore" preferred to seek the company of "jeunes filles," and made a gesture of annoyance. It was also apparent that the Giantess had observed her husband's pursuit of Blackie, because when White Eye trailed after Blackie, without fail, trailing behind him would be the Giantess—grave and serene. This situation lasted a while until Blackie broke it off definitively, as she gave me to understand.]

Aldao cannot resist using adverbs like *visibly* when she discusses the one-eyed Ojo blanco, nor does she blush when she labels her own gossip as *discreet*. Her prose is the playful malice of the accomplished gossip, and she is equally ruthless in her descriptions of everyone, regardless of gender or rank. Aldao does show slightly more sympathy for women, as in the case of a man who lectures her on the nature of the ideal marriage: "Me dijo, que él, era el Dios de su mujer—no agregó, si ella era una diosa para él" [He told me that he was God for his wife—he did not add that she was a goddess for him].[13]

Mientras ruge el huracán is not a novel, rather it is a series of episodes connected by a place (the Hotel Flora) and a vague theme (love as pursuit). Nor is the book a traditional memoir, since Aldao does nothing much herself; she only reports what others do. It does not have the coherent frame structure or didactic purpose of *El libro de buen amor*, the medieval frame tales of love. In fact, *Mientras ruge el huracán* resembles nothing more than a scandal sheet, a tabloid-like wallow in upper-class gossip. This is love as market commodity, more titillation than inspiration, more calculation than idealism, more demythification than romanticizing. There are echoes of the language of sentimental romances; for example, there is the aristocrat who succeeds, over his parents' objections, in marrying a beautiful commoner. But since his beloved made a deliberate plan to win his affections, the sentiment is tarnished. Throughout the book, the boiling of romantic entanglements is presented as parallel to the war: while men employ military strategy on their battlefields, women employ romantic strategy on theirs.

The Language of Love: Seduction and Betrayal

One of the fundamental reasons that nineteenth-century women authors did not trust love was that they considered the medium of conveying it—language—to be an illusion. The silence generally expected of women could acceptably be broken with the language of sentiment, but this freedom was a volatile one. Repeatedly in their works, the writers show that the language of love traps lovers in a web of desire and deceit.

Suppose that one wanted to assemble a typical love poem from nineteenth-century Argentina. The imagery would draw on a vocabulary of flowers, gems, music, stars, clouds, eyes, voices, and most of all, souls. The content of the poem could be yearning for an absent lover, praising a dear one's beauty, exclaiming that two souls are now one, or lamenting a broken heart. Add an exclamation mark or two. The resulting poem would look something like this one, "Nuestras almas" [Our Souls] (1878) by Agustina Andrade:

> Dos suspiros que se juntan
> En el camino del cielo,
> Por que brotan de dos pechos
> Que sienten el mismo anhelo;
> Dos blancas perlas del alba
> Que en el cáliz de las flores
> Que buscan, para volverles
> Sus perfumes y colores;
> Dos azules nubecillas
> Que se unen allá en los cielos
> Para contemplar la luna
> Y envolverla entre sus velos;
> Dos arpas que alegres riman
> De amor iguales poemas,
> Y tristes, si una está triste,
> Buscan siempre iguales temas;

Dos aves que a un tiempo cantan,
Dos arroyos que murmuran,
Eso son nuestras dos almas
Que eterna dicha se auguran![14]

[Two sighs that meet/ On the way to heaven,/ For they rise to form two breasts/ That feel the same desire;/ Two white pearls of the dawn/ That in the flower's calyx/ Seek one another, to exchange with each other/ Their fragrances and colors;/ Two small clouds/ That join there in the heavens/ In order to contemplate the moon/ And envelope it with their veils;/ Two harps that joyously rhyme/ Equal poems of love/ And both sad, if one is sad,/ Seeking always the same themes;/ Two birds that sing as one,/ Two babbling brooks/ Those are our souls/ That foretell eternal happiness!]

Andrade's poem, and the legions like it, could have been written by either a man or a woman. Her friend Gervasio Méndez, the poet and editor of *El Album del Hogar*, cranked out one weekly for his magazine. The equally praised poet Carlos Guido y Spano wrote poems even more sentimental than those of Andrade and Méndez. Judging from their regular appearance in periodicals of every sort and the praise they brought to their authors, love poems such as Andrade's must have responded to the taste of the Argentine public.

The poetic revolutions that began in the late 1880s so thoroughly rejected the kind of language used by Andrade, that reading her poem is difficult for readers today. However, if the present-day reader can resist the urge to dismiss such poetry as sentimental "goop," and try to read it seriously as readers from the 1800s did, then certain undercurrents become apparent. Principal among these generational commonalities is the longing for companionate love, that is, a spiritual experience superior to the usual economic or biological concerns of traditional marriage. In a country with no provision for divorce and little means for women to earn their living respectably, love could hardly be an entirely emotional issue. When a woman's love led to marriage, she lost all control over her own money and property as well as custody of her children. Remaining single was not a realistic option for most women, both for reasons of social pressure and the difficulty of earning a living. Marriages of economic convenience were still common, particularly among the moneyed classes, in the last century. The novelist Emma de la Barra really did marry her uncle, an arrangement approved by her society and by the family's bankers. Moreover, childhood upbringing produced such separate, gendered spheres for men and women that they often had little in common. In this setting, the ideal of companionate love, an egalitarian relationship based on sentiment and similarity of spirits, seemed far superior to the shabbiness of institutional love and marriage. It also seemed remote. Thus, the many variations on the idea that "two souls become one" seem evidence that two separate souls were more usual practice.

Existing alongside the poems of exalted language are others that distrust that same language. From the same 1870s that saw the publication of Andrade's *Nuestras almas*, came the poem *El y ella* [He and She] by Silvia Fernández, herself a practitioner of sentimental love poetry:

> —Adiós, luz de mi vida, mi sirena,
> Mujer de tez de rosa y azucena,
>   Mi bello serafín.
> Mañana volveré, y mientre ausente
> Estoy de ti, ángel puro e inocente,
>   Acuérdate de mí.
> —Adiós, dueño absoluto de mi vida,
> Mi esperanza más bella y bendecida,
>   Acuérdate de mí.
> No olvides que te adoro con locura,
> No olvides que tu amor y tu ternura
>   Alientan mi existir.
> —Me aburre esta mujer con su terneza,
> No vale dos cominos su belleza,
>   Qué cutis! ¡qué color!
> Mas yo la he de decir, sin inmutarme,
> Aunque tal vez se muera por amarme,
>   Que todo se acabó.
> —Al fin, gracias a Dios, libre me veo!
> ¡Oh! cómo me empalaga el galanteo
>   De este hombre aburridor!
> Y él me ama con delirio, soy su anhelo;
> Mas lo he de despedir, aunque recelo
>   Que muera de dolor.[15]

["Goodbye, light of my life, my mermaid,/ Lady of rose and lily complexion,/ My beautiful seraph./ I shall return tomorrow, and while absent/ I am from you, pure and innocent angel,/ Remember me."/ "Goodbye, supreme master of my life,/ My most beautiful and blessed hope,/ Remember me./ Do not forget that I adore you madly,/ Do not forget that your love and gentleness/ Inspire my existence."/ "That woman's clinginess bores me,/ Her beauty is worthless,/ What skin! What a color!/ But I will tell her, without hesitation,/ Even if she should die of love for me,/ That it is all over."/ "At last, thank God, I am free!/ Oh! how I am annoyed by the courting/ Of this boring man!/ And he loves me deliriously, I am his passion;/ But I will tell him goodbye, although I fear/ That he will die of sorrow."]

The contrast between the elevated language of the couple's adieu with the clumping reality of their true feelings is funny, but the message is pointed: language is illusion and dangerously misleading. Ready-made endearments and automatic passions create a mask for actors playing a part. (The reaction to Fernández' laughter at love is discussed in Chapter 5).

The perils of love's language are also a frequent theme in prose. For example, another exploration of miscommunication and conflicting desires is found in the vignette *El y ella* published by Lola Larrosa in 1878. As in Fernández' *El y ella*, the scene is structured around the alternating comments of a man and a woman; in this case, however, the couple never directly address each other. The woman wants to be able to love the man freely, but she does not trust his weak character. He is afraid that he will lose her, yet he does not want to give up his escapades with other, less virtuous women. He is aware of her angry silence, which he reassures himself is just temporary. She, on the other hand, asks herself:

> ¿Qué juicio se hará de mi silencio? ¿Creerá que soy tan tonta que no lo comprendo? El hace como que no le importa mi resentimiento; esto demuestra la bella índole de su carácter.[16]

> [What does he make of my silence? Could he think that I am so stupid that I don't understand him? He acts like my resentment doesn't matter to him; that shows the lovely nature of his character.]

The scene ends with the woman's decision to let fate take its course. The couple never break their silence, never reach an understanding. Their miscommunication—her silence as well as his evasions—dooms their feelings for each other.

The novels written about the legendary Lucía Miranda, however, are the most outstanding examples of dangerous language.[17] Lucía's conversation does not make a clear distinction between the romantic love she feels for her husband, the religious love God and Christians have for others, and the affectionate companionship between friends. This failure to distinguish between different kinds of love has tragic results: the *cacique* Mangoré falls in love with Lucía, thinking that she returns his love. When he discovers the truth, he attacks the Spanish fort and massacres those within.

Anything But Love:
The Poetry of Ida Edelvira Rodríguez

It was not easy for a woman writer to avoid love as a theme. The literary possibilities available to her were limited, both through social taboos and the taste of her readers. In spite of the pressures to write only about love, however, some authors explored other areas of human experience. For example, the poet Ida Edelvira Rodríguez did not write about romantic love in personal terms, a highly unusual move for the nineteenth century. By not adopting the role of the lovesick poet, Rodríguez rejected the most common poetic authorial self of her day. Moreover, since it was a cliché of the time to say that women were "born to love," refusing to write about her own romantic impulses was tantamount to denying the traditional female role. In light of this widespread belief that love was part of women's nature, Rodríguez' choice to follow a different path is thought-provoking.

One likely reason to avoid the cliché of love is precisely that it was a cliché. Perhaps Rodríguez was simply bored with all the sentimental romance that cluttered the pages of journals. Maybe she was more interested in literary innovation. After all, the 1880s saw the first stirrings of the Modernist movement that sought inspiration in art, exoticism, and unusual verse forms. Indeed, a case can be made for considering Rodríguez one of those interested in Modernist experimentation. However, if today's readers examine her work in light of her ethnicity, the mulatta Rodríguez' avoidance of personalized love poems may be a reflection of the limited vocabulary available to her. Conventional love imagery depended almost entirely on blond hair and blue eyes; it was daring to write odes to brown hair and eyes. In the same *El Album del Hogar* where Rodríguez published most of her poems, a debate over the relative merits of blondes and brunettes went on for months. In such a climate, it is doubtful that a poem extolling African-style beauty would have been published. If Rodríguez was attracted to women, there was no possibility at all of publishing a poem in praise of lesbian love.

If not love, then, what could a mulatta poet who wanted to hide her race and class write about? One authorial role she could choose was that of the patriot. The patriotic voice was primarily a male one, but women also adopted the patriot's pose occasionally. The poet Silvia Fernández, for instance, combined conventional national symbols, such as the flag, with religious ones, particularly the Virgin of Luján, the patroness of Argentina. Rodríguez wrote three poems of national destiny that I have been able to find: *Canto a Serbia* [Song to Serbia] (one of her first, published in 1876), *El mundo de Colón* [The World of Columbus] (1877); and *¡Noventa y tres!* [Ninety-three!] (1878). The first, *Canto a Serbia,* is a call to arms for Serbians fighting Turkish rule and a rebuke to European nations for not coming to their aid. Her poem *¡Noventa y tres!* expresses horror at the violence of the French Revolution. Her most popular poem was *El mundo de Colón,* which praises Columbus as a "genio colosal" [colossal genius].[18] She even puts into Columbus' mouth the words of Moses who was forbidden to enter the Promised Land:

> ¡Dios mío! si no me es dado
> Contemplarla en esta vida . . .
> Con esta ilusión querida
> Que baje al sepulcro helado.

[My God! if it is not given to me/ To see it in this life . . . / With this/ cherished hope/ May I descend to the icy grave.]

The sentiments expressed in these poems were common ones at the time, and it is not difficult to find similar poems written by men in the pages of *La Nación* or *La Prensa.* Although Rodríguez' poems do not explicitly refer to Argentina, their general themes—rebellion against unjust power, nostalgia for the original edenic vision of America, and revulsion at civil violence mingled with anticlericalism—were real and present issues in Argentina. Indeed, they define the intellectual project of the Generation of 1880: to rebuild the nation after the devastation of the Independence struggle, the Rosas tyranny, and the ensuing civil wars; to create a vision of material progress as inspirational as Columbus's search for an earthly paradise; to unite the often violent factions of Argentine society; and to secularize social institutions while still recognizing the unique role of the Catholic Church in Hispanic culture.

Rodriguez' veiled references to actual Argentine political issues overstepped women's bounds in the view of at least one critic. In the same journal that published *¡Noventa y tres!* Oscar Weber took aim at women writers in general and at Rodríguez in particular, saying that women had made Argentine literature effeminate, melancholy, and degenerate.[19] Weber's diatribe is more than disagreement with Rodríguez' politics—he is furious that a *woman* dared to write about such matters. Silvia Fernández' patriotic poems never inspired such hysteria because they were unrelated to unpleasantness or specific issues; they were "happy poems" suitable for consumption by women and children. The ugliness of Weber's attack on Rodríguez evidently warned her of the dangers of her stance: after the publication of *¡Noventa y tres!* she published no more politically conscious poetry that I have been able to find. If she did continue to write on political issues, she must have published them in newspapers that I have not read, under a pseudonym, or anonymously. In any event, they no longer appeared in the journals where her earlier poems had been published and where Rodríguez continued to publish after Weber's attack.

If not love, if not politics, then what? Apparently, Rodríguez was moved by music; she wrote a lovely poem about the last aria in the opera *Lucia de Lammermoor*, ending in the cry of Edgardo at the death of his "pálida reina de la noche umbría"[20] [pale queen of the shadowy night]. In another poem about an opera, she describes Bellini's sleepwalker:

> La dulce heroina del sublime idilio
> Que el genio de Bellini idealizara,
> Pasa sola y dormida, semejando
> Visión de melancólica esperanza![21]

[The sweet heroine of sublime idyll/ That the genius of Bellini idealizes,/ Passes alone and asleep, like/ A vision of melancholy hope!]

Rodríguez also writes about the undines, water spirits similar to mermaids, whose beautiful song is a hymn: "Y lo cantan las olas que rodando/ Van a morir a la desierta playa"[22] [And the rolling waves sing it/ As they go to die on the deserted beach]. The voice of legend and exoticism was, like that of music, sufficiently impersonal to attract Rodríguez, as in her long poem *La fugitiva (Fragmento de una leyenda Oriental)* [The Fugitive: Fragment from an Oriental Legend], an Arabian fantasy about two separated lovers. Rodríguez' small book, *La flor de la montaña* [Flower of the Mountain], is about a young prince who searches for the "flower of the ideal, of hope," but he loses his way, and seeks fame instead of the inspiration of his love for Clelia. In all these poems, Rodríguez draws on a vocabulary of sorrow, loneliness, and the night, which is repeated in almost all her works. The consistent use of nocturnal imagery is, I believe, a kind of masking; it is a cloak that covers her from the sight of others.

The night, loneliness, and sorrow appear again in *Desencanto* [Disenchantment], the last poem by Rodríguez that I have been able to find published in a newspaper. After this, as far as I know, she published only her book, *La flor de la montaña*.

> La bóveda infinita tiene estrellas,
> La inmensa mar sus olas argentadas,
> La triste tierra sus divinas flores,
> El corazón anhelos y esperanzas!
> Dios da luz en la esfera a las estrellas,
> Dios agita en el mar las ondas bravas,
> El da perfumes a las dulces flores,

El pone la ilusión dentro del alma!
　　Pero estrellas y flores, y ondas puras,

Todo encanto perece, Dios reemplaza;
Sólo una vez perdida en la existencia
No vuelve más al pecho la esperanza![23]

[The infinite vault has stars,/ The immense sea its silvery waves,/ The sad earth its divine flowers,/ The earth desires and hopes!/ God gives light in the sphere to the stars,/ God moves in the sea the brave waves,/ He gives perfumes to the sweet flowers,/ He puts hope inside the soul!/ But stars and flowers, and pure waves,/ Every enchantment that dies, God replaces it;/ Only hope, once lost to existence,/ Never again returns to the breast!]

Desencanto is a sad poem no matter how it is read, but if it is read in light of Rodríguez' situation as an Afro-Argentine struggling to lead an intellectual life in the midst of poverty and prejudice, it is especially poignant. She says that hope, once lost, cannot be revived, a theme she will return to later in *Flor de la montaña*. One wonders if Rodríguez herself lost hope, if she gave up writing, or maybe gave up writing for the public. Given the restrictions placed on her by her marginalization—walls constructed by her race, class, and gender—it is possible that she could no longer write behind a mask. If one is constantly on guard not to reveal oneself, the poetic possibilities run out rather quickly. She was warned off of writing patriotic themes, and she explored other ones, but how long can a poet repeat odes to the night or to the opera? Finally, Rodríguez seems to have run out of impersonal themes, and her society did not permit her the freedom to write personal ones. It is hard to say which barrier—her race, her class, or her gender—was the most restrictive, but the combination must have been formidable indeed.

Elvira Aldao's Childhood Memoirs

At the opposite end of the economic spectrum from Ida Rodríguez was Elvira Aldao de Díaz, who came from a family of wealth and influence. Aldao did something that few women writers of her time did: she wrote a memoir of her childhood, *Recuerdos de antaño* [Memories of Yesteryear] (1931). The second half of the 1800s saw many travel memoirs (Aldao and Eduarda Mansilla were among the authors of these popular and often charming books), and quite a few male authors wrote autobiographical works, the most noted being Miguel Cané's *Juvenilia* (1884). However, women shied away from autobiography; their society frowned on women "calling attention to themselves." To speak of oneself was to invite criticism of that self, a risk that few women cared to take. An older woman, however, who has reached the blessed age when others' opinions count for little, might be inclined to remember a distant childhood. It is not surprising, therefore, that the two major female memoirists were Juana Manuela Gorriti, who wrote *Lo íntimo* in 1892 (the year of her death) at the age of seventy-six, and Elvira Aldao, who wrote *Recuerdos de antaño* when she was seventy-three. Cané, on the other hand, wrote his famous autobiography at the age of thirty-two.

It is likely that Aldao had Cané's *Juvenilia* in mind when she wrote her own autobiography. Like *Juvenilia, Recuerdos de antaño* is a rambling series of anecdotes, in loose chronological order, that include many famous people. The overall effect of the two memoirs is, as David William Foster points out, "synecdochical," speaking "on behalf of a generation."[24] However, Cané speaks for the male half of his generation, the half who participated in national politics. A woman could not have attended the Colegio Nacional, the setting of *Juvenilia*, nor could she have had access to decision-making in the way that Cané and his schoolmates did. Aldao, therefore, can speak only for the female half of her generation (which was that of Cané's; he was only seven years older than Aldao). She, unlike Cané, is aware that she is writing only for her own sex. After confusing the recipe for preparing a traditional dish, she wonders if a reader will make fun of her, but then dismisses the danger, doubting

> que haya lectora que continúe leyendo este libro hasta llegar a esta página (lo que es lector . . . ni uno solo; el que llegue a abrirlo . . . a las primeras de cambio lo arrojará lejos)"[25]
>
> [that there is a female reader who has continued reading this book so as to arrive at this page (as for a male reader . . . not a one; he who might have opened it . . . at the first few pages he would have thrown it far away)]

This book, then, is a woman's life, written for women readers, who know how to read and appreciate its contents.

While Cané is going on about elite education and future national politicians, Aldao write about her own education based on dolls, hats, maids, fashion, parties, houses, and hordes of relatives and friends. One of the more delightful scenes occurs when a very young Aldao is trying to squeeze into a room filled with women wearing hoop skirts. The hoops sway up and down as the women move, swallowing the small child in the immense globes of fabric (98-101). The restrictions of women's lives are much in evidence. For example, as a child, Aldao accompanied her mother on her social visits, because a woman could not walk alone in public (28); and a friend's beautiful singing voice is displayed only at private parties, because a woman of her class does not sing professionally (283). There are also discreet references in women's coded language to subjects that could not been discussed frankly. One instance occurs when Aldao is in school, and the priest asks her questions in confession that she does not understand:

> Fue necesario dar el salto transcendente en la vida femenina, la transformación de la joven soltera en la mujer casada, para que comprendiera el sentido de las preguntas del anciano sacerdote. (17)

> [It was necessary to take the transcendent leap in feminine life, the transformation from a young spinster to a married woman, to understand the sense of the questions of the old priest.]

This veiled reference to loss of virginity is embedded in a larger anecdote about young Aldao's refusal to confess, and then the subject is quickly changed. The episode is obliquely summed up as one that had an influence on her spiritual life. The reader is left to wonder what that influence was.

Like Cané's memoir, *Recuerdos de antaño* documents the changes Argentine society experienced in the post-Rosas boom: Aldao's father builds the first three-story house in Rosario, a break with the traditional Hispanic style of house (272); Aldao and her husband return from England with new ideas about hygiene, and install a complete English-style bathroom (324-27); and Aldao botches the recipe for mazamorra simply because no one prepares it anymore (244-45). Unlike Cané, Aldao's window on national events is one step removed from the sphere of action. For instance, she brings up her uncle, a governor of Santa Fe who was assassinated, but the event she narrates is a family visit (63). Indeed, political figures are everywhere in the book, but not as politicians; they are family members or friends. Aldao was constantly in the midst of the ruling class of Argentina, but she was an observer only.

The abundance of Aldao's memories hides one omission: love. Aldao, like Ida Rodríguez, is willing to write about others' romances, but not her own. Her husband appears in passing references, but she is silent about their meeting, courtship, and marriage. Aldao is indiscreet enough about other women, such as her cousins who were deceived by the same man (44), but utterly discreet about herself, even though her marriage was a proper one, lacking the scandal that marked Juana Gorriti's. (In *Lo íntimo*, Gorriti also omitted her husband—a notable omission indeed, one that has disappointed generations of sensation-seeking readers). It is possible that Aldao, who described others' entanglements with dry wit, did not have the vocabulary to describe her own. Lofty sentiment was not her style, but one could hardly be ironic about one's own love.

Obligatory Romance

The dangers and limitations of romance were well understood by Argentine women. In novels, reading romances is commonly presented as the first step in a woman's downfall into illicit relationships. In life as well, sentimental novels were felt to be destructive. María Echenique, for example, believed that they were an obstacle in women's emancipation:

> Nuestro corazón se rebela contra las ideas de espiritualidad, de sensibilidad, de poesía que cultivadas por la mujer han contribuido insensiblemente hasta el día, a su retraso en el camino del progreso y al mejoramiento de su condición.[26]
>
> [Our heart rebels against the ideas of spirituality, of sensibility, of poetry that, as cultivated by women, have to this day contributed callously to their backwardness on the road of progress and the improvement of their condition.]

Yet, in spite of such warnings, romance shadowed women writers of the 1800s, forcing them into conventions that gave them very little creative leeway. Since matters of love were thought to be women's realm, even their very nature, authors were obligated to deal with it in some way, whether by embracing it, as Josefina Pelliza did, or conspicuously omitting it, as Aldao did. Once a writer decided to write about romance, however, she was further obligated to uphold "proper" standards of love: female characters who stray must be punished, and the main character must be rewarded for virtue with a happy ending. Ultimately, women writers had little opportunity to create a plot that departed from the cliché of the imperiled but virtuous heroine who finally finds happiness with a noble and handsome husband. Efforts to expand the possibilities of this plot, such as those by Lola Larrosa, were not entirely successful, because to question the plot was to explode it. If the romance plot is a metaphor for the system of gender roles as a whole, as Rachel Blau DuPlessis maintains, questioning it is tantamount to challenging women's identity in society—as only the fearless such as Echenique were willing to do.

Endnotes

[1] Rachel Blau DuPlessis, *Writing beyond the Ending: Narrative Strategies of Twentieth-Century Women Writers* (Bloomington: Indiana University Press, 1985), 5.

[2] Doris Sommer, *Foundational Fictions: The National Romances of Latin America* (Berkeley: University of California Press, 1991), 7.

[3] Josefina Pelliza de Sagasta, *Margarita* (Buenos Aires: El Orden, 1875), 21.

[4] See Pelliza's serialized attack on nuns, beginning with "¿Reclusa o hermana de caridad? Ni lo uno, ni lo otro," *La Alborada del Plata* (17 February 1878): 108-109.

[5] César Duayen [Emma de la Barra], *Stella* (Barcelona: Maucci, 1909), 222.

[6] Lola Larrosa de Ansaldo, *Los esposos* (Buenos Aires: Compañía Sud-Americana de Billetes de Banco, 1895), 31-32.

[7] See David William Foster, *The Argentine Generation of 1880* (Columbia: University of Missouri Press, 1990), 104-107, for a discussion of the best known stock market novel, *La Bolsa*.

[8] Lola Larrosa de Ansaldo, *El lujo: novela de costumbres* (Buenos Aires: Juan A. Alsina, 1889), 17-18. Further references to this work appear in the text.

[9] DuPlessis, 3.

[10] Eduarda Mansilla de García, "Sombras," *Creaciones* (Buenos Aires: Juan A. Alsina, 1883), 283.

[11] Elvira Aldao de Díaz, *Mientras ruge el huracán* (Buenos Aires: Balder Moen, 1922), 49-50.

[12] Ibid., 89.

[13] Ibid.

[14] Agustina Andrade, *Lágrimas* (Buenos Aires: La Tribuna, 1878), 22-23.

[15] Silvia Fernández, *Armonías del alma* (Buenos Aires: La Nación, 1876), 31-32.

[16] Lola Larrosa, "El y ella," *El Album del Hogar* (11 August 1878): 44.

[17] See the complementary, extended discussion on this subject in Francine Masiello, *Between Civilization and Barbarism* (Lincoln: University of Nebraska Press, 1992), 36-43.

[18] Ida Edelvira Rodríguez, "El mundo de Colón," *El Album poético argentino* (Buenos Aires: La Ondina del Plata, 1877), 88.

[19] Oscar Weber, "Resultados inmediatos," *El Album del Hogar* (29 December 1878): 203.

[20] Rodríguez, "La aria final de 'Lucía'," *El Album del Hogar* (14 July 1878): 12.

[21] Rodríguez, "La sonámbula," *El Album del Hogar* (3 August 1879): 34.

[22] Rodríguez, "El canto de las ondinas," *El Album del Hogar* (4 January 1880): 111.

[23] Rodríguez, "Desencanto," *La Alborada Literaria del Plata* (29 February 1880): 57.

[24] David William Foster, *The Argentine Generation of 1880* (Columbia: University of Missouri Press, 1990), 34.

[25] Elvira Aldao de Díaz, *Recuerdos de antaño* (Buenos Aires: Peuser, 1931), 244. Further references to this work will be included in the text.

[26] María Eugenia Echenique, "Pinceladas," *La Ondina del Plata* (7 May 1876): 217.

Readers Then and Now

In death as in life, Juana Manso attracted both admiration and enmity. By the time of her death in 1875, she had gathered such public honor that the newspaper *La Prensa* described her as "esta distinguida escritora argentina"[1] [this distinguished Argentine writer], but she had also outraged enough influential people to be denied burial in the municipal cemetery. *La Ondina del Plata* believed that her memory would be venerated by generations to come;[2] but by 1904, her name had become a coded warning, as when the budding writer Delfina Bunge was criticized by her family for her ambitions:

> Entre otras cosas, llamábanla Juana Manso, lo que parecía ser el colmo del ridículo: Juana Manso, que fue amiga de Sarmiento, era una maestra gorda, fea y muy "tipa" y sus novelas, que nadie leía, tenían fama de cursis y abominables.[3]

> [Among other things, they called her Juana Manso, which seemed the ultimate in ridicule: Juana Manso, who was a friend of Sarmiento, was a fat, ugly, and vulgar schoolteacher, and her novels, which nobody read, had the reputation of being pretentious and awful.]

In 1967, however, the Argentine government issued a stamp in Manso's honor, and contemporary literary critics such as Francine Masiello consider her "one of the most interesting figures among nineteenth-century women intellectuals."[4]

Clearly, Juana Manso's literary reputation lies in the eye of the beholder. It is not unusual that strong, crusading women provoke mixed public reactions, but the varying assessments of Manso's and other women's works also raise fundamental questions about literary history and criticism. Once a piece of writing is published, it is no longer within the author's control; only the readers have the responsibility to appreciate it, integrate it into the literary tradition, and pass along its memory. Women's works are especially vulnerable to distortion at each of these stages. It has been documented how breakdowns in this process have doomed Anglo-American women's writing to oblivion,[5] and there is a growing body of similar evidence in Hispanic American literary criticism.[6] In the case of Argentine women writers of the 1800s, their literary reputation can be studied in three temporal stages: their reception by contemporaries, their codification into the margins of formal literary history in the 1920s, and their rediscovery by today's readers.

In her study of Teresa de la Parra's readers, Elsa Krieger Gambarini concludes that critical reaction often has less to do with the work itself than with the critic's search for recognizable events and values in the work. Drawing on Barthes' concept of the *texte lisible*, she points out that many critics cannot read a new text without transforming it into a conventional one. This is especially true when a male critic reads a woman's text:

> Clearly there is nothing less objective than this type of reductive critical reading, because in it the reader simply rediscovers him or herself, confirming his or her intellectual and cultural tradition in endless repetition. That which the male critic understands, that which is significant because it is recognizable in de la Parra's work, that which is rediscovered, is the feminine as understood by traditional culture. Unconsciously, in directing his discourse to the novel/novelist, the male critic *attributes to it what he understands as the feminine*[7] [my italics].

Thus, the reader's reactions are not controlled entirely by the text. Rather, the reader filters perceptions of the text through previously-determined ideas of gender roles. This filtered reading discards those elements that do not belong to the reader's gender concepts, and even inserts characteristics of traditional gender that may not actually exist in the text.

Gambarini's comments about de la Parra's critics are also useful in understanding the reception of nineteenth-century Argentine women's works, particularly how unconventional features were often simply ignored, and why these women were not seriously incorporated into literary history. Moreover, the idea that a patriarchal critic reads a woman's work according to his own concept of the feminine can be extended by pointing out that he reads according to his own vision of what is "literary," a definition which may exclude women's works.

A striking example of how a critic's notions of the feminine and the literary can distort his reading occurs in Francisco Bilbao's review of the novel *Un ángel y un demonio o el valor de un juramento* [An Angel and a Demon or the Value of an Oath] (1857) by Margarita Rufina

Ochagavia.[8] A clue to Bilbao's literary concerns can be seen in the language with which he opens the review:

> Joven de 17 años, [Ochagavia] ha osado subir a la montaña para desde allí dirigir el plan de su batalla. Pasa revista de sus tropas, mide el campo, observa la posición del enemigo y da la señal.[9]

> [A 17-year-old young woman, (Ochagavia) has dared to climb the mountain to direct from there her plan of battle. She reviews the troops, surveys the field, observes the position of the enemy, and gives the signal.]

This military rhetoric is an odd choice for a review of a love story, but more importantly, it is a highly gendered language that imposes masculine culture on the reading of a woman's text. As the review continues, Bilbao specifies what the American novel ought to be:

> Los elementos del drama en América están en el pueblo, están en la lucha de la religión de la edad media con la filosofía, y más que todo, en las aspiraciones de la inmortal juventud que busca el camino de la verdad. . . . La novela penetrando en los salones de las ciudades de América, solo puede dar lugar a la *comedia*:—penetrando en la historia en el foro, en la vida política del día, presenta elementos de *tragedia*. (332-33)

> [The elements of drama in America reside in its villages, in the struggle between medieval religion and philosophy, and most of all, in the aspirations of immortal youth that seek the path of the truth. (...) The novel that penetrates the salons of America's cities can only give rise to *comedy*:—when it penetrates history in the forum, in the political life of the day, it presents elements of *tragedy*.]

Thus, Bilbao values public over private, rural over urban, idealism over disenchantment, and tragedy over comedy. Ochagavia's novel is a domestic romance, it takes place in the city, it deals with personal rather than nationalist themes, its young characters find their aspirations threatened by corruption, and it lacks a religious-philosophical interpretation. Ergo, according to Bilbao's scheme of things, it is a failure.

Bilbao's review reveals that he did not read the novel for what it was (a love story) but for what he wanted it to be (a Byronesque political work); indeed, the novel is unrecognizable in the review. The author is equally unrecognizable; Bilbao refers to her as "this child" who writes with "admirable innocence" (332). Another reader, not wedded to Bilbao's notions of gender, might be struck by Ochagavia's cynical asides and direct language, as when the character Alicia is dreaming about her beau's gallantries: "No sabía que los hombres juran por costumbre inveterada y sin darle valor a lo que dicen"[10] [She didn't know that men vow out of inveterate habit and without attaching any importance to what they say]. Bilbao says that when he reads about youth's disenchantment, he stifles a smile out of "human respect," (332) but his smile is anything but respect. It smugly dismisses the author, her novel, and what she hoped to achieve.

Although Bilbao was a particularly obtuse and self-absorbed reader, he was not alone in imposing a universal, one-size-fits-all filter of conventional ideas of femininity and literariness onto women's works. Indeed, at all three stages of critical reception studied here, readers' reactions—both favorable and disapproving—reveal as much about themselves as about the texts.

Contemporaries' Reactions to Women's Writing, 1870–1910

Nineteenth-century readers of women's writing generally did perceive the works through strongly gender-defined filters. However, such a filter does not necessarily imply a negative response; on the contrary, many women's works of the 1800s received positive, enthusiastic reviews by both men and women in contemporary newspapers and journals. Since visible conformity to traditional femininity was expected, works that fell within those boundaries were often praised with fanfare. Outbursts of undiluted misogyny were rare, although when they did occur, they were memorable. Oscar Weber, for example, was so distressed by the proliferation of women writers that he wrote an essay about them in *El Album del Hogar* in 1878. He, like Bilbao and others, conceived of literature in military-nationalistic terms. However, into that current of "normal" literature, a "deviant" factor had intervened: women writers had caused Argentine literature to be "effeminate" and "degenerate." Citing a sixteenth-century Spanish monk as his authority on female psychology, Weber believed that women were incapable of producing "viril" literature and that they were "más ignorante que sus colegas del sexo barbudo"[11] [more ignorant than their colleagues of the bearded sex]. Weber's search for virility among a group of women must have disappointed him more often than not, but most male critics did not expect virility from female writers. Weber's hysterical brand of imperiled masculinity was an aberration, not the norm.

Instead, most male critics sought traditionally defined feminine qualities in women's writings. The word *delicadeza* [delicacy] appears constantly in their reviews, no matter what the topic might be, and the imagery of flowers and songbirds is rampant. This insistent reading can be called the "Delicacy Imperative." It seeks out and praises the aspects of a work that correspond to the critic's concept of women as tenderly emotional, morally superior, and unrelentingly prim. Melancholy, for instance, is not only permissible but desirable in the tender emotions of a lady poet—so long as it is not allowed to stray into more profound or angry emotions. Moreover, a lady's writing, according to the Delicacy Imperative, is supposed to come from innate inspiration rather than from deliberate craft; it should be the spontaneous expression of sensibility, not the careful labor of the conscious mind. If a writer departs from this role and creates scenes that lack delicacy, sweetness, or lyricism, or if she discusses writing as a profession or an artifice, she is either ignored or reproved by the enforcers of delicacy.

This gender concept is not just a male creation; women writers of the period often espoused the Delicacy Imperative and strove to live up to it. Both Josefina Pelliza and Lola Larrosa, for instance, included collected critical praise in the prefaces of their books, and, judging by what they chose to include, they were proud to be considered delicate. In Pelliza's *Pasionarias* [Passion Flowers] (1887), the first critic included in the preface is none other than Carlos Guido y Spano, one of the most respected poets of the day, who began his letter thus: "Versos como los que vd. ha tenido la amabilidad de obsequiarme, no se juzgan, se sienten. Espira de ellos ese místico aroma guardado como en una urna inviolable en el fondo de las almas tiernas"[12] [Verses such as the ones that you have had the kindness to bestow upon me, cannot be judged, they must be felt. They exude that mystic aroma kept as in an inviolable urn in the depth of tender souls]. Some of the other critics liked Guido y Spano's phrase "not judged but felt" so well that they repeated it in their own reviews. Similar manifestations of the Delicacy Imperative are found in the preface to Larrosa's *Los esposos* [Husband and Wife] (1895), where she includes excerpts from reviews such as this one:

> ¡Cuánta sencillez, cuánta delicadeza! Esas páginas sólo puede escribirlas una mujer. . . . Sólo la naturaleza ha reservado para el sentimiento y la inteligencia femenina ese don de presentar aunados los rayos de oro y reflejos de luna. . . . Una mujer que escribe, siempre goza de nuestras simpatías. Hay, por lo menos, allí el coraje suficiente para afrontar las creencias de una sociedad que piensa que sólo la aguja debe ser el objetivo de la mujer.[13]

> [So much simplicity, so much delicacy! Only a woman could write those pages. (...) Nature has reserved solely for the feminine sentiment and intelligence that gift of presenting joined together rays of gold and reflections of the moon. (...) A woman who writes always enjoys our sympathies. There is in her, at the very least, sufficient courage to confront society's beliefs that women's only objective should be the needle.]

This passage alerts us to why Pelliza and Larrosa would be willing to collaborate with the demands of delicacy: it gave them a socially acceptable authorial voice that mitigated their unconventional choice to become a writer. If the act of becoming a professional writer was indelicate, at least their works could not be accused of lacking feminine sensibility.

Even so, obeying the Delicacy Imperative could be a limitation as well as a tool for finding a sympathetic audience. This duality is clearly seen in Rafael Obligado's lengthy and enthusiastic review of Silvia Fernández' *Armonías del alma* [Harmonies of the Soul] in *La Ondina del Plata* of 1876. He warmly praises many of her poems precisely because they reflect the "natural suavidad de su inspiración, que ilumina sin deslumbrar, asociándose a su ternura y delicadeza de mujer" [natural gentleness of her inspiration that illuminates without blinding, drawing on her womanly tenderness and delicacy]. That is, he praises the poems that conform to his previously conceived ideas of what a feminine text should be. When Fernández fails to meet his expectations, he adopts a fatherly tone of disappointed reproof:

> La poesía titulada *Los recuerdos de la infancia* es una de las más bellas del libro; pero no obstante esta afirmación, séanos permitido, a nombre de la imparcialidad que debe ser el alma de la crítica para que sus conclusiones tengan algun valor, observar a su autora que no debiera haber hecho resaltar la nube del dolor sobre la frente del alba de la vida, esa nube que *"hace que todo nos parezca odioso."* Cuando las aves perciben la primera vibración del día, no gimen: aletean de placer, cantan de entusiasmo. Un himno a la infancia debe tener la entonación expansiva del hosanna.[14]

> [The poetry entitled *Memories of Childhood* is one of the loveliest in the book; but in spite of this affirmation, let us be permitted, in the name of the impartiality that must be the soul of the critic if his conclusions are to have any validity, to observe to the author that she should not have emphasized the cloud of sorrow above the dawn of life, that cloud that *"makes everything seem hateful to us."* When the birds perceive the first vibration of the day, they do not sigh: they flutter their wings with pleasure, they sing with enthusiasm. A hymn to childhood should have the expansive intonation of a hosanna.]

Obligado was not pleased with the suggestion that childhood could be painful rather than carefree; that a woman would do so seemed particularly shocking to him. His rhetoric of birds and religion becomes especially thick in this passage, which is overlaid with the "more in sorrow than in anger" voice of the disappointed patriarch. For Obligado and other upholders of traditional concepts of ideal womanhood, there are certain things a woman should not write about, not because they do not exist, but because they are "indelicate" and thus "unwomanly."

At least Obligado did explain why he did not like certain lines in *Memories of Childhood*. Another poem, *El y ella* [He and She], inspired an ominous silence. For Obligado, "ser poeta es saber cantar el amor! Y la Señorita Silvia Fernández sabe cantarlo" [to be a poet is to know how to sing of love! And Miss Silvia Fernández knows how to sing it]. He then enumerates the pieces about love: "*A una estrella, Tú y yo, ¡Qué importa!, Vivo en ti, Su imagen* y otras, con excepción de *El y ella*, son composiciones de mérito"[15] [*To a Star, You and I, What Does it Matter!, I Live in You, His Image*, and others, with the exception of *He and She*, are compositions of merit]. Why did Obligado single out *El y ella* but fail to explain his dislike? The answer is that *El y ella* is funny. The other poems are conventional, sentimental pieces of romantic longing. *El y ella* makes fun of a couple whose true, mundane feelings are at odds with their exalted language. (The poem is quoted in its entirety in the previous chapter.) As modern critics such as Hélène Cixous know, humor is not delicate, it is subversive. Fernández' humorous poems, which she tucked without warning in between religious and romantic ones, are snakes in the garden. They imply that she found respectable codes of behavior flawed and—more shocking by far—ridiculous. Obligado was not prepared to discuss a poem written by a woman who found the customs of love absurd. His belief in traditional concepts of female sensibility blocked his ability to transform *El y ella* into a *texte lisible*.

A few male readers did escape the Delicacy Imperative. Alberto Navarro Viola, who compiled the influential *Anuario bibliográfico de la República* [Bibliographic Annual of the Republic] (1880–89), is one male reader who seems remarkably free of notions of idealized femininity.[16] Indeed, he ruthlessly skewered Josefina Pelliza's poetry precisely because of its "artless," "delicate" qualities. Navarro was not in favor of women authors as a group, but neither was he necessarily opposed to them. A comparison of his responses to Eduarda Mansilla's works over four years reveals that he was willing to accept her work with relative fairness. His favorable reviews of *Cuentos, Creaciones*, and *Lucía Miranda* are balanced by his criticism of her drama, *La marquesa de Altamira*. He points out that the dialogue is engaging but that there is little physical movement; Mansilla had failed to allow for the differences in visual spectacle and written prose.[17] His comments do not seem unfair—physical movement *is* important in theatrical works—but in addition, they are gender-neutral; they are based on criteria that a male writer would have to meet as well. Navarro's review of Mansilla's *Recuerdos de viaje* [Travel Memories] is also reasonable. It points out that the book has not received the notice it deserves nor has it been appreciated for what it is: "Convengo en que esos *Recuerdos* se presentan exageradamente sujetivas; pero veo también que llevan el título de *Recuerdos*, y no los concibo de otra manera"[18] [I agree that these *Memories* are presented in an exaggeratedly subjective manner; but also I see that they carry the title of *Memories*, and I do not consider them to be anything else]. Unlike Bilbao, who insisted that all works fit one literary mold, Navarro was willing to adjust his reading to fit the work. The word *delicadeza* does not appear at all in the review.

Navarro was not a typical reader, however. More usually, knowledge of the author's sex distorted the reading of a work and undermined the effusive words of apparent praise. The double-edged language of the Delicacy Imperative can be seen, for instance, in Edmundo de Amicis' prologue to Emma de la Barra's *Stella*. The novel had originally been published under a male pseudonym, and, even though the author's identity was soon revealed, the novel was first read as a man's work. Evidently, this brief suspension of gender identity confused De Amicis's confidence in how to read the work, thus producing statements such as this one: "No existe casi una página en la que no se sienta la mujer; pero son pocas aquellas en las cuales deja de sentirse que la mano delicada nos da el apretón de una mano viril"[19] [Scarcely a page exists in which one does not perceive the woman; but there are few in which one fails to feel that the delicate hand gives us the grip of a viril hand]. Delicate or viril? De Amicis could not decide, because he thought that the novel was too well written to be a woman's work. It did not "cae en los defectos y en las debilidades a que inclina el ánimo del ingenio feminil"[20] [fall into the defects and weaknesses to which the soul of feminine talent is inclined]. Here De Amicis reveals his belief that a woman's talent is naturally defective and weak; therefore, a woman who writes well is masculine, not feminine. The muddled polarity of delicacy and virility found in *Stella*'s prologue reveals that *delicate* was just another way of saying "not as good as a man's work."[21] De Amicis and others did indeed praise women's works effusively, but their praise simultaneously marginalized the authors and belittled their creations.

This double-edged "praise" dominated the response to women's works by their contemporaries. By far, the majority of book reviews in nineteenth-century Argentina were written by men; even women's periodicals tended to give the job of literary criticism to male writers. As a result, it is difficult to find enough woman-authored reviews to make considered judgments about how women's reading differed from men's. Among existing women's responses, however, the gendered values of delicacy and virility also persist. Raymunda Torres y Quiroga describes Germaine de Staël as "el *hombre femenino* y la más viril y célebre escritora de su tiempo"[22] [the *feminine man* and the most viril and celebrated author of her time], while Carlota Garrido de la Peña praises Emilia Pardo Bazán for "su ingenio varonil y cultivadísimo, aunque delicadamente femenino"[23] [her manly and extremely cultured, though delicately feminine, talent]. In one sentence, Garrido unwittingly sums up the dilemma of the nineteenth-century woman writer: to be recognized for excellence, she must be simultaneously masculine and feminine. The wonder is that so many women continued to write anyway—and that so many chose *not* to write under a male pseudonym.

When Argentine women wrote about other women writers, the one unmistakable commonality was pride that a woman had written and published at all. There is almost always a defensiveness in their pride, a desire to answer their critics. In the same article in which Carlota Garrido discusses the Spanish writer Pardo Bazán's "manly femininity," she raises the accusation that no great scientific discovery had been made by a woman, then replies that Pardo Bazán's scientific studies were serious enough to convince the critic Menéndez Pelayo that women did indeed have an aptitude for scientific speculations. Garrido goes further and says that

> La señora Bazán ha tratado con lucidez de espíritu y galanísima dicción las materias más árduas y espinosas del mundo moral como del mundo físico, en sus estrechas relaciones, teorías abstrusas, donde suelen estrellarse e incurrirse en error aquellos talentos masculinos, poco cuidadosos de beber en las fuentes de las ciencias.

> [Mrs. Bazán has treated with lucidity of spirit and elegant diction the most arduous and thorny issues in the moral world as well as in the physical world, in the narrow relations, obstruse theories, where those masculine talents tend to crash and fall into error, careless in drinking from the fountains of the sciences.]

That is, Pardo Bazán could not only equal male scientific writers, she could surpass them, precisely because of her feminine judgment. This belief that female culture is different from men's, but a necessary complement to it, is the basis of women's identity and pride in the 1800s. Garrido was not ashamed to own up to delicacy, nor was she concerned that public talent was considered manly, because she believed that women's delicate, moral, and emotional natures were the source of strong roles for women, that men would run amok without the moderating influence of women's better souls. Far from rebelling against the Delicacy Imperative, she embraced it and defended it as her natural territory.

Garrido and others experienced genuine pleasure that women were writing and publishing so visibly in the late 1800s. They were quite conscious of the enforced silence of the decades under the dictator Rosas, and therefore, their freedom to write still seemed new and marvelous. The number of periodicals specifically directed to women was considered proof of women's progress, and every book published by a woman seemed to open opportunities for others. Moreover, it was believed that women authors were filling a need previously left unaddressed: to write about women, their issues and experiences, and in particular to highlight the connection between the home and the national destiny. This gender-specific reader response is evident, for example, in the poem "A las señoritas argentinas que escriben en la *Ondina del Plata*" [To the Ladies Who Write for *La Ondina del Plata*] published by that journal in 1876:

> Preciosas hijas del bello Plata,
> Flores nacidas para brillar:
> Con cuánto orgullo siempre "la Ondina"
> Vuestros cantares publicará!
> Vuestros cantares tan deliciosos
> En donde el genio brilla sin par,
> Esos cantares que ensalzan tiernos
> La amada patria y el dulce hogar.[25]

[Precious daughters of the beautiful Plata,/ Flowers born to be brilliant:/ With what pride "la Ondina" always/ Your songs will publish!/ Your songs so delicious/ In which genius shines without par,/ Those songs that tenderly exalt/ The beloved country and the sweet home.]

In this and other poems like it, the periodical itself was as praised as the women who wrote in its pages. *La Ondina* satisfied a hunger that the readers felt for works written by and for women. Similarly, grateful poems dedicated to a specific writer are commonly found in the numbers following the publication of the author's work. Shortly after the publication of Silvia Fernández' first poems, for instance, "Tórtola" [Agustina Andrade] wrote about how her feelings echoed those of Fernández, and thus she felt less alone.[26]

The pattern of womanly pride in *La Ondina del Plata* was no different from that in *El Album del Hogar* and *La Alborada del Plata*. There was a special awareness of women writers in *El Album del Hogar* following the debate by Josefina Pelliza and Da Freito on women's right to write. In one article, the otherwise anti-emancipationist columnist "Luciérnaga" lists her favorite writers and then asks them to write even more:

¿Por qué esa poca fe en el porvenir? Si es verdad que para conquistar el nombre de escritora es necesario afrontar obstáculos y sufrir las críticas consiguientes, también es cierto que un día nuestra perseverancia por el trabajo intelectual es recompensada.[27]

[Why this little faith in the future? If it is true that in order to win the name of writer it is necessary to confront obstacles and suffer the consequent criticism, it is also certain that one day our perseverence on behalf of intellectual work will be compensated.]

Support for women writers was so widespread among Argentine women of the 1800s that it crossed political lines, uniting emancipationists and anti-emancipationists in the belief that a new age for women had dawned.

Pride in women's publications as well as the belief in a separate female culture led to the first tentative efforts at creating women's literary history. Women's periodicals of the time are permeated with a sense of history, both a consciousness of the past and an awareness of current changes. Clorinda Matto de Turner's *El Búcaro Americano*, for instance, is a treasure trove of biographical sketches, reviews, and essays surveying the field of women's literature. In such articles, it is assumed that future generations will remember and value women writers. *La Ondina del Plata* confidently writes in a biographical note about Eduarda Mansilla that "la inmortalidad, la vida después de la muerte, está también reservada a las inteligencias femeninas"[28] [immortality, life after death, is also reserved for feminine intelligences]. Yet the same journal announced that soon it would reprint some of Rosa Guerra's works because, just eleven years after Guerra's death, they were in danger of being forgotten.[29] They were not published, however, and no explanation was given for the omission.

The Centennial of Independence in 1910 sparked a variety of historical works, many of them amateurish albums of the social register, but others with valuable data. For example, Mercedes Pujato Crespo wrote a knowledgeable article on the history of women's journalism; however, already by 1910, she realized that the journals and their editors were being forgotten. She called the editors "heroines" and concluded her piece with a request that they be remembered.[30] In the end, the articles that contained bits of women's history were never brought together into one coherent overview; the formal history of women's literature of the 1800s was not written by those who participated in it. Thus, their memory was put in jeopardy, and their works were left vulnerable to the caprices of future readers.

Ricardo Rojas and the Creation of the Literary Canon

In particular, the fate of nineteenth-century women's literature was left in the hands of Ricardo Rojas (1882–1957). It is curious but true that the literary history of Argentina was created and institutionalized by just one man. In 1912, Rojas was named the first professor of Argentine literature at the University of Buenos Aires, and from the beginning he understood his duties to include the creation of a formal history. Just five years later, in 1917, the first volume of his fundamental work, *La historia de la literatura argentina* [The History of Argentine Literature] was published; three more volumes appeared periodically until 1922. After 1922 and until now, new editions have been published regularly. Other literary histories of Argentina have been written since that of Rojas, but no other is as frequently cited. Rarely challenged, routinely consulted, Rojas' is the defining canon of literary history in Argentina.[31]

Unlike many literary critics, Ricardo Rojas was sufficiently conscientious to include women writers in his history. Moreover, he gave them more than a footnote or an aside; he dedicated an entire chapter, titled "Las mujeres escritoras," to women writers in his *Historia de la literatura argentina*. His personal library, preserved at his house (now a museum) on Charcas street in Buenos Aires, contains a substantial collection of women's works; María Echenique's *Colección literaria*, for example, can be found there but not at the National Library. Jottings in the margins are evidence that he read what he owned. Rojas' recognition of women authors should not be underestimated. For women writers and critics such as Noemí Vergara de Bietti, the chapter is a reminder that "no escribimos sin tradición, sin un ayer"[32] [we do not write without a tradition, without a yesterday].

Rojas' chapter on "Las mujeres escritoras" has a laudable premise; he believed that women writers were a sign of a country's progress and modernity:

> la mujer emancipada que se mezcla libremente a la vida, que estudia a la par del hombre, colabora en los periódicos y saca a luz sus libros, es un fenómeno propio del siglo XIX y de la atmósfera liberal de las sociedades modernas. Conocida ya la evolución de nuestra cultura, se comprende que en la Argentina anterior a la independencia la mujer haya vegetado silenciosa, al margen de la vida intelectual y civil.[33]

> [the emancipated woman who mingles freely in life, who studies on a par with men, who collaborates on periodicals and brings to light her books, is a phenomenon unique to the nineteenth century and to the liberal atmosphere of modern societies. Given the evolution of our

culture, it is understood that, in Argentina prior to Independence, women vegetated silently on the margins of intellectual and civic life.]

Since, according to Rojas, emancipated women are a sign of social evolution in the Darwinian sense, then it becomes necessary to sketch out the stages in the course of this progress.[34] Therefore, he begins with "barbarism": the Conquest of the Americas, the rough society that followed it, and the decadence of the viceroyalty. Since there were few, if any, women writers at that time, he refers instead to women who gained fame for their erotic adventures or their saintly works. The next stage he discusses is the Independence era, in which women take a nobler role in support of the political cause. The most outstanding woman in intellectual, artistic, and political circles of the time was Mariquita Sánchez, whom Rojas considers the precursor of the modern Argentine woman. He devotes considerable space to Sánchez, who indeed was a remarkable woman. Her letters to friends and relatives make fascinating reading; however, she did not write creative works. In the absence of literary women, Rojas proposes the substitute of a famous character.

At last Rojas arrives at the post-Rosas period in which he believed that women had left the margins of intellectual life. He mentions an impressive number of women. It is clear that Rojas was unusually well informed about women writers of the time. Those who receive passing mentions include Juliana Gauna, Ida Edelvira Rodríguez, Rufina Margarita Ochagavia, Manuela Rosas, Celestina Funes, and Silvia Fernández. He also alludes to some distinguished foreigners who resided and published in Buenos Aires: Carolina Freyre de Jaimes, Clorinda Matto de Turner (whose name he misspells), and Gabriela de Laperrière. Short paragraphs are devoted to Rosa Guerra, Juana Manso, and Agustina Andrade. Longer descriptions of several paragraphs are dedicated to Josefina Pelliza de Sagasta and Eduarda Mansilla de García; the longest study, comprising a separate cameo section, is about Juana Manuela Gorriti. When grouped this way, the value of Rojas' inclusion of women becomes evident: he preserved a number of names that otherwise might have been forgotten altogether. Simply listing so many authors produces the effect that Noemí Vergara mentions, that is, the proud knowledge that women writers are not "without a tradition, without a yesterday."

However, a mention is not the same as a serious study. In fact, a mention is as much as most of these women are given. Of those who are discussed rather than just listed, Andrade receives one-and-a-half inches of text in the edition I consulted, Manso receives two inches, and Guerra three. Emma Berdier, a hoax created by other writers, is discussed in a nine-inch footnote, more space than is given to the authentic

Andrade, Guerra, and Manso combined. The section on Pelliza is seventeen inches long, more than the twelve inches given to Mansilla. Gorriti earns thirty inches of text. If these numbers seem generous, they should be compared with the space dedicated to male writers. For instance, Lucio Mansilla, Eduarda's brother, receives a discussion twelve pages long: a page of Lucio for an inch of Eduarda. In simple quantitative terms, then, Rojas' inclusion of women writers in his history is little more than a gesture or a token. It is not a serious, equitable study of their works.

What Rojas said about the writers is even more damaging than the small attention he gave them. He said that Pelliza had "más vocación que talento" [more vocation than talent]; that Guerra "fue menos afortunada en su carrera que la aplaudida Eduarda Mansilla" [was less fortunate in her career than the acclaimed Eduarda Mansilla]; that Manso resembled Domingo Sarmiento in her masculine face and pedagogical interests, but that her works "muy estimados en su época, han vivido menos que su nombre" [well regarded in her time, have endured less than her name]; and that Andrade's poetry was the expression of "una ingenua sensibilidad" [an ingenuous sensibility] (787, 792). These comments are deadly. Few readers, after hearing Rojas' summary, would want to read the works of these writers. It is particularly appalling that Manso's physical appearance is presented as a literary judgment. Pelliza, who Rojas admits was not the original thinker that Manso was, receives a longer, more detailed study in which her beauty is mentioned several times. One wonders if Manso had been pretty, would she have received equal consideration? Just as Rojas found Manso's face more important than her writing, he found Gorriti's life more interesting than her fiction. Rojas says that Gorriti has "no obstante su mal gusto literario, el más raro temperamento de mujer que haya aparecido en nuestras letras" (796) [in spite of her bad literary taste, the most uncommon woman's temperament that has appeared in our letters]. He repeats several times the words *raro* (which is more than just *uncommon*; it also implies *strange* or *peculiar*) and *temperamento* as he reviews Gorriti's melodramatic life. The few comments about her works are not praise; he thinks that she does not have "el don de la emoción perdurable ni de la forma feliz" (798) [the gift of enduring emotion or felicitous form]. The only woman author who does not suffer a belittling remark is Mansilla.

In themselves, Rojas' remarks are patronizing and dismissive, but they would not be so damaging if it were not for the unique role of his *Historia de la literatura argentina*. Historians and critics often simply repeat the judgment of Rojas or use it as a point of departure; his work is so fundamental that it is frequently quoted without attribution. When he makes a mistake, such as identifying Rosa Guerra's death date as 1894 instead of the correct 1864, the error is incorporated—uncorrected—into subsequent histories. Thus, it is especially important to understand the double-edged content of Rojas' famous chapter. In essence, the way that he included women amounts to a kind of exclusion. Rojas taught his readers that, while women's writing did exist, it was not good or important, and thus it could be ignored without apology. By segregating women into the ghetto of their own chapter, Rojas removed them from the context of their male contemporaries, and left the impression that women did not participate in mainstream (i.e., male) literary movements. By giving more importance to the authors' gender than to their works, he provided an example of how biography could be used to ignore an author's works. While it is doubtful that Rojas intended to marginalize women, the boomerang effect of his inclusion of women's works has removed them from the canon of texts that students of literature are required to study.

In the 1930s and 1940s, when Rojas was at the height of his career, nineteenth-century women writers faded from public memory. Only an occasional note, short and written as a curiosity, appears, usually in a women's magazine.[35] Emma de la Barra, whose life did not end until 1947, was still in the public eye because her novel *Stella* was made into a hit movie in 1945. Silvia Fernández published a second wave of poetry in her later years, but it was not as widely read as the poetry of her youth. Elvira Aldao, the last to die of the writers studied here, continued to publish into the 1950s; yet, her most popular book, *Cartas íntimas*, did not carry her name on the title page. Instead, it carried the name of her correspondent, Lisandro de la Torre. Most important, a new generation of women authors, such as Alfonsina Storni and María Luisa Bombal (a Chilean living in Buenos Aires), was astonishing Argentine readers, and Victoria Ocampo was staking out women's claim to literary criticism through her journal *Sur*. To the post-World War I generation, the women of the 1800s seemed hopelessly outdated.

The Rediscovery: Today's Readers

As feminism entered the academy in the 1970s both in Argentina and in the United States, literary scholars began to question the history they had been taught. In the rare moments when it included women, it emphasized stock characters such as the "lone woman" (for example, Sappho and Sor Juana), the "pants wearer" (George Sand and Juana Manuela Gorriti), or the "doomed romantic" (Gabriela Mistral and Alfonsina Storni). However, new literary theories were downplaying biographical criticism, emphasizing the continuity of tradition, and redefining which written texts were worthy of study. This first generation of feminist historians asked questions such as "Was Sor Juana the only woman writer of her time?" and "What would we think about George Sand's writing if we did not know her biography?" Equally important, they were not embarrassed that a work was a "woman's novel" or "feminine poetry." These historians became literary archaeologists, intent on restoring the memory of women's past.

Once lost texts are rediscovered, however, readers of the late twentieth century find that it is not always easy to read them. The distance of time and cultural change can make old texts difficult to understand in an emotional, if not intellectual, way. It is impossible to read texts from the 1800s as readers then responded to them; try as they may, today's readers cannot divorce themselves from their own cultural context. Even the most conscientious scholar reads from a double perspective of time, simultaneously respecting the integrity of the past while reacting in terms of the tastes, ideology, and theories of the present. Thus, in scholarly terms, Lola Larrosa can be valued for her historical significance and certain interesting features of her novels, but her works are not pleasing to today's literary aesthetics. They are too sentimental and moralizing, and they have improbable happy endings —precisely the characteristics that nineteenth-century readers liked about Larrosa's writing. Similarly, Eduarda Mansilla's short story "El ramito de romero," with its cadaverous femme fatale, provides fodder for Freudian fun that the author certainly never intended; and Emma de la Barra's novel *Stella*, feminist in a genteel sort of way, includes racist comments that were commonplace at the time, but make today's readers cringe. Josefina Pelliza's poetry is, frankly, awful by today's standards, and her prose is a mess of clauses with no identifiable antecedents. Her attitude toward punctuation can politely be described as eccentric. Pelliza earns a special status for her seething anger in *Conferencias*, but she will never enjoy the same critical regard that more "accessible" (i.e., pleasing to today's aesthetic standards) writers such as Juana Manuela Gorriti and Eduarda Mansilla enjoy.

Mary Berg addresses this issue in terms of the "translating reader." She points out that

> As more and more fiction by 19th-century Latin American women writers is rediscovered, reread, and reestablished as part of the panorama of cultural life of the last century, it becomes increasingly evident that these literary works require translation into 20th-century terms. Or, rather, that inevitably we translate the past into our own present range of perceptions and uses of language, into the context of our

current concerns with issues of gender, identity, how fictional and autobiographical realities overlap or intermesh, and how fictional theory and practice are related.[36]

She chooses the example of Gorriti's *Peregrinaciones de una* [sic] *alma triste* [Peregrinations of a Sad Soul] (1876) to show how today's readers are challenged by popular works of the past: "Whether this text is read now as a feminist account, a commentary on historical and social circumstances in 1875, or a work of autobiographical fiction…depends upon the translating reader."[37] Berg's "translating reader" is engaged in the same quest that Elsa Krieger Gambarini described in her discussion of the *texte lisible*. Today's readers, male and female, cannot help but read nineteenth-century works through the lens of our contemporary preoccupations.

Of the interpretive possibilities that Berg identifies, the reading that seeks "commentary on historical and social circumstances" is the most common and accessible. Nineteenth-century women authors were indeed concerned with the issues of their time, and they freely commented on them in their writing. The novel *Stella*, for instance, is critical of upper-class family structure, education, the role of gauchos, conspicuous consumption, political indifference, religious hypocrisy, and more. Such works provide historians with rich material in their reconstruction of nineteenth-century women's culture, ideas, and concerns. Francine Masiello, for example, has traced women's national imaginings, as expressed in their literature, in her award-winning *Between Civilization and Barbarism: Women, Nation, and Literary Culture in Modern Argentina*; Kathryn Lehman has examined patriotic imagery in Juana Manso's works; and Graciela Batticuore has analyzed Gorriti's political genealogies. Not all socio-historical studies are political, though. Gorriti's recipe book, *Cocina ecléctica*, has inspired studies by Josefina Iriarte, Claudia Torre, and Nina Scott on the role of cookery in women's culture; and Lola Larrosa's novels provide information on economic issues in the unstable 1890s. As women's journalism becomes more available to scholars, their essays will help rewrite history in many areas, from national identity to the cultural construction of motherhood.

Almost as popular as reading literature for its historical significance is, as Berg points out, reading for the convergence of fiction and autobiography. Certainly this is true of Gorriti's writing; her life was as novelesque as her writing, and few critics have been able to resist retelling its dramatic events. But other women writers are also assumed to include autobiographical material in their works. Emma de la Barra's *Stella*, for instance, is considered, by Carmelo Bonet and others, to be a description of the social milieu in which the author herself lived.

Larrosa's own poverty is probably reflected in her novels, particularly in the character of María in *El lujo* who, like Larrosa, tries desperately to earn her living by translating works for rich patrons. Elvira Aldao's ten volumes of memoirs are a goldmine of material for documenting the customs and attitudes of the Argentine upper class.

Ida Edelvira Rodríguez presents a special problem to the translating reader who examines the close ties between literature and autobiography. She was Afro-Argentine and desperately poor, but she never addressed these issues in her poetry.[38] Yet today's readers instinctively feel that the issues of race, gender, and class do influence a writer's work in some way. Should readers respect her silence or look for a hidden text, the palimpsest of her own life? Apparently, Rodríguez communicated with her editors by mail,[39] thus hiding her race from them; the editors seem to have assumed that she was white, since there is no mention otherwise in the references to her. (In Argentina of the 1800s, it is certain that the editors would have mentioned her race if they had known it.) When Bernardo González Arrili included his friend's visit to Rodríguez in his *Mujeres de nuestra tierra*, the visit was marked by surprise at her race, her poverty, and her intellect.[40] The first poem that I have been able to find by Rodríguez is dated 1876 and the last, her book *La flor de la montaña*, is dated 1887. After this date, I have no more information about her. Although Rodríguez' race was not generally known in Euro-Argentine society, it was known in the Afro-Argentine community, where she was regarded with pride. An article from *La Broma*, an Afro-Argentine newspaper, uses her as an example of the community's progress:

> Qué dice [el crítico], al leer los preciosos versos de la gran poetiza argentina Ida Edelvira Rodríguez, autora del *Himno a Colón* que con aplauso universal se ha escuchado en los certámenes literarios del Coliseum y del teatro Colón. ¿No es esto progreso?[41]

> [What does (the critic) say, on reading the precious verses of the great Argentine poetess Ida Edelvira Rodríguez, author of the *Hymn to Columbus* that was heard with universal applause in the literary competitions held at the Coliseum and the Colón theater. Isn't this progress?]

I assume that someone else read the poem for Rodríguez, since that was the custom for presenting women's poetry in public. Again, I make this assumption from the absence of comment on her race.

Does Rodríguez' race matter? For the Afro-Argentine community represented by *La Broma*, the answer is an unequivocal yes. In terms of literary history a hundred years later, again, yes. Rodríguez was able to gain widespread respect for the quality of her poetry, in spite of the fact that there was little Argentine literary tradition for her as a person of color and only a nascent one for her as a woman. It is important to recognize that achievement; moreover, she is a reminder that there were voices from outside the upper class, which history texts should include.

Does Rodríguez' race matter in literary terms? The answer here is not so clear.[42] In many ways, it does not matter. She deserves a place in the history of Argentine poetry for the merits of her writing alone; her poetry is thematically interesting and as aesthetically good as the best of the day. Besides, white writers do not have to write about being white, so black writers should not be obligated to write about being black. Rodríguez has the same right to write about the last aria of the opera *Lucia di Lammermoor* as any other member of the audience. Suppose the author of *Ode to a Grecian Urn* had been black; would readers criticize him for not writing *Ode to an African Urn*? In this sense, today's readers should respect Rodríguez' choices as a creative artist and do her the courtesy of a color-blind reading. That Rodríguez herself was interested in such a reading is evident from her choice to publish in journals aimed at Euro-Argentine readers.

And yet, today's readers cannot help feeling that Rodríguez' race and class do matter in literary, not just biographical or historical, terms. I agree with Richard L. Jackson when he says that "I have always thought that black writers who choose to say little or nothing overtly about the black experience in Latin America are, at the same time, telling us much about it."[43] From this point of view, one way to read her works is to assume that all of them are about being Afro-Argentine, without saying so. This approach has a certain justice—after all, Eduarda Mansilla wrote about the white Argentine experience without saying so—but it also can add an overlay of meaning to some of her poems. Here, for example, is part of her poem, *Voces de la noche* [Voices of the Night], published in 1878:

> —¿Qué expresas con tu música divina,
> Nocturno trovador de la enramada,
> Que en el silencio de la noche inmensa
> Odas o idilios en la sombra cantas? . . .
> —¿Qué acento misterioso es el que escuchas,
> Alma, cuando la noche se adelanta,
> Y envuelta entre su manto tenebroso
> Cruza el cielo de estrellas coronada?
> —El acento divino que desciende
> De lo alto de la esfera constelada,
> En las desgracias de la vida triste:
> ¡El acento inmortal de la esperanza![44]

[What do you express with your divine music,/ Nocturnal troubadour
of the arbor,/ What in the silence of the immense night/ you sing odes
or idylls in the shadows?/(...) What mysterious accent is that which you
hear,/ Soul, when the night approaches,/ And enveloped in its gloomy
mantel/ And crowned with stars, crosses the sky?/ The divine accent
that descends/ From the heights of the constellationed sphere,/ To the
misfortunes of sad life:/ The immortal accent of hope!]

In this poem, the nightbird's song could be read as Rodríguez' own
desire to write. Her joy in the night and the stars becomes more
significant when the reader realizes that, while above were her beloved
stars, surrounding her were the stinking, crowded, noisy slums. While
she was hearing music and poetry in the night of her imagination, the
actual noises in the *conventillo* were much less divine and mysterious.
Most poets of the late 1800s included lines referring to life's misfortunes, but in Rodríguez' case, the line contains echoes of more than just
Romantic sensibility. The poem does not have to be read as a black-
consciousness work, but it certainly gains an extra poignancy when it
is read that way. Yet, a century later, the known facts about Rodríguez'
life are so few that biographical interpretations of her work are mostly
speculative. This is the case with most women authors of the 1800s.

The third of Berg's reading possibilities, and not the least problematic, is that of the feminist account. Many of today's readers hope to
find examples of early feminism in writing of the 1800s. In its worst
form, this "Feminist Imperative" is the modern-day equivalent of the
Delicacy Imperative of a century ago. The Feminist Imperative concludes that any female writer must be feminist; thus, even the most
virulent of anti-emancipationists, such as María Pilar Sinués de Marco,
could be labeled feminist. Successful writers, such as Mansilla and
Gorriti, are assumed to be emancipationists in spite of the writers'
claims to the contrary. It is much easier to enjoy openly emancipationist
writers such as María Eugenia Echenique than to puzzle over anti-
emancipationist sentiments written by strong, worldly women. Yet
anti-emancipationist writers and their accomplishments cannot be dismissed just because they do not fit present-day ideas of professional
women. Did Larrosa really believe—without irony or sarcasm—that a
wife's main duty was to please her husband and that women should not
seek employment outside the home? It must be concluded, however
reluctantly, that yes, she did believe it, and that she did not consider her
own career as a journalist and novelist to be a contradiction. How could
Pelliza demand legal and economic rights for women, but in the same
breath refuse political rights? Conscientious scholars must try to grasp
the nineteenth-century concept of complementary, but not overlapping,

gender roles that Larrosa and Pelliza espoused, and understand how they used such roles to create public careers. Certainly, there are many examples of feminist sentiments deliberately hidden under a submissive rhetoric; Nancy Saporta Sternbach examines the example of Rosa Guerra in this light.[45] The challenge today is to recognize such examples but to refrain from imposing irony on all "womanly" rhetoric.

While not all women writers were emancipationists, they all do reveal a striking strength and energy. They could manipulate with skill the rhetoric of modesty, but they were hardly timid themselves. Even those who opposed emancipation, such as Larrosa, Mansilla, and Pelliza, were advocates of forceful civic motherhood; they demanded respect for women who chose traditional roles and proposed extension of those roles into intellectual and creative areas. Those who did advocate emancipation—most notably, Echenique and Manso—dazzle today's readers with their vision, willingness to express unpopular opinions, and eloquence. The struggles of those in poverty, such as Rodríguez, Larrosa, and Gorriti, seem nothing less than heroic. Thus, all the writers studied here, regardless of political persuasion, fulfill one of present-day feminism's goals: to reconstruct women's past, rewriting it in terms of strength and struggle.

Most readers today approach nineteenth-century women's works with historical, rather than literary, purposes in mind (although there is much literary pleasure to be found). This seeking after historical knowledge reflects a century's change in cultural standards, but it also indicates that, after years of being forgotten, women of the 1800s have found a new readership. This new audience interprets their works in ways that the authors could not have anticipated. The delicacy, for instance, that they were so careful to cultivate is held in low esteem today, while passages of anger, which they tried to suppress, are sought after and prized. In spite of readings that shift over time, however, women's works still speak to female readers in a unique voice, and remind women that they have a proud yesterday.

Endnotes

[1] "La señora Manso," *La Prensa* (25 April 1875): 2.

[2] "Juana Manso," *La Ondina del Plata* (2 May 1875): 145.

[3] Manuel Gálvez, *Amigos y maestros de mi juventud* (1904; reprint, Buenos Aires: Hachette, 1961), 89.

[4] Francine Masiello, *Between Civilization and Barbarism* (Lincoln: University of Nebraska Press, 1992), 70.

[5] Two well-known examples are Joanna Russ, *How to Suppress Women's Writing* (Austin: University of Texas Press, 1983) and Jane Tompkins, *Sensational Designs: The Cultural Work of American Fiction 1790–1860* (New York: Oxford University Press, 1985).

[6] See, for example, Velia Bosch, ed. *Teresa de la Parra ante la crítica* (Caracas: Monte Avila, 1980) and Elsa Krieger Gambarini, "The Male Critic and the Woman Writer: Reading Teresa de la Parra's Critics," Bernice Hausman, trans., *In the Feminine Mode: Essays on Hispanic Women Writers*, Noël Valis and Carol Maier, eds. (Lewisburg: Bucknell University Press, 1990), 177-94.

[7] Gambarini, "The Male Critic," 178.

[8] In the introduction to her novel, Ochagavia says that she has just turned 17, thus she must have been born ca. 1840. She is mentioned as one of the founding members of El Ateneo de La Plata by Sara Jaroslavsky and Estela Maspero, "La cultura argentina en el decenio 1852–1862," *Cursos y Conferencias* 31 (1947): 116. I have been unable to discover more than these meager biographical facts nor have I found evidence of other novels.

[9] Francisco Bilbao, "Literatura," *La Revista del Nuevo Mundo* (11 July 1857): 331. Further references to this essay appear in the text.

[10] Margarita Rufina Ochagavia, *Un ánjel y un demonio o el valor de un juramento* (Buenos Aires: Imprenta de Mayo, 1857), 20.

[11] Oscar Weber, "Resultados inmediatos," *El Album del Hogar* (29 December 1878): 203.

[12] Carlos Guido y Spano, "Hojas de roble," *Pasionarias* (Buenos Aires: Imprenta Europea, Morena y Defensa, 1887), 3.

[13] "Dos palabras sobre la autora," *Los esposos* (Buenos Aires: Compañía Sud-Americana de Billetes de Banco, 1895), 8.

[14] Rafael Obligado, "Crítica literaria: Armonías del alma," *La Ondina del Plata* (12 November 1876): 541.

[15] Ibid., 543.

[16] The *Anuario*'s importance in the history of Argentine literary criticism is discussed in Antonio Pagés Larraya's "La crítica literaria de la generación argentina del 80," *Cuadernos Hispanoamericanos* 390 (December 1982):

676-83. Most of the other critics discussed in this article solved the problem of how to read women's works by ignoring them altogether.

[17] Alberto Navarro Viola, "La marquesa de Altamira," *Anuario bibliográfico de la República* (1881) 3:400-401. The review of *Cuentos* is in (1880) 2:284-86; *Creaciones* in (1883) 5:299-300; and *Lucía Miranda* is in (1882) 6:295-96.

[18] Navarro Viola, *Anuario bibliográfico*, (1882) 4:289.

[19] Edmundo de Amicis, "Prólogo," *Stella* (Barcelona: Maucci, 1909), ix.

[20] Ibid.

[21] This attitude was so prevalent that it even appeared in women's magazines. A review of the Spanish poet Patrocinio de Biedma in *La Ondina del Plata* says that "no merece el efeminado título de poetisa, sino que ha conquistado el de poeta" [does not deserve the effeminate title of poetess, but rather she has won that of poet] and that "piensa como hombre y siente como una mujer" [she thinks like a man and has feelings like a woman]. J.R. de Mendoza, "Patrocinio de Biedma," *La Ondina del Plata* (29 October and 5 November 1876): 520-21, 530.

[22] Raymunda Torres y Quiroga, "Madama Staël," *La Ondina del Plata* (10 December 1876): 595.

[23] Carlota Garrido de la Peña, "Letras femeninas: Emilia Pardo Bazán," *El Búcaro Americano* (1 March 1896): 58.

[24] Ibid., 59.

[25] Hortencia Bustamante de Baeza, "A las señoritas argentinas que escriben en la *Ondina del Plata*," *La Ondina del Plata* (27 August 1876): 411.

[26] Tórtola [Agustina Andrade], "A Silvia Fernández," *La Ondina del Plata* (29 October 1876): 519.

[27] Luciérnaga, "Plumadas," *El Album del Hogar* (30 November 1879): 174-76. See also her "Plumadas," (8 June 1879): 391, and "Arco-Iris," *El Album del Hogar* (28 December 1879): 106.

[28] "Eduarda Mansilla de García," *La Ondina del Plata* (9 May 1875): 157.

[29] *La Ondina del Plata* (2 January 1876): 12.

[30] Mercedes Pujato Crespo, "Historia de las revistas femeninas y mujeres intelectuales que les dieron vida," *Primer Congreso Patriótico de Señoras en América del Sud* (Buenos Aires: Imprenta Europa, 1910): 157-79.

[31] For an overview of Rojas' many literary activities, see Antonio Pagés Larraya, "Ricardo Rojas: fundador de los estudios universitarios sobre literatura argentina," *La Revista de la Universidad de Buenos Aires* 5 (1959): 349-67; reprinted in his *Juan María Gutiérrez y Ricardo Rojas: Iniciación de la crítica argentina* (Buenos Aires: Facultad de Filosofía y Letras, 1983), 57-80. For an idea of the regard in which Rojas is held, see *Testimonios sobre Ricardo Rojas* (Buenos Aires: Instituto de Literatura Argentina "Ricardo Rojas," 1984).

[32] Noemí Vergara de Bietti, "De cómo fui y no fui alumna de Ricardo Rojas," *Testimonios sobre Ricardo Rojas*, 193.

[33] Ricardo Rojas, *La literatura argentina*, *Los modernos* (Buenos Aires: Juan Roldán, 1925) 2:768. There are many editions of this work, so scholars who wish to examine the original text should use whichever edition is available, turning to the chapter "Las mujeres escritoras" in the second volume, *Los modernos*. Further references to this work will appear in the text.

[34] For a discussion of Rojas' theory of history, see Ana María Zubieta, "La historia de la literatura: Dos historias diferentes," *Filología* 22 (1987): 191-213.

[35] See, for example, Zulma Núñez, "Mercedes Rosas, La primera novelista argentina," *Atlántida* (November 1946): 30, 94; "Hace 50 años que murió la poestisa Josefina Pelliza de Sagasta, figura olvidada," *Democracia* (Concordia) (11 August 1938): n.p.; or María Velasco y Arias, "Eduarda Mansilla de García," *Boletín del Colegio de Graduados de la Facultad de Filosofía y Letras* 28-29 (August–December 1939): 91-94.

[36] Mary Berg, "Rereading Fiction by 19th-Century Latin American Women Writers: Interpretation and Translation of the Past into the Present," *Translation Perspectives* 6 (1991): 127.

[37] Ibid., 132-33.

[38] It is possible that Rodríguez wrote about race in articles for the Afro-Argentine newspapers under a pseudonym that I am unaware of.

[39] See, for example, the note in *La Alborada Literaria del Plata* (9 May 1880): 142, in which Rodríguez communicates with the editor by letter, saying that she will submit more poetry when her tasks permit more free time.

[40] Bernardo González Arrili, "Ida Edelvira Rodríguez: La poetisa negra," *Mujeres de nuestra tierra* (Buenos Aires: Ediciones La Obra, 1950), 106-10. The visit was made by the poet Joaquín Castellanos and possibly Emma de la Barra.

[41] Redacción, "Sobre el mismo tema. *El folleto de D. Zenon*." *La Broma* (8 February 1878): 1. I am indebted to George Reid Andrews for informing me of this article, and to Lea Fletcher for tracking it down. For information about the Afro-Argentine community, see George Reid Andrews, *The Afro-Argentines of Buenos Aires 1800–1900* (Madison: University of Wisconsin Press, 1980).

[42] For a good summary of current discussion of this question, see Richard L. Jackson, "Introduction: Recent Trends in Afro-Spanish American Literary Criticism," *The Afro-Spanish American Author II: The 1980s* (West Cornwall, Connecticut: Locust Hill Press, 1989), xiii-xxiii. Also see the conflicting opinions about Phillis Wheatly (1753–84), the United States poet who rarely wrote about her race, in William H. Robinson, ed. *Critical Essays on Phillis Wheatley* (Boston: G.K. Hall, 1982).

[43] Richard L. Jackson, *Black Writers in Latin America* (Albuquerque: University of New Mexico Press, 1979), 6.

[44] Ida Edelvira Rodríguez, "Voces de la noche," *El Album del Hogar* (15 December 1878): 186.

[45] Nancy Saporta Sternbach, "'Mejorar la condición de mi secso': The Essays of Rosa Guerra," *Reinterpreting the Spanish American Essay: Women Writers of the Nineteenth and Twentieth Centuries*, Doris Meyer, ed. (Austin: University of Texas Press, 1995), 46-56.

Biographical Notes

As any genealogist knows, it is not easy to find reliable life information about women. One encyclopedia lists all of Camilo Aldao's sons but none of his daughters; another names Manuel García Mansilla's father, but omits his mother Eduarda. Margarita Rufina Ochagavia mentions in the introduction to her novel, *Un angel o un demonio* (1857), that she is seventeen years old and that is the extent of our knowledge about her. Even Rosa Guerra, who was more prolific than Ochagavía and more visible publicly, lacks a reliable biography: her birthdate is unknown, and her death occurred in 1864, not 1894 as Ricardo Rojas (and those who quote him) have reported.[1] Of the biographical references that are available, Lily Sosa de Newton's *Diccionario biográfico de mujeres argentinas* is the most reliable and extensive. Vicente Cutolo's *Nuevo diccionario biográfico argentino*, on the other hand, is not always reliable—Rodríguez' name is written as Ida Elvira, Lola Larrosa's *Ecos del corazón* is listed as *Suspiros del corazón*, and he accepts Ricardo Rojas as infallible—but if the reader is wary and consults other sources, this dictionary is usable. Occasionally an anthology, such as the one edited by José Carlos Maubé and Adolfo Capdevielle, will provide some useful biographical information, as will social notes in magazines. One such note states that Lola Larrosa's birthday falls on the anniversary of the battle of Ituzaingó;[2] a quick look at a historical dictionary pinpoints that date as February 20. Of the various reference works on pseudonyms, Mario Tesler's recent *Diccionario argentino de seudónimos* includes more women than most. Unfortunately, most women's pseudonyms are unrecorded and lost to today's readers.

In the following entries, the symbol [LSN] indicates that the 1986 edition of Sosa de Newton's *Diccionario biográfico de mujeres argentinas* is a major source of information; [LSN72] refers to the 1972 edition. [VOC] refers to Cutolo's *Nuevo diccionario biográfico argentino*.

The Authors

Elvira Aldao de Díaz (1858–1950) [LSN72]. Born at Rosario into a family of both wealth and influence, Aldao's long life in the elite circles of Rosario and Buenos Aires made her a witness to an extraordinary amount of Argentine history. While her father and brothers pursued public careers, she led the life of a daughter of privilege: she received a smattering of formal education but intense training in manners and dress, and made perpetual visits to female relatives and family friends. Unlike many women of her class, however, she read books with more substance than romances, and although she disclaims intellectual pretensions, it is clear from the references in her memoirs that she read widely. She married Manuel Díaz, a relative who was as wealthy as the Aldaos and with whom she shared a taste for innovation in such luxuries as a private carriage (the first in Rosario) and English-style bathrooms (which allowed both indoor toilets and year-round bathing). Late in her life, she travelled often in Europe, spending the World War I years in France, Italy, and Spain. In 1922, she published *Mientras ruge el huracán*, which recounts her observations of life in an Italian hotel during the war. She was 64 years old at the time. Whatever had been pent up inside her now came pouring out, the books—ten in all—appearing at regular intervals until her death. She never wrote fiction; instead, she wrote about her childhood (*Recuerdos de antaño*); summers in Mar del Plata, which the Aldaos helped develop into a resort (*Veraneos marplatenses*); another memoir of the war (*Horas de guerra y horas de paz*); and great men she knew and admired (*Reminiscencias sobre Aristóbulo del Valle* and *Cartas íntimas*). When she died at the age of 92 in Mar del Plata, *La Nación* published a sympathetic obituary in her honor, calling her "la testigo capaz de discernir qué correspondía a la historia y qué iba formando la historia pequeña"[3] [the witness capable of discerning what corresponded to history and what formed intimate history].

Agustina Andrade (1858–91) Pseudonym: La Tórtola. [LSN, VOC]. Born in Gualeguaychú, Andrade was the daughter of one of Argentina's most famous poets, Olegario V. Andrade. By the age of sixteen, she was already publishing poems in newspapers and magazines, both those edited by her father and by others. She is included in *El Album poético argentino* (1877), and her previously published poems were collected in 1878 in the much-praised *Lágrimas: ensayos poéticos*. At the age of 18, Andrade married the explorer and celebrity Ramón Lista with whom she had two daughters. Evidently, she ceased to write after her marriage.

Her biographer, Horacio Romero, implies that the marriage was un-happy due to the infidelities of Lista.[4] For whatever reason, Andrade ended her life with a gunshot to the heart at the age of 33.

Emma de la Barra (1861–1947) Pseudonym: César Duayen. [LSN]. Married young to her paternal uncle, Emma Barra de la Barra led the quiet life of a wealthy woman in Buenos Aires, organizing charity projects, receiving praise for her singing at private gatherings, and writing nothing more than an article or two for the newspapers about musical activities.[5] Then, in 1904, her husband died. To distract herself during the period of mourning, she wrote the novel *Stella: novela de costumbres argentinas*, which was published under the pseudonym of César Duayen in 1905. From the first, the novel was an enormous success, meriting a long and perceptive review in *La Nación*.[6] It also provoked speculation about its author, who finally was revealed in *La Nación* on September 26, 1905.[7] Within two months of its appearance more than 9,000 copies of *Stella* had been sold,[8] with editions continu-ing to appear into the 1940s; in an interview in 1932, the author mentions that more than 300,000 copies of *Stella* had been sold.[9] No Argentine novel, by a man or a woman, had ever sold so many copies, and few have sold as many since. Shortly after the publication of *Stella*, Barra married Julio Llanos, with whom she shared interests in both journalism and travel; their most notable joint project was a series of dispatches from Europe during World War I. Other novels appeared, but without the enormous success of the first: *Mecha Iturbe* (1906); *Eleonora* (1933); and *La dicha de Malena* (1943), the latter two appearing first in serial form. Barra also wrote a collection of children's stories, *El manantial* (1908), along with many articles and stories for the daily press. Shortly before Barra died, *Stella* became a success once again, this time as a film directed by Benito Perojo in 1943.[10]

María Eugenia Echenique (1851–78) [VOC]. It was not easy for a writer living in Córdoba to break into the circles of Buenos Aires, but Echenique was the exception. When she died at the age of just 26, probably of cancer, she was mourned in both cities. *La Nación* called her a "joven de extraordinario talento" [a young woman of extraordi-nary talent]; her old debating foe, Josefina Pelliza, praised the "fuerza dulce y persuasiva de su palabra siempre profunda y medida" [sweet and persuasive force of her always profound and measured words]; and Juana Manuela Gorriti laid a wreath on her tomb.[11] Echenique, having studied law,[12] had more formal education than most women of her day, as her intelligent, insightful essays reflect. Two series of articles in particular brought her both respect and çontroversy: the first was

"Cartas a Elena" (1874), in which she found the contemplation of nature to be an inspiration for meditations about science, education, the future of women, and even space travel. The second was a much read and commented on debate with Pelliza in the pages of *La Ondina del Plata* (May 7–October 15, 1876) about the emancipation of women. Although many writers wrote about the emancipation of women, Echenique's essays stand out for their intellectual depth and for her understanding of the economics of the issue; for example, she pointed out the irony of the government's support of immigrant workers while native-born Argentine women were unable to find employment.[13] Her sister Rosario edited a collection of Echenique's essays under the title of *Colección literaria*, the second edition appearing in 1926.

Silvia Fernández (1857–1945) [LSN]. Fernández was just 19 when she published her first collection of poems, *Armonías del alma*, most of which had already appeared in newspapers and journals. Although this first book was very well received, she did not publish again until 37 years later, when *Versos* appeared in 1913. A third collection, also called *Versos*, was published in 1922. Fernández never married, living a quiet life among her family.[14] Many of her poems are religious in nature, but some reveal a delightful sense of humor that sets her apart from her contemporaries.

Juana Manuela Gorriti (1816–92) [LSN]. Gorriti was born in 1816 (not 1818 or 1819 as stated in many biographies), to a distinguished family that was forced into exile to Bolivia by Rosas. While still a teenager, she married Isidoro Belzú, a charismatic military man who became President of Bolivia. It was a tempestuous marriage. Eventually the couple separated, and Gorriti moved to Lima, Peru, with her two daughters. Later, she had two illegitimate children. Tragically, she outlived all of her children. Faced with little income, Gorriti began to write and teach for a living. Through her *tertulias*, which became centers of intellectual life in Lima, she encouraged many others to write. Her anecdotal memoir, *Lo íntimo* (1892), reveals an abiding kindness toward other authors, especially women. Gorriti continued her role as mentor when she returned to Buenos Aires in 1875. She was a model of the disciplined, professional author at a time when women were beginning to view writing as a profession instead of a pastime. From the time she began to write in the early 1840s until a few days before her death in 1892, she produced a steady and varied stream of essays, vignettes, stories, translations, biographies, and novels. She even compiled a cookbook with recipes from friends that is strikingly similar to those of women's organizations so popular today in the United States.

Gorriti's literary works fall squarely within the first wave of Romanticism in Hispanic America. Her stories, such as "La novia del muerto" [Dead Man's Bride] or "El guante negro" [The Black Glove], are still a pleasure to read. It is not surprising that among the first movies made in Argentina were film versions of her stories. All but forgotten during the first half of this century, Gorriti is the subject of much attention these days. Feminist literary historians are preparing new editions of her work. This new analysis of her work is restoring Gorriti to her place among Hispanic American authors.[15]

Lola Larrosa de Ansaldo (1857–95) [VOC].[16] Born in Uruguay, Larrosa came to Buenos Aires as a young woman and spent her professional career there until her death from tuberculosis at the age of 38. Unlike wealthy women who wrote for their own pleasure or for intellectual satisfaction, Larrosa earned her living by writing conventional newspaper stories,[17] numerous essays for women's journals, and four novels; she also edited the literary magazine *La Alborada del Plata* in 1880. After her marriage, she continued to write to support her husband and son, since her husband suffered from mental illness.[18] Her novels are curious hybrids, containing idyllic scenes of domestic bliss alongside vivid descriptions of female poverty. Perhaps she knew more about poverty than about bliss; Matto de Turner says that Larrosa's novels "le dieron pan escasísimo, pero, cuando ella también comenzó a enfermar . . . las más desesperantes exigencias sitiaron ese hogar infortunado"[19] [earned her very little daily bread, and when she also became ill (...) her unfortunate home was besieged by the most desperate suffering]. Judging from the numerous mentions of Larrosa in the social notes of women's journals and the moving elegies after her death, she must have been well-liked. The Sociedad Proteccionista Intelectual, a women's literary group of which Larrosa was a member, paid for her funeral and commemorative plaque.

Eduarda Mansilla de García (1838–92) Pseudonyms: Daniel, Alvar, Eduarda, and possibly others. [LSN]. The niece of the dictator Rosas, the daughter of the noted general Mansilla and his famously beautiful child-bride Agustina Rosas, the sister of the dandy and writer Lucio Mansilla, and the mother of the talented García boys, Eduarda Mansilla was destined to be noticed. Fortunately, in addition to the famous men in her life, she possessed intelligence and talent of her own. She was married at age 16 to Manuel García, son of a prominent anti-Rosas family, prompting the newspapers to dub them Romeo and Juliet. Soon after, she began writing, maintaining a prodigious output until her last years when ill health finally silenced her. She wrote countless newspaper articles, four novels, a book of short stories, Argentina's first book of children's stories, three plays, a travel memoir, and even music for the piano.[20] She accompanied her diplomat husband to the United States, where she knew President Lincoln (whom she admired and described with sympathy) and Mrs. Lincoln (whom she found chubby, vulgar, and pretentious).[21] When her husband was assigned to European duties, Mansilla flourished in the salons of Paris and wrote a novel in French. The couple had separated, however, by the time García died from a bone caught in his throat; Mansilla had to travel from Florence to Vienna to be at his deathbed. When she returned to Buenos Aires for the last time in 1890, her children, who had spent most of their lives in Europe, had trouble adjusting to a city that, to them, was a backwater.[22] Mansilla's struggles to sustain a genuine career as a writer helped open doors for other women, and in her writing, within the limits of her class ideology, she advocated improvements in women's roles. Yet she rejected friendship with other women writers, including overtures from Juana Manuela Gorriti, her rival as most influential woman writer of the day.[23] Mansilla's writings are currently undergoing something of a revival, and certainly some of her works are deserving (her *Recuerdos de viaje* are especially enjoyable), but it would be a mistake to overstate her role as a protofeminist. She herself said that "no soy partidaria de la emancipación de la mujer"[24] [I am not a believer in the emancipation of women].

Juana Paula Manso (1819–75) [LSN]. A fighter and a rebel, Manso also was a one of the outstanding thinkers of her day. These were not endearing qualities to a society that disapproved of women who are both smart and outspoken. Marriage to a shiftless musician, who soon abandoned her, left Manso on her own to earn a living for herself and her children. She founded coeducational schools—a scandalous innovation—and carried out a distinguished career in education and educational reform. She gave Chataqua-style public lectures to audiences that often were unsympathetic. At some of her lectures in 1866–67, for instance, the audience shouted her down, splashed asafoetida on her clothes, and threw stones at her. Yet she also earned much applause, and even managed to gain the respect of the generally misogynist newspaper, *La Prensa*. Manso converted to a Protestant belief, which fed the animosity of some aspects of Buenos Aires society. As she lay dying, a priest and some society women tried repeatedly to extract confession and communion from her, but Manso's will was as strong as ever: "La Sra. Manso, sin conmoverse, señalándoles la Biblia que tenía a su lado, les informó que en el evangelio de Jesucristo, había estudiado los principios en que descansaba su fe y que esta fe era inconmovible." [25] [Unmoved, Mrs. Manso, pointing to the Bible that she had at her side, informed them that in the gospels of Jesus Christ, she had studied the principles on which her faith rested and that this faith was unshakable.] Refused burial in the municipal cemeteries, Manso was buried instead in the British cemetery through the intervention of the British ambassador.

Manso published two novels, *Los misterios del Plata* and *La familia del Comendador*, as well as the newspaper, *El Album de Señoritas* before giving up literature to focus on pedagogical and other non-literary writings. Her ideas about the emancipation of women were not taken up by large segments of society until after her death. Her lasting contributions to Argentine women were in educational reform, in breaking barriers to women's writing, and in providing an example of unswerving feminism.[26]

Clorinda Matto de Turner (1852–1909) [LSN]. This Peruvian author figures in a study of nineteenth-century Argentina because she, like Juana Manuela Gorriti, came to Buenos Aires late in life, founded a women's literary magazine, and was a crusading mentor to women writers. Born in Cuzco, Matto was fluent in Quechua and knowledgeable about the customs of the Indians in that region. Married to an English doctor and unsuccessful businessman, she lived in a small Andean town that later would provide the setting for her novel *Aves sin nido* [Birds without a Nest]. There she began to write occasional works such as historical vignettes, short essays for newspapers, and translations from Quechua. Matto's financial situation worsened following her husband's death, forcing her to turn to writing and editing in earnest in order to earn a living. She eventually moved to Lima and established a reputation for seeking rights for women and Indians and for criticizing the Catholic Church. Her writings, particularly her novels *Aves sin nido* and *Indole*, scandalized and infuriated many Peruvians to the extent that, in 1895, a mob destroyed her house and press. She escaped to Buenos Aires where she lived for the remainder of her life. Matto had lost her country but not her nerve. When speaking at the all-male Ateneo, shortly after arriving in Buenos Aires, she took the opportunity to chide the audience for not supporting women writers. Within a few months, Matto began publishing *El Búcaro Americano*, a magazine dedicated to women's issues, that endured until shortly before her death in 1909.[27] More than any other figure of the day, Matto educated her readers about the many active women writers throughout Latin America. She left no doubt that women authors were not alone and that their literature was thriving and valuable.

Josefina Pelliza de Sagasta (1848–88) Pseudonyms: Figarillo, Judith, and possibly others. [LSN, VOC]. This writer was born underneath a wagon while her parents were moving to Concordia to be at a safe distance from the dictator Rosas. Pelliza left Concordia as a young woman for Buenos Aires, where she married Félix Sagasta, had several children, and continued to write poetry for a variety of newspapers and journals. She also wrote novels and essays, engaged in several debates on women's issues, and edited *La Alborada del Plata* in 1878.[28] Pelliza's fiction and poetry were conventionally Romantic, which earned her much public praise, but also some scathing reviews. The evolution from the preface of *Lirios silvestres* (1877) to that of *Conferencias* (1885) reveals an increasingly bitter and defiant tone. In her opinions about emancipation, too, there is an evolution from the fierce anti-emancipationist of the debate with Echenique in 1876, to the equally fierce campaigner for women's rights in *Conferencias* in 1885, though she never wavered in her opposition to woman suffrage. Her particular causes were the right to education, legal reform to give women custody of their children and a role in managing family finances, and the defense of women writers. When Pelliza died at the age of 40 (the Recoleta Cemetery records list uremia as the cause of death), Juana Manuela Gorriti tried to organize an album of poetry in her honor, but the effort failed.[29] Gorriti suggested that Pelliza's admirers were more attracted by her beauty than by her writing, and lamented how quickly her friend was forgotten.

Ida Edelvira Rodríguez (ca. 1860–?) Pseudonym: Everardo and probably others [LSN]. In the series of profiles written about contributors to *El Album del Hogar* in 1879, that of Rodríguez offers a few bare facts about her: she was "sin bienes de fortuna y nacida en modesto hogar" [without fortune and born in an humble home], yet "cuenta apenas 19 años de edad y ya su nombre ha repercutido allende el Plata"[30] [she is barely 19 years old and already her name has reverberated beyond the River Plate]. This meager note at least indicates her age; on the back of her photo filed in the Archivo General Nacional in Buenos Aires is a hand-written inscription that says, "Literata argentina vive en lo del Sr. Angel Estrada, donde fue criada" [Argentine writer living at the house of Mr. Angel Estrada, where she was raised]. (Estrada was the editor and owner of a press that is still in existence. Perhaps Rodríguez was the child of a servant in the Estrada household). Beyond these two references, the only other biographical material I have been able to find is in Bernardo González Arrili's *Mujeres de nuestra tierra*.[31] In it, he records a visit to Rodríguez' apartment in a slum on Venezuela Street. The surprise of the visitors at the poverty of the dwelling was supplanted by their discovery of the poet's race: Rodríguez was the daughter of former slaves. In spite of her poverty, Rodríguez spoke knowledgeably about current national and foreign writers and with animation about the classics. Unable to afford her own books, she read those that a friend loaned her. She preferred to read about ancient Greece, but had to be satisfied with ancient Rome, since her friend's library did not include works on Greece. "Tenía escrita 'inútilmente', según advirtió con sonrisa entristecida, una tragedia en verso cuya acción se desarrollaba en la Roma de los Emperadores"[32] [She had written 'uselessly,' she told us with a sad smile, a tragedy in verse with the action set in Imperial Rome]. Rodríguez' poems were included in *El Album poético argentino* (1877), in *El Album del Hogar* from 1878 to 1880, and in *La Alborada Literaria del Plata* (1880); according to González Arrili, she also wrote "social notes" which were probably unsigned or signed with a pseudonym. As far as I have been able to determine, she was able to publish only one small book, *La flor de la montaña* (1887). Nowhere in her poetry will readers find reference to her poverty, her surroundings in the slums, or her race. Today's readers may regret that she did not write about these subjects, but it is not difficult to see that she would have good reasons to avoid them.

Endnotes

[1] Néstor Tomás Auza found the only published announcement of Guerra's death in *El Nacional* (23 August 1864), five days after the event. See his *Periodismo y feminismo en la Argentina* (Buenos Aires: Emecé, 1988), 187.

[2] "Miscelánea," *La Alborada Literaria del Plata* (29 February 1880): 63.

[3] "Elvira Aldao de Díaz falleció en Mar del Plata," *La Nación* (15 May 1950): 4.

[4] Horacio Romero, *La poesía en la tierra de Andrade* (Gualeguachú: Imprenta Gutenberg, 1946), 70. Lista himself was murdered for failure to pay a debt. See *La Nación* (24 February 1898): 5.

[5] See, for example, Emma de la Barra, "Concierto del círculo Santa Cecilia," *La Nación* (20 June 1893): 3. Barra founded this musical society.

[6] "Bibliografía: Stella," *La Nación* (15 September 1905): 5.

[7] "Stella: Una Revelación del Exito," *La Nación* (26 September 1905): 8. To follow both the success of the novel and the speculations about its author, see previous articles (19 September 1905): 3 and (24 September 1905): 9.

[8] "Biblioteca de la Nación," *La Nación* (25 December 1905): 1.

[9] "Una novela y una vida," *Noticias Gráficas* (24 October 1932): 9.

[10] "Stella," *Heraldo del Cinematografista* (13 October 1943): 189. Still photos from the movie are included in "Personajes de papel y tinta," *Sintonía* (1 September 1943): 56-57. My thanks to the kind staff at the Museo del Cine for their help in finding these sources.

[11] "Maria Eujenia Echenique." *La Nación* (31 January 1878): n.p.; Josefina Pelliza de Sagasta, "María Eugenia Echenique," *La Alborada del Plata* (3 February 1878): 89; and *Colección literaria* (Córdoba: "La Elzeviriana," 1926), 15-16.

[12] "Mosáico," *La Alborada Literaria del Plata* (21 March 1880): 95.

[13] María Eugenia Echenique, "Necesidades de la mujer argentina," *La Ondina del Plata* (16 January 1876): 25-27; in *Colección literaria*, 183-88.

[14] "Falleció Ayer Doña Silvia Fernández," *La Nación* (26 June 1945): 14.

[15] A notable example of this new scholarship on Gorriti is *El ajuar de la patria*, Cristina Iglesia, comp. (Buenos Aires: Feminaria, 1993). This collection of essays provides an excellent starting point for understanding Gorriti's life and work. For a more detailed biography of Gorriti, see the entry by Mary Berg in *Spanish American Women Writers: A Bio-Bibliographical Source Book*, Diane Marting, ed. (New York: Greenwood, 1990), 227-40.

[16] Although Cutolo is often careless about his information, this entry is particularly error ridden. More reliable are the speeches given at Larrosa's memorial service and reported in "Social," *El Búcaro Americano* (1 and 15 February 1896): 17-22, 44-46.

[17] For example, see "25 de Mayo de 1810," *La Nación* (25 May 1877): 2. The content is conventional patriotism.

[18] Clorinda Matto de Turner delicately identifies Larrosa's husband's illness as the same one that killed Guy de Maupassant, i.e., syphilis. *El Búcaro Americano* (1 February 1896): 18.

[19] Ibid.

[20] See Lily Sosa de Newton, "Eduarda Mansilla de García: narradora, periodista, música y primera autora de literatura infantil," *Mujeres y cultura en la Argentina del siglo XIX*, Lea Fletcher, ed. (Buenos Aires: Feminaria, 1994), 87-95.

[21] Eduarda Mansilla de García, *Recuerdos de viaje* (Buenos Aires: Alsina, 1882), 80-81.

[22] See the memoirs of Daniel García Mansilla, *Visto, oído y recordado* (Buenos Aires: Kraft, 1950), 184, 196-97.

[23] Juana Manuela Gorriti, *Lo íntimo* (Buenos Aires: Ramón Espasa, 1892), 73-74.

[24] Eduarda Mansilla de García, "America literaria: educación de la mujer," *La Nación* (28 July 1883): 1. This essay is also notable for its defense of sewing as a means of making a good living, a case of class-induced blindness.

[25] "Entierro de la señora Manso," *La Prensa* (27 April 1875): 1.

[26] See the excellent article by Lea Fletcher, "Juana Manso: una voz en el desierto," *Mujeres y cultura en la Argentina del siglo XIX* (Buenos Aires: Feminaria, 1994), 108-20. Fletcher describes how Manso's physical appearance has distorted her reputation in the eyes of many Argentines, who even today dismiss Manso because she was not pretty.

[27] Additional biographical information is found in Mary Berg's entry in *Spanish American Women Writers*, 303-15.

[28] A notice in the 30 May 1876, issue of *La Nación* announced that she was going to publish a monthly magazine to be called *La Mujer*, but Néstor Tomás Auza was unable to find evidence that the plan was carried out: *Periodismo y femenismo en la Argentina 1830-1930* (Buenos Aires: Emecé, 1988), 26.

[29] *Lo íntimo*, 100-101.

[30] Luciérnaga, "Retratos a la pluma: Ida Edelvira Rodríguez," *El Album del Hogar* (19 October 1879): 127.

[31] Bernardo González Arrili, "Ida Edelvira Rodríguez: la poetisa negra," *Mujeres de nuestra tierra* (Buenos Aires: Ediciones La Obra, 1950), 106-10. My thanks to Lily Sosa de Newton for pointing out this source, and my thanks to Lea Fletcher for loaning it to me.

[32] Ibid., 109.

Fig. 1. Eduarda Mansilla de García. (Photo: Archivo General de la Nación, Buenos Aires.) [Observe Mansilla's gown and see page 78, note 71, for a detailed description of dressmaking in the 1850s.]

Fig. 2. María Eugenia Echenique.
(Photo: frontispiece of her book,
Colección literaria.)

Fig. 3. Rosa Guerra.
(Photo: Archivo General de la Nación, Buenos Aires.)

Fig. 4. Lola Larrosa de Ansaldo. (Photo: frontispiece
of her book, *Obras de misericordia.*)

Fig. 5. Agustina Andrade.
(Photo: archives, *La Prensa*.)

Fig. 6. Ida Elvira Rodríguez.
(Photo: Archivo General de la
Nación, Buenos Aires.)

Fig. 7. Silvia Fernández. (Photo, left: archives, *La Prensa*.)

Fig. 8. Juana Manuela Gorriti. (Photo, bottom: Archivo General de la Nación.)

CARICATURAS CONTEMPORÁNEAS
Señora EMMA DE DE LA BARRA, por CAO

Escribió un brillante libro que ha tenido la virtud,
en unas cuantas semanas, de hacer célebre á su autora,
gracias á la cual el cielo es más luminoso ahora,
pues se la debe una *Stella* de primera magnitud.

Fig. 9. Emma de la Barra (Cameo
photo: Archivo General de la Nación,
Buenos Aires.)

Fig.10. Emma de la Barra (carica-
ture: *Caras y Caretas*, 7 octubre 1905).

Fig. 11. Clorinda Matto de Turner, 1890. (Photo, top: courtesy, Mary Berg).

Fig. 12. Juana Paula Manso. (Photo, left: archives, *La Prensa*).

Fig. 13. Josefina Pelliza de Sagasta. (Photo, right: *El Sud-Americano*, 1888:73, at Biblioteca Nacional.).

a.

b.

c.

d.

Fig. 14. Argentine postal stamps hon-
oring Argentina's women writers:
  a. Cecilla Grierson.
  b. Alfonsina Storni.
  c. Juana Azurduy de Padilla.
  d. Juana Manuela Gorriti.
  e. Juana Paula Manso.

e.

Chronology of Selected Events Concerning Women's Writing in Argentina 1810–1985

1810. Overthrow of the Viceroyalty, leading to independence from Spain. Much of the pre- and post-Independence intellectual and political activity occurs at salons held by women; the most famous one is that of Mariquita Sánchez, where, among other notable events, the national anthem is sung for the first time.

1823. President Bernardino Rivadavia creates the Sociedad de Beneficencia, under the direction of 13 women from the social elite, to establish elementary schools for girls.

1829. Juan Manuel Rosas is elected governor of Buenos Aires, thus consolidating his political hold over the country. Rosas rejects the values of the Enlightenment that had guided the Independence movement, and imposes the traditional Spanish values of church, military, and patriarchal family.

1830. The first Argentine women's newspaper, *La Aljaba*, debuts on November 16. It is edited by the Uruguayan poet, Petrona Rosende de Sierra, who is a fervent advocate of education for women. The newspaper is closed down after just three months of publication.

1832. George Sand publishes *Indiana*, which is widely read in Latin America in spite of disapproval of the author's personal life.

1838. Eduarda Mansilla is born. Her aunt, the wife of Rosas, dies, and Rosas declares two years of national mourning for her. Rosas' daughter, Manuelita, becomes hostess at official gatherings; Rosas refuses to allow her to marry, enforcing the custom that the unmarried daughter take care of her parents. Rosas withholds funding from the Sociedad de Beneficencia, effectively halting its educational activities.

1839. As the terror under Rosas increases, thousands of writers and intellectuals seek haven in exile, among them Mariquita Sánchez and the families of Juana Manuela Gorriti and Juana Manso.

1848. Josefina Pelliza is born under a wagon during her parents' move to Entrerríos. Camila O'Gorman and her lover are shot on orders from Rosas.

1851. María Eugenia Echenique is born.

1852. The dictator Rosas is defeated in the Battle of Caseros on February 3 and flees to England; there, his daughter, Manuelita, defies her father and marries. Thousands of exiles begin returning to Argentina. The Sociedad de Beneficencia is re-established. Rosa Guerra and others publish the thrice-weekly newspaper *La Camelia* from April 11 to May 11. Harriet Beecher Stowe's *Uncle Tom's Cabin* is published in book form, and becomes known to many Argentine women who either read it in imported copies or hear about it through newspaper reports.

1854. Juana Manso publishes *El Album de Señoritas* from January 1 to February 17. Her novel, *La familia del Comendador*, unfinished in the newspaper, is published separately.

1856. The novel *La gaviota* by Fernán Caballero (Cecilia Böhl de Faber) becomes a best seller in Spain.

1857. Margarita Rufina Ochagavia's novel, *El ángel o el demonio o el valor de un juramento*, is published. Silvia Fernández and Lola Larrosa are born.

1858. Elvira Aldao and Agustina Andrade are born. In Madrid the play *Baltasar*, by Cuba's Gertrudis Gómez de Avellaneda, sets a new performance record.

1859. Juana Manso scandalizes Buenos Aires by establishing its first coeducational elementary school.

1860. Rosa Guerra and Eduarda Mansilla both publish novels called *Lucía Miranda*. Mansilla also publishes *El médico de San Luis*, reprinted in 1879 and 1962. Ida Edelvira Rodríguez is born.

1861. Slavery is abolished in Buenos Aires, and the slaves are emancipated; previous laws had emancipated slaves in the provinces in 1853. Mercedes Rosas, sister of the dictator, publishes *María de Montiel* under the pseudonym of M. Sasor. Emma de la Barra is born.

1862. *Clemencia: Drama en 3 actos y en verso* is published by Rosa Guerra. Juana Manso's school text, *Compendio de la historia de las Provincias Unidas del Río de la Plata* appears in its first edition.

1863. Rosa Guerra publishes *Julia o la educación: Libro de lectura.* Mercedes Rosas, still using the pseudonym M. Sasor, publishes *Emma.* In Spain, Rosalía de Castro captures the beauty of the Galician language in her collection of folk-inspired poems, *Cantares gallegos.*

1864. Rosa Guerra's last work, *Desahogos del corazón: Poesías*, is published. Guerra dies in August of this year.

1865. Juana Manso assumes the editorship of *Los Anales de Educación Común.* Though still living in Lima, Juana Manuela Gorriti publishes *Sueños y realidades* in Buenos Aires.

1867. Manso publishes *Los misterios del Plata*, written ca. 1846. Jorge Isaacs of Colombia publishes *María*, Latin America's most popular Romantic novel.

1868. Mariquita Sánchez dies. Her death represents the passing of the idealistic generation that fought for independence from Spain, only to lose their freedom to Rosas.

1869. In Paris, Eduarda Mansilla publishes *Pablo ou la vie dans les Pampas.*

1870. Bartolomé Mitre founds a daily newspaper, *La Nación*. It includes women's writing and announces their latest works; it is generally more hospitable to women than its rival, *La Prensa*, established the previous year.

1872. José Hernández publishes *Martín Fierro*, probably the most widely read Argentine book of the nineteenth century.

1875. The most influential pro-emancipationist journal, *La Ondina del Plata*, is founded by Luis Telmo Pintos; the first issue appears on February 7. Juana Manso dies on April 24. Her enemies, citing her membership in a Protestant religion, prevent her burial in the municipal cemetery, thus defying the cemetery's written policy of being open to all faiths. Manso is buried instead in the British cemetery. Josefina Pelliza de Sagasta's first novel, *Margarita*, is published and announced on the front page of *La Nación*. Juana Manuela Gorriti arrives in Buenos Aires and establishes literary salons as she had done in Lima.

1876. María Eugenia Echenique and Josefina Pelliza de Sagasta engage in a widely read debate concerning women's rights in *La Ondina del*

Plata. Echenique articulates the moderate emancipationist stance that will gain acceptance over the next decades. Silvia Fernández publishes her first book of poetry, *Armonías del alma*. Gorriti publishes *Panoramas de la vida*.

1877. Gorriti's *La Alborada del Plata* begins publication on November 18. *La Ondina del Plata* publishes *El Album poético argentino*, which features women's writing alongside men's. Josefina Pelliza publishes *La chiriguana* and *Lirios silvestres*.

1878. *La Alborada del Plata* ceases publication on May 1. On July 7, *El Album del Hogar*, edited by Gervasio Méndez, begins publishing. Its first *época* of 1878–84 is hospitable to women's writing; its second era does not include any women. Agustina Andrade publishes a collection of her poetry, *Lágrimas*. Lola Larrosa de Ansaldo publishes *Ecos del corazón*, a collection of her essays. María Eugenia Echenique dies in Córdoba at the age of 26. Gorriti's *Misceláneas* is published.

1879. On December 28, *La Ondina del Plata* ceases publication.

1880. Lola Larrosa de Ansaldo resuscitates *La Alborada del Plata*, calling it *La Alborada Literaria del Plata*, from January 1 to May 9. Eduarda Mansilla publishes the first Argentine collection of children's stories, *Cuentos*.

1881. Eduarda Mansilla publishes the drama *La marquesa de Altamira*. Josefina Pelliza publishes *Canto inmortal*.

1882. Larrosa's first novel, *Las obras de misericordia*, appears. Mansilla publishes *Recuerdos de viaje*, her memoirs of life in the United States during the Lincoln administration. Her 1860 novel, *Lucía Miranda*, is republished under her own name. Pelliza publishes *El César*. Gorriti publishes *El mundo de los recuerdos*.

1883. Mansilla publishes *Creaciones*, a collection of short stories. Celestina Funes publishes yet another *Lucía Miranda*, this one in verse. In Spain, Emilia Pardo Bazán sparks controversy with *La cuestión palpitante*, a defense of Naturalism.

1884. On April 6, *El Album del Hogar* ceases publication.

1885. Mansilla publishes *Un amor*. Pelliza publishes a collection of essays called *Conferencias: el libro de las madres*. It includes a passionate plea to modify the legal principle of *patria potestad*, which denied women legal custody of their children.

1887. Pelliza publishes *Pasionarias*, a collection of poetry and short stories. Ida Edelvira Rodríguez publishes *La flor de la montaña*, her first and perhaps only work published outside of periodicals. The 1887 census lists 42 women ranchers, but no women in the professions. There are 789 primary school teachers, then the only respectable job for women. In contrast, there are 29,570 women employed as washerwomen or maids.[1]

1888. *El lujo*, Lola Larrosa's novel about a prodigal daughter, is published. Josefina Pelliza dies at the age of 40; Gorriti tries to put together a commemorative album, but the effort fails. Gorriti publishes *Oásis en la vida*.

1889. Cecilia Grierson becomes the first woman to be graduated from an Argentine medical school; she begins a distinguished career in public health for women and children. Other female "firsts" follow, but the professions continue to be virtually all male. Gorriti publishes *La tierra natal*. In Peru, Clorinda Matto de Turner's novel, *Aves sin nido*, is published. The reaction to the novel is stormy: Matto is excommunicated by the Church and burned in effigy. Her friend, Mercedes Cabello de Carbonera, publishes *Blanca Sol*, a novel in the style of Zola.

1890. Gorriti gathers recipes from friends and relatives, and publishes them in a collection called *Cocina ecléctica*.

1891. Agustina Andrade commits suicide by shooting herself in the heart.

1892. Juana Manuela Gorriti and Eduarda Mansilla de García die. Both deaths inspire large public funerals and lengthy newspaper coverage.

1893. Rubén Darío arrives in Buenos Aires, where he will stay until 1898. His circles establish *modernismo* in Argentina; women are not invited. Excluded from the new Ateneo founded by Rafael Obligado, literary women organize their own Sociedad Proteccionista Intelectual, which grows to 800 members. Larrosa publishes her last novel, *Los esposos*.

1895. Clorinda Matto de Turner, fleeing violent persecution in Peru, arrives in Buenos Aires. The Ateneo invites her to give a speech, something no woman has been invited to do before. She takes the opportunity to chide the men for not knowing or supporting women's writing. Lola Larrosa dies of tuberculosis.

1896. The first issue of *El Búcaro Americano*, edited by Clorinda Matto de Turner, appears on February 1; in the first and second numbers, it publishes the elegies to Larrosa at the dedication of her commemorative plaque. The text of Matto's speech to the Ateneo is reprinted in the first issue. Drawing on a very different audience, the anarchist women's periodical, *La Voz de la Mujer*, begins publication; it appears whenever funds permit, and internal struggles cause a rapid turnover of editors.

1897. Matto de Turner publishes the textbook *Analogía: Segundo año de gramática castellana en las escuelas normales, según el programa oficial*.

1901. Clorinda Matto de Turner publishes a translation into Quechua of the Biblical books Luke and Acts.

1902. Matto de Turner publishes *Boreales, miniaturas y porcelanas*.

1903. Lola Mora's sculpture of female nudes causes such public uproar that it is moved from a popular park to a less visible spot among the trees in a remote plaza.

1905. Emma de la Barra publishes her first novel, *Stella*, under the pseudonym of César Duayen. The novel becomes an overnight sensation, and editions continue into the 1940s.

1906. Barra publishes *Mecha Iturbe*, which does not have *Stella's* success.

1907. During the bitter Tenants' Strike, women take an active part in protesting rent increases by slumlords. *Afectos*, a book of poetry, is published by Edelina Soto y Calvo, who is 63 at the time. Published at the insistence of her brother, the poet Francisco Soto y Calvo, the book is well received, and she continues to publish into her eighties.

1908. As Matto de Turner's health fails, *El Búcaro Americano* publishes its last issue on May 16. Barra publishes a collection of children's stories, *El manantial*.

1909. Clorinda Matto de Turner dies on October 25. Her *Cuatro conferencias sobre América del Sur* is published in Buenos Aires and *Viaje de recreo* in Valencia.

1912. Ricardo Rojas is named first professor of Argentine literature at the University of Buenos Aires, giving him a unique opportunity to establish the literary canon.

1913. Silvia Fernández, after a silence of 37 years, publishes *Versos*. In Montevideo, Delmira Agustini publishes *Los cálices vacíos*, a pioneering work of female erotic imagery.

1914. The census of this year counts 517 women in the professions, 5,848 primary school teachers, and 93,000 domestic servants or washerwomen.

1916. Alfonsina Storni publishes her first book, *La inquietud del rosal*. In the next 20 years, she will produce an astonishing body of work that establishes her as one of Argentina's finest poets. She also represents the extraordinary generation of the 1930s, a group of women who, unlike the women of the Ochenta, has left a lasting literary memory.

1918. "En la sierra," based on a Gorriti story, is filmed by the pioneering Argentine production company Martínez y Gunche. The two men who found the company plan to film more Gorriti stories, but the company goes bankrupt.

1922. Elvira Aldao de Díaz publishes *Mientras ruge el huracán*, her first book, at the age of 64. Fernández publishes another book called *Versos*. Ricardo Rojas publishes a chapter on women writers in his *La literatura argentina* that institutionalizes critical opinion about them.

1923. Aldao publishes *Horas de guerra y horas de paz*. Leopoldo Torre Ríos directs "El puñal del mazorquero," a silent film based on a Gorriti story.

1924. In Venezuela, Teresa de la Parra publishes *Ifigenia*, signaling a new generation of women novelists.

1926. Aldao remembers the hardships of war in *París 1914–1919*.

1928. Aldao publishes a memoir of a friend, his politics, and the country in revolution in *Reminiscencias sobre Aristóbulo del Valle*.

1930. Silvia Fernández publishes *La Virgen de Luján y la bandera de la patria*.

1931. Aldao remembers her childhood in *Recuerdos de antaño*. Apparently there is some indiscretion in the book; at least her brother, the novelist Martín Aldao, thinks so. He burns his own copy and tries to buy all the copies in the bookstores in order to burn them also. Victoria Ocampo establishes the magazine *Sur,* thereby claiming women's right to literary criticism.

1933. Aldao publishes *Recuerdos dispersos*. Emma de la Barra's *Eleonora*, which had appeared previously as a magazine serial, is published as a book.

1935. Aldao publishes *Cartas de dos amigas*. María Luisa Bombal's surrealist novel, *La última niebla*, portrays women's sexual and social oppression.

1943. Emma de la Barra's *La dicha de Malena*, a novel previously published in *Caras y Caretas*, is published as a book. Her novel *Stella* becomes a hit again, this time as a film. Although made in Argentina, the film is directed by the Spanish director Benito Perojo. The role of Alex makes a star of the Argentine actress Zully Moreno.

1945. Silvia Fernández dies and is buried at Luján. Gabriela Mistral of Chile becomes the first Latin American writer to win the Nobel Prize for Literature.

1947. Emma de la Barra dies in Buenos Aires on April 15. In a campaign guided by Evita Perón, Argentine women receive the right to vote on September 23.

1948. Juan Perón dissolves the Sociedad de Beneficencia, which has snubbed his wife Evita, and places the responsibility for girls' education under government control.

1950. Elvira Aldao de Díaz dies in Mar del Plata. Before her death, she publishes *Cartas íntimas*, the collected letters that the politician Lisandro de la Torre wrote to her. The collection is reprinted in 1951, 1952, and 1959.

1967. Argentina issues a commemorative stamp in honor of Juana Manso.

1985. One hundred years after the publication of Josefina Pelliza's *Conferencias*, the legal principle of *patria potestad* is changed to give women equal custody of their children.

---

[1]Census information for 1887 and 1914 is from James R. Scobie, *Buenos Aires: Plaza to Suburb, 1870–1910* (New York: Oxford University Press, 1974), 216.

Bibliography

Abeijón, Carlos and Jorge S. Lafauci. *La mujer argentina antes y después de Eva Perón*. Buenos Aires: Editorial Cuarto Mundo, 1975.

Adelfa. "La violeta." *La Ondina del Plata* (20 February 1876): 91-92.

Aldao de Díaz, Elvira. *Cartas de dos amigas*. Mar del Plata: De Falco, 1935.

———. *Cartas íntimas a Elvira Aldao de Díaz*. Buenos Aires: Futuro, 1951, 1952, 1959.

———. *Horas de guerra y horas de paz: impresiones*. Buenos Aires: Balder Möen, 1923.

———. *Mientras ruge el huracán*. Buenos Aires: Balder Möen, 1922.

———. *París 1914–19 (Impresiones)*. Buenos Aires: Agencia General de Librería y Publicaciones, 1926.

———. *Recuerdos de antaño*. Buenos Aires: Peuser, 1931.

———. *Recuerdos dispersos*. Buenos Aires: Peuser, 1933.

———. *Reminiscencias sobre Aristóbulo del Valle*. Buenos Aires: Jacobo Peuser, 1928.

———. *Repercusiones sobre el libro Reminiscencias sobre Aristóbulo del Valle*. Buenos Aires: Jacobo Peuser, 1929.

———. *Veraneos marplatenses 1887–1923*.

Aldaraca, Bridget. "El ángel del hogar: The Cult of Domesticity in Nineteenth-Century Spain," *Theory and Practice of Feminist Literary Criticism*. Eds. Gabriela Mora and Karen S. Van Hooft. Ypsilanti: Bilingual Press, 1982. 62-87.

Amicis, Edmundo de. "Prólogo." *Stella* (Barcelona: Maucci, 1909).

Andrade, Agustina ["Tórtola"]. "A Silvia Fernández." *La Ondina del Plata* (29 October 1876): 519.

———. *Lágrimas: ensayos poéticos*. Buenos Aires: La Tribuna, 1878.

Andrews, George Reid. *The Afro-Argentines of Buenos Aires 1800–1900*. Madison: University of Wisconsin Press, 1980.

Angelina, Eva [Zoila Aurora Cáceres]. "La emancipación de la mujer." *El Búcaro Americano* (1 June 1986): 127-30.

Arciniegas, Germán. "Don Ricardo Rojas." *El Mundo* (10 June 1956): 24.

"Arco-Iris." *El Album del Hogar* (28 December 1879): 106-107.

Ardener, Edwin. "Belief and the Problem of Women" and "The 'Problem' Revisited." *Perceiving Women.* Shirley Ardener, ed. New York: John Wiley & Sons, 1975. 1-27.

Argentine Bibliography: A Union Catalog of Argentine Holdings in the Libraries of the University of Buenos Aires. Boston: G. K. Hall, 1980.

Arteaga Alemparte, Justo. "Mujeres y flores." *La Ondina del Plata* (27 February 1876): 104-106.

Auza, Néstor Tomás. *Periodismo y feminismo en la Argentina, 1830–1930.* Buenos Aires: Emecé, 1988.

Barra, Emma de la ["César Duayen"]. "Concierto del círculo Santa Cecilia." *La Nación* (20 June 1893): 3.

———. *La dicha de Malena.* Buenos Aires: Tor, 1943. Published in abbreviated form in *Caras y Caretas* (25 January–15 March 1913): n.p.

———. *Eleonora.* Buenos Aires: Tor, 1933.

———. *El manantial.* Buenos Aires: Angel Estrada, 1908.

———. *Mecha Iturbe.* Buenos Aires: Maucci, 1906. Editions continuing into the 1940s.

———. *Stella: novela de costumbres argentinas.* Buenos Aires: Möen, 1905. Many editions extending into the 1940s.

Barrancos, Dora. *Anarquismo, educación y costumbres en la Argentina de principios de siglo.* Buenos Aires: Contrapunto, 1990.

Berg, Mary. "Rereading Fiction by 19th-Century Latin American Women Writers: Interpretation and Translation of the Past into the Present." *Translation Perspectives* 6 (1991): 127-33.

Biagini, Hugo Edgardo. *Cómo fue la generación del 80.* Buenos Aires: Plus Ultra, 1980.

———. *El movimiento positivista argentino.* Buenos Aires: Belgrano, 1985.

———. "El progresismo argentino del Ochenta." *Revista Interamericana de Bibliografía* 28 (1978): 373-84.

Bibliografía Argentina de Artes y Letras. *Artes y letras en "La Nación" 1870–1899.* Buenos Aires: Fondo Nacional de las Artes, 1968.

"Biblioteca de la Nación." *La Nación* (25 December 1905): 1.

Bilbao, Francisco. "Literatura." *La Revista del Nuevo Mundo* (11 July 1857): 331-36.

Bonet, Carmelo. "*Stella* y la sociedad porteña de principios de siglo." *Cursos y Conferencias* 44 (1953): 303-16.

Bosch, Velia, ed. *Teresa de la Parra ante la crítica* (Caracas: Monte Avila, 1980).

Bullrich, Silvina. *La mujer argentina en la literatura*. Buenos Aires: Ministerio de Cultura y Educación, 1972.

Bustamante de Baeza, Hortencia. "A las señoritas argentinas que escriben en la *Ondina del Plata*." *La Ondina del Plata* (27 August 1876): 411.

Cabello de Carbonera, Mercedes. "Miss Nightingale." *La Alborada del Plata* (3 and 10 February 1878): 94-95; 101-103.

Campanella, Hebe N. *La generación del 80: su influencia en la vida cultural argentina*. Buenos Aires: Tekné, 1983.

Cané, Miguel. *Charlas literarias*. Buenos Aires: Sceaux, 1885.

Carlson, Marifran. *¡Feminismo! The Women's Movement in Argentina from its Beginnings to Eva Perón*. Chicago: Academy, 1988.

Chaney, Elsa M. *Supermadre: Women in Politics in Latin America*. Austin: University of Texas Press, 1979.

Cixous, Hélène. "The Laugh of the Medusa." Keith and Paula Cohen, trans. *Signs* 1 (1976): 875-93.

"Conversación." *La Nación* (12 January 1876): 1.

Coronado, Martín. "*Lágrimas*: Poesías de la señorita Agustina Andrade." *El Album del Hogar* (4 August 1878): 32-35.

Cutolo, Vicente Osvaldo, ed. *Nuevo diccionario biográfico argentino*. Buenos Aires: Elche, 1975.

Da Freito [Antonio Argerich]. "A la señora de Sagasta." *El Album del Hogar* (5 January 1879): 209.

———. "Autopsia de un artículo." *El Album del Hogar* (22 December 1878): 193-94.

———. "Escepticismo y fe." *El Album del Hogar* (19 October 1879): 123-25.

———. "La mujer en la naturaleza y la civilización." *El Album del Hogar* (8 December 1878): 177-78.

———. "Párrafos de Da Freito a la comendadora Tijerita." *El Album del Hogar* (2 November 1879): 143-44.

———. "Sin nombre." *El Album del Hogar* (24 November 1878): 163-64.

Darío, Rubén. *Obras completas: Autobiografía*. Madrid: Mundo Latino, 1920.

Di Carlo, Adelia. "El periodismo femenino literario en la República Argentina, hasta el año 1907." *Caras y Caretas* 1762 (1932): n.p.

Díaz de Guzmán, Ruy. *La Argentina*. Buenos Aires: Espasa-Calpe, 1945.

Dresner, Zita. "Domestic Comic Writers." *Women's Comic Visions*. June Sochen, ed. Detroit: Wayne State University Press, 1991. 93-114.

DuPlessis, Rachel Blau. *Writing Beyond the Ending: Narrative Strategies of Twentieth-Century Women Writers*. Bloomington: Indiana University Press, 1985.

Echenique, María Eugenia. "Cartas IX (en una quebrada)." *La Ondina del Plata* (14 November 1875): 486-68.

———. *Colección literaria*. Rosario Echenique, ed. Córdoba: La Elzeviriana, 1926.

———. "La emancipación de la mujer." *La Ondina del Plata* (25 June, 13 August, 27 August, 8 October, 15 October 1876): 318-20, 385-87, 409-11, 481-83, 493-95.

———. "Necesidades de la mujer argentina." *La Ondina del Plata* (16 January 1876): 25-27.

———. "Pinceladas." *La Ondina del Plata* (7 May 1876): 217-18.

"Eduarda Mansilla de García." *La Ondina del Plata* (9 May 1875): 157-59.

"Elvira Aldao de Díaz falleció en Mar del Plata." *La Nación* (15 May 1950): 4.

"Ema [*sic*] de la Barra de Llanos (César Duayen) falleció ayer en esta capital." *La Nación* (6 April 1947): 4.

Emma. "Mosaico." *La Alborada del Plata* (30 December 1877): 56.

Etchepareborda, Roberto. "La estructura socio-política argentina y la Generación del Ochenta." *Latin American Literary Review* 13 (1978): 127-34.

"Falleció Ayer Doña Silvia Fernández." *La Nación* (26 June 1945): 14.

Fernández, Silvia. *Armonías del alma: poesías*. Buenos Aires: La Nación, 1876.

———. *Versos*. Luján: La Perla del Plata, 1913.

———. *Versos*. Buenos Aires: Bayardo, 1922.

———. *La Virgen de Luján y la bandera de la patria: poesía*. Buenos Aires: 1930.

Ferrari, Gustavo and Ezequiel Gallo, eds. *La Argentina del ochenta al centenario*. Buenos Aires: Sudamericana, 1980.

Fletcher, Lea. "Juana Manso: una voz en el desierto." *Mujeres y cultura en la Argentina del siglo XIX*. Buenos Aires: Feminaria, 1994. 108-20.

———. *Modernismo: sus cuentistas olvidados en la Argentina.* Buenos Aires: Ediciones del 80, 1986.

———, ed. *Mujeres y cultura en la Argentina del siglo XIX.* Buenos Aires: Feminaria, 1994.

Foster, David William. *The Argentine Generation of 1880: Ideology and Cultural Texts.* Columbia: University of Missouri Press, 1990.

Frederick, Bonnie. *La pluma y la aguja: las escritoras de la Generación del '80.* Buenos Aires: Feminaria, 1993.

———. "Reading the Warning: The Reader and the Image of the Captive Woman." *Chasqui* 18 (1989): 3-11.

———. "A State of Conviction, a State of Feeling: Scientific and Literary Discourses in the Works of Three Argentine Writers, 1879–1908." *Latin American Literary Review* 9 (July–December 1991): 48-61.

———. "El viajero y la nómada: los recuerdos de viaje de Eduarda y Lucio Mansilla." *Mujeres y cultura en la Argentina del siglo XIX.* Lea Fletcher, ed., Buenos Aires: Feminaria, 1994. 246-51.

Funes, Celestina. *Lucía Miranda: episodio nacional.* Rosario: Imprenta El Mensajero, 1883.

Galerstein, Carolyn L., ed. *Women Writers of Spain: An Annotated Bio-Bibliographical Guide.* New York: Greenwood, 1986.

Gálvez, Manuel. *Amigos y maestros de mi juventud.* Reprint of 1904. Buenos Aires: Hachette, 1961.

Gambarini, Elsa Krieger. "The Male Critic and the Woman Writer: Reading Teresa de la Parra's Critics." Bernice Hausman, trans. *In the Feminine Mode: Essays on Hispanic Women Writers.* Noël Valis and Carol Maier, eds. Lewisburg: Bucknell University Press, 1990. 177-94.

García Mansilla, Daniel. *Visto, oído y recordado.* Buenos Aires: Kraft, 1950.

Garrels, Elizabeth. "La nueva Eloísa en América o el ideal de la mujer de la generación de 1837." *Nuevo Texto Crítico* 2 (1989): 27-38.

Garrido de la Peña, Carlota. "Letras femeninas: Emilia Pardo Bazán." *El Búcaro Americano* (1 March 1896): 58.

———. "Tarea patriótica." *El Búcaro Americano* (1 April 1896): 100-101.

González Arrili, Bernardo. "Ida Edelvira Rodríguez: la poetisa negra." *Mujeres de nuestra tierra.* Buenos Aires: Ediciones La Obra, 1950. 106-10.

Gorriti, Juana Manuela. "Algo sobre la muger." *La Alborada del Plata* (9 December 1877): 25.

———. *Lo íntimo.* Buenos Aires: Ramón Espasa, 1892.

——. "Prospecto." *La Alborada del Plata* (18 November 1877): 1.

——. "¿Qué es el génio?" *La Alborada del Plata* (2 December 1877): 17.

Greenblatt, Stephen. *Renaissance Self-Fashioning*. Chicago: University of Chicago Press, 1980.

Guerra, Rosa. *Lucía Miranda*. Buenos Aires: EUDEBA, 1956.

Guerrero, César H. *Mujeres de Sarmiento*. Buenos Aires: n.p., 1960.

Guy, Donna. *Sex and Danger in Buenos Aires*. Lincoln: University of Nebraska Press, 1991.

"Hace 50 años que murió la poetisa Josefina Pelliza de Sagasta, figura olvidada." *Democracia* (Concordia) (11 August 1938): n.p.

Hedges, Elaine. "The Needle or the Pen: The Literary Rediscovery of Women's Textile Work." *Tradition and the Talents of Women*. Florence Howe, ed. Urbana: University of Illinois, 1991. 338-64.

Iglesia, Cristina, ed. *El ajuar de la patria: Ensayos críticos sobre Juana Manuela Gorriti*. Buenos Aires: Feminaria, 1993.

Ingemanson, Birgitta. "The Political Function of Domestic Objects in the Fiction of Aleksandra Kollantai." *Slavic Review* 48 (1989): 71-82.

Jackson, Richard L. *The Afro-Spanish American Author II: The 1980s*. West Cornwall, Connecticut: Locust Hill Press, 1989.

——. *Black Writers in Latin America*. Albuquerque: University of New Mexico Press, 1979.

Jaroslavsky, Sara and Estela Maspero. "La cultura argentina en el decenio 1852-1862." *Cursos y Conferencias* 31 (1947): 109-51.

Jitrik, Noé. *El 80 y su mundo*. Buenos Aires: Jorge Alvarez, 1968.

"Juana Manso." *La Ondina del Plata* (2 May 1875): 145.

"Juana Manuela Gorriti." [obituary] *La Prensa* (7 November 1892): 5.

"Juana Manuela Gorriti." [funeral] *La Prensa* (8 November 1892): 5.

Kirkpatrick, Susan. "On the Threshold of the Realist Novel: Gender and Genre in *La gaviota*." *PMLA* 98 (1983): 323-40.

——. *Las Románticas: Women Writers and Subjectivity in Spain, 1835–1850*. Berkeley: University of California Press, 1989.

Knaster, Meri. *Women in Spanish America: An Annotated Bibliography from Pre-Conquest to Contemporary Times*. Boston: G. K. Hall, 1977.

Lacau, María Hortensia and Mabel Manacorda de Rosetti. "Antecedentes del modernismo en la literatura argentina." *Cursos y Conferencias* 31 (1947): 163-92.

Lafleur, Héctor René, Sergio D. Provenzano, and Fernando P. Alonso. *Las revistas literarias argentinas, 1893-1967.* Buenos Aires: Centro Editor de América Latina, 1968.

Lanser, Susan Sniader. *Fictions of Authority: Women Writers and Narrative Voice.* Ithaca: Cornell University Press, 1992.

Larrosa, Lola. *Ecos del corazón: colección de artículos literarios.* Buenos Aires: 1878.

——. *Los esposos.* Buenos Aires: J.A. Berra, 1893.

——. *¡Hija mía!* Buenos Aires: Alsina, 1888.

——. "La misión de la muger." *La Prensa* (21 October 1882:1.

——. "La mujer en el hogar." *La Ondina del Plata* (24 September 1876): 464-65.

——. *El lujo.* Buenos Aires: Alsina, 1889.

——. *Las obras de misericordia.* Buenos Aires: Oswald, 1882.

——. "25 de mayo de 1810." *La Nación* (25 May 1877): 2.

Lavrin, Asunción. *The Ideology of Feminism in the Southern Cone, 1900–1940.* Latin American Program Working Papers no. 169. Washington, D.C.: Wilson Center, Smithsonian Institute, 1986.

Leavitt, Sturgis. *Argentine Literature: A Bibliography of Literary Criticism, Biography, and Literary Controversy.* Chapel Hill: University of North Carolina, 1924.

Leguizamón, Martiniano. "La leyenda de Lucía de Miranda." *Revista de la Universidad de Córdoba* 6, 1 (March 1919): 3-11.

Lichtblau, Myron I. *The Argentine Novel in the Nineteenth Century.* New York: Hispanic Institute, 1959.

——. "El tema de Lucía Miranda en la novela argentina." *Armas y Letras* 2, 1 (January, March 1959): 23-31.

Little, Cynthia Jeffress. "Moral Reform and Feminism: A Case Study." *Journal of Interamerican Studies and World Affairs* 17 (1975): 386-97.

Lozano de Vílchez, Enriqueta. "La modestia." *La Ondina del Plata* (16 January 1876): 34-35.

Luciérnaga. "Plumadas." [Women writers] *El Album del Hogar* (8 June 1879): 391.

——. "Plumadas." [Eduarda Mansilla] *El Album del Hogar* (22 June 1879): 406-407.

——. "Plumadas." [Women writers] *El Album del Hogar* (30 November 1879): 174-76.

——. "Retratos a la pluma: Ida Edelvira Rodríguez." *El Album del Hogar* (19 October 1879): 127.

M. [Bartolomé Mitre]. "Bibliografía: 'Stella.'" *La Nación* (15 September 1905): 5.

Mansilla de García, Eduarda. "América literaria: educación de la mujer." *La Nación* (28 July 1883): 1.

——. *Un amor* (novela). Buenos Aires: El Diario, 1885.

——. *Creaciones*. Buenos Aires: República, 1883.

——. *Cuentos*. Buenos Aires: República, 1880.

——. "Educación de la mujer." *La Nación* (28 July 1883): 1.

——. *Lucía Miranda. La Tribuna* (10 May–4 July 1860). Buenos Aires: Alsina, 1882. Buenos Aires: J.C. Rovira, 1933.

——. *El médico de San Luis*. Buenos Aires: La Paz, 1860. Buenos Aires: 1879. Buenos Aires: Editorial Universitaria, 1962.

——. *La marquesa de Altamira*. Buenos Aires: Imprenta de la Universidad, 1881, 1887.

——. *Pablo ou la vie dans les Pampas*. Paris: E. Lachaud, 1869.

——. *Recuerdos de viaje*. Buenos Aires: Alsina, 1882.

Mansilla, Lucio V. "Bibliografía y juicio crítico." *La Revista de Buenos Aires* 2 (1864): 351-75.

——. *Entre-nous: causeries de un jueves*. Juan Carlos Ghiano, ed. Buenos Aires: Hachette, 1963.

Manso de Noronha, Juana. *La familia del Comendador*. Buenos Aires: J.A. Bernheim, 1854.

——. "La redacción." *Album de Señoritas* (1 January 1854): 1.

"Maria Eujenia [*sic*] Echenique." [obituary] *La Nación* (31 January 1878): n.p.

Martínez, Elia. "Evolución femenina." *El Búcaro Americano* (15 February 1897): 169-70.

——. "Reminiscencias patrióticas." *El Búcaro Americano* (15 May 1897): 217-18.

Marting, Diane, ed. *Spanish American Women Writers: A Bio-Bibliographical Source Book*. New York: Greenwood, 1990.

——. *Women Writers of Spanish America: An Annotated Bio-Bibliographical Guide*. New York: Greenwood, 1987.

Masiello, Francine. *Between Civilization and Barbarism: Women, Nation, and Literary Culture in Modern Argentina*. Lincoln: University of Nebraska Press, 1992.

———, ed. *La mujer y el espacio público: el periodismo femenino en la Argentina del siglo XIX*. Buenos Aires: Feminaria, 1994.

Matto de Turner, Clorinda. "Bautismo." *El Búcaro Americano* (1 February 1896): 2-3.

———. "Doctora Cecilia Grierson." *El Búcaro Americano* (1 June 1896): 126-27.

———. "Las obreras del pensamiento en la América del Sud." *El Búcaro Americano* (1 February 1896): 5-14; reprinted in *Boreales, miniaturas y porcelanas*. Buenos Aires: J.A. Alsina, 1902. 245-66.

———. "Social." [Elegy to Lola Larrosa.] *El Búcaro Americano* (1 February 1896): 17-22.

Maubé, José Carlos and Adolfo Capdevielle, eds. *Antología de la poesía femenina argentina*. Buenos Aires: Ferrari, 1930.

McGee, Sandra F. "The Visible and Invisible Liga Patriótica Argentina, 1919-28: Gender Roles and the Right Wing." *Hispanic American Historical Review* 64 (1984): 233-58.

Meehan, Thomas C. "Una olvidada precursora de la literatura fantástica argentina: Juana Manuela Gorriti." *Chasqui* 10 (1981): 3-19.

Meléndez, Concha. "La leyenda de Lucía de Miranda en la novela." *La novela indianista en Hispanoamérica* in *Obras completas*. Vol. 1. San Juan, Puerto Rico: Instituto de Cultura Puertorriqueña, 1970. 169-77.

Mendoza, J.R. de. "Patrocinio de Biedma." *La Ondina del Plata* (29 October, 5 November 1876): 520.

Meyer, Doris. *Reinterpreting the Spanish American Essay: Women Writers of the 19th and 20th Centuries*. Austin: University of Texas Press, 1995.

———. *Victoria Ocampo: Against the Wind and the Tide*. New York: George Barziller, 1979.

"Miscelánea," *La Alborada del Plata* (29 February 1880): 63.

Molyneux, Maxine. "No God, No Boss, No Husband: Anarchist Feminism in Nineteenth-Century Argentina." *Latin American Perspectives* 13 (1986): 119-45.

Montserrat, Marcelo. "La mentalidad evolucionista: una ideología del progreso." *La Argentina del Ochenta al Centenario*. Gustavo Ferrari and Ezequiel Gallo, eds. Buenos Aires: Sudamericana, 1980. 785-818.

"Mosáico." *La Alborada del Plata* (21 March 1880): 94-95.

Nari, Marcela. "Alejandra: Maternidad e independencia femenina." *Feminaria* 6, 10 (April 1993) Sec. 2: 7-9.

Navarro Viola, Alberto. *Anuario bibliográfico de la República Argentina*. Buenos Aires: n.p., 1880–89.

Nisbet, R. *History of the Idea of Progress*. New York: Basic Books, 1980.

"Una novela y una vida: César Duayen recuerda los días que escribiera las páginas de *Stella*." *Noticias Gráficas* (24 October 1932): 9.

"Una nueva colaboradora." *La Alborada del Plata* (21 March 1880): 95.

Núñez, Zulma. "Mercedes Rosas: La primera novelista argentina." *Atlántida* 29 (November 1946) 30, 94.

Obligado, Rafael. "Crítica literaria: Armonías del alma." *La Ondina del Plata* (12 November 1876): 541-44.

Ochagavia, Margarita Rufina. *Un ánjel y un demonio o el valor de un juramento*. Buenos Aires: Imprenta del Mayo, 1857.

Offen, Karen. "Defining Feminism: A Comparative Historical Approach." *Signs* 14 (1988): 119-57.

Oreggioni, Alberto F., ed. *Diccionario de literatura uruguaya*. Montevideo: Arca, 1987.

Pagés Larraya, Antonio. "La crítica literaria de la generación argentina del 80." *Cuadernos Hispanoamericanos* 390 (1982): 676-83.

———. *Juan Gutiérrez y Ricardo Rojas: Iniciación de la crítica argentina*. Buenos Aires: Facultad de Filosofía y Letras, 1983.

———. "Ricardo Rojas: fundador de los estudios universitarios sobre literatura argentina." *La Revista de la Universidad de Buenos Aires* 5 (1959): 349-67.

Palouse Translation Project. "The Emancipation of Women: Argentina 1876." *Journal of Women's History* 7 (Fall 1995): 102-26.

Parker, Rozcika. *The Subversive Stitch*. London: Women's Press, 1986.

Passicot, María Emilia. "Social." *El Búcaro Americano* (15 February 1896): 44-46.

Peden, Margaret Sayers, trans. and comp. *A Woman of Genius: the Intellectual Autobiography of Sor Juana Inés de la Cruz*. Salisbury, Conn: Lime Rock Press, 1982.

Pelliza, M.A. *Críticas y bocetos históricos*. Buenos Aires: Imprenta del Mayo, 1879.

Pelliza de Sagasta, Josefina ["Judith"]. *Canto inmortal*. Buenos Aires: Imprenta Colón, 1881.

———. *El César*. Buenos Aires: Imprenta Colón, 1882.

———. *La chiriguana*. Buenos Aires: La Ondina del Plata, 1877.

———. *Conferencias. El libro de las madres.* Buenos Aires: Jeneral Lavalle, 1885.

———. "La emancipación de la mujer." *La Ondina del Plata* (23 July, 10 September 1876): 349-52, 434-37.

———. *Lirios silvestres.* Buenos Aires: Imprenta del Porvenir, 1877.

———. *Margarita.* Buenos Aires: El Orden, 1875.

———. "María Eugenia Echenique." *La Alborada del Plata* (3 February 1878): 89.

———. "La mujer." *La Ondina del Plata* (4 June 1876): 267-68.

———. "La mujer literata en la República Argentina." *El Album del Hogar* (15 December 1878): 185-86.

———. "La mujer literata en la República Argentina: Al señor Da Freito." *El Album del Hogar* (1 December 1878): 169.

———. *Pasionarias.* Buenos Aires: Imprenta Europea, 1887.

———. "¿Reclusa o hermana de caridad? Ni lo uno, ni lo otro." *La Alborada del Plata* (17 February 1878): 108-109.

———. "Ultima palabra." *El Album del Hogar* (29 December 1878): 202.

Pérez Amuchástegui, A.J. *Mentalidades argentinas (1860–1930).* 6th ed. Buenos Aires: Editorial Universitaria de Buenos Aires, 1984.

"Personajes de papel y tinta." *Sintonía* (September 1943): 56-57.

Pintos, Luis Telmo. "El hombre y la mujer." *La Ondina del Plata* (14 March 1875): 61-62.

———. "La mujer: habilitada para la enseñanza." *La Ondina del Plata* (1 August 1875): 302-302.

"Plumadas." *El Album del Hogar* (22 June 1879): 407.

Polo y Peyrolón. "La mujer y la flor." *El Album del Hogar* (13 July 1879): 11-13.

Poovey, Mary. *The Proper Lady and the Woman Writer.* Chicago: University of Chicago Press, 1984.

Prieto, Adolfo. *El discurso criollista en la formación de la Argentina moderna.* Buenos Aires: La Sudamericana, 1988.

Pujato Crespo, Mercedes. "Historia de las revistas femeninas y mujeres intelectuales que les dieron vida." *Primer Congreso Patriótico de Señoras en América del Sud.* Buenos Aires: Imprenta Europea, 1910. 157-79.

Redacción. "Sobre el mismo tema. *El folleto de D. Zenon." La Broma* (8 February 1878): n.p.

Las Redactoras. "Las mujeres." *La Camelia* (11 April 1852): 2.

Rivarola, E.E. "Bibliografía." *La Nación* (19 September 1905): 3.

Rivera, Jorge. *Los bohemios*. Buenos Aires: Centro Editor de América Latina, 1971.

Robinson, William H., ed. *Critical Essays on Phillis Wheatley*. Boston: G. K. Hall, 1982.

Rodríguez, Ida Edelvira. "La aria final de 'Lucía'" *El Album del Hogar* (14 July 1878): 12.

——. "El canto de las ondinas." *El Album del Hogar* (4 January 1880): 111.

——. "Desencanto." *La Alborada Literaria del Plata* (29 February 1880): 57.

——. *La flor de la montaña*. Buenos Aires: La Sudamericana, 1887.

——. "El mundo de Colón." *El Album poético argentino*. Buenos Aires: La Ondina del Plata, 1877. 88.

——. "La sonámbula." *El Album del Hogar* (3 August 1879): 34.

——. "Voces de la noche." *El Album del Hogar* (15 December 1878): 186.

Rodríguez Alcalá, Hugo, ed. *On the Centennial of the Argentine Generation of 1880*. Latin American Studies Program, no. 4. Riverside: University of California, 1980.

Rojas, Ricardo. *La literatura argentina*. Buenos Aires: Juan Roldán, 1925.

Romero, Horacio. *La poesía en la tierra de Andrade*. Gualeguachú: Imprenta Gutenberg, 1946.

Rosende Sierra, Petrona. "Prospecto." *La Aljaba* (1830) n.p.

——. "Felicidad de las señoras." *La Aljaba* (19 November 1830): 3.

——. "Educación de las hijas." *La Aljaba* (23 November 1830): 1.

——. "A las que se oponen a la instruccion de las mugeres." *La Aljaba* (30 November 1830): 2.

Ruiz, Elida, ed. *J. M. Gorriti, C. Duayen, M. de Villarino y otras: Las escritoras, 1840–1940*. Buenos Aires: Centro Editor de América Latina, 1980.

Russ, Joanna. *How to Suppress Women's Writing*. Austin: University of Texas Press, 1983.

Saez de Melgar, Faustina. "Estudios sociales sobre la mujer: la abnegación." *La Ondina del Plata* (7 November 1875): 471-73.

Sánchez de Thompson de Mendeville, María. *Cartas de Mariquita Sánchez*. Clara Vilaseca, ed. Buenos Aires: Peuser, 1952.

——. *Recuerdos del Buenos Aires virreynal*. Buenos Aires: Ene, 1953.

Sarlo, Beatriz. *El imperio de los sentimientos: narraciones de circulación periódica en la Argentina, 1917–1927.* Buenos Aires: Catálogos Editora, 1985.

Sarmiento, Domingo F. *Obras de D. F. Sarmiento.* Vol. 46. Buenos Aires: Mariano Moreno, 1900. 276.

Schade, George D. "Los viajeros argentinos del Ochenta." *Texto Crítico* 10 (1984): 82-103.

Scobie, James R. *Buenos Aires: Plaza to Suburb, 1870–1910.* New York: Oxford University Press, 1974.

Scott, Nina M. "Juana Manuela Gorriti's *Cocina ecléctica*: Recipes as Feminine Discourse." *Hispania* 75 (1992): 310-14.

Seminar on Feminism and Culture in Latin America. *Women, Culture, and Politics in Latin America.* Berkeley: University of California Press, 1990.

"La señora Manso." *La Prensa* (25 April 1875): 2.

Showalter, Elaine. "Feminist Criticism in the Wilderness." *Writing and Sexual Difference.* Elizabeth Abel, ed. Chicago: University of Chicago Press, 1982. 9-36.

———. "Introduction: The Rise of Gender." *Speaking of Gender.* Elaine Showalter, ed. New York: Routledge, 1989. 1-13.

Sinués de Marco, María del Pilar. "Las armas de la mujer." *La Ondina del Plata* (21 May 1876): 242-44.

Smith, Sidonie. *A Poetics of Women's Autobiography: Marginality and the Fictions of Self-Representation.* Bloomington: Indiana University Press, 1987.

"Social." [Funeral orations for Lola Larrosa.] *El Búcaro Americano* (1, 15 February 1896): 17-22, 44-46.

Sommer, Doris. *Foundational Fictions: The National Romances of Latin America.* Berkeley: University of California Press, 1991.

Sosa de Newton, Lily. *Las argentinas de ayer a hoy.* Buenos Aires: Zanetti, 1967.

———. *Diccionario biográfico de mujeres argentinas.* Buenos Aires: n.p., 1972.

———. *Diccionario biográfico de mujeres argentinas.* Buenos Aires: Plus Ultra, 1986.

———. "Eduarda Mansilla de García: narradora, periodista, música y primera autora de literatura infantil," *Mujeres y cultura en la Argentina del siglo XIX.* Lea Fletcher, ed. Buenos Aires: Feminaria, 1994. 87-95.

——. "Incorporación de la mujer al periodismo en la Argentina." *Evaluación de la literatura femenina de Latinoamérica, siglo XX: II Simposio International de Literatura.* Juana Alcira Arancibia, ed. San José, Costa Rica: n.p., 1985. 263-70.

Soto y Calvo, Edelina. *Afectos.* Paris: Durand, 1907.

——. *Emociones.* Buenos Aires: J. Samet, 1927.

——. *Parque vetusto.* Buenos Aires: Juan Toia, 1929.

"Stella." *Heraldo del Cinematografista* (13 October 1943): 189.

"Stella: Una Revelación del Exito." *La Nación* (26 September 1905): 8.

Sternbach, Nancy Saporta. "'Mejorar la condición de mi secso': The Essays of Rosa Guerra." *Reinterpreting the Spanish American Essay: Women Writers of the Nineteenth and Twentieth Centuries.* Doris Meyer, ed. Austin: University of Texas Press, 1995. 46-56.

Suárez, José Bernardo. *El tesoro de las niñas: coleccion de articulos estractados i traducidos de los mejores autores, i publicada para servir de texto de lectura en los colejios y escuelas.* Buenos Aires: Pablo E. Coni, 1868.

Szuchman, Mark D. *Order, Family, and Community in Buenos Aires, 1810–1860.* Stanford: Stanford University Press, 1988.

Teresa de Jesús, Sor. "Educación del hogar." *La Ondina del Plata* (26 March 1876): 150-52.

Tesler, Mario. *Diccionario argentino de seudónimos.* Buenos Aires: Galerna, 1991.

Testimonios sobre Ricardo Rojas. Buenos Aires: Instituto de Literatura Argentina "Ricardo Rojas," 1984.

Tijerita. "Cortes y recortes." *El Album del Hogar* (26 October 1879): 130-31.

——. "Crónica de Palermo." *El Album del Hogar* (16 February 1879): 261-63.

Todd, Janet. *Feminist Literary History.* New York: Routledge, 1988.

Tompkins, Jane. *Sensational Designs: The Cultural Work of American Fiction 1790–1860.* New York: Oxford University Press, 1985.

Torres y Quiroga, Raymunda. "Madama Staël." *La Ondina del Plata* (10 December 1876): 595.

——. "La mujer y la sociedad." *La Ondina del Plata* (26 March 1876): 147-49.

——. "Progreso." *La Ondina del Plata* (15 October 1876): 497-98.

Tuttle, Lisa. *Encyclopedia of Feminism.* New York: Facts on File, 1986.

Una Suscritora. "Educación de la mujer." *La Ondina del Plata* (12 March 1876): 124-25.

Varas Marín, Quiteria. "A una violeta." *La Ondina del Plata* (2 April 1876): 162.

Velasco y Arias, María. "Eduarda Mansilla de García." *Boletín del Colegio de Graduados de la Facultad de Filosofía y Letras*. 28, 29 (August–December 1939): 91-94.

Vergara de Bietti, Noemi. "De cómo fui y no fui alumna de Ricardo Rojas." *Testimonios sobre Ricardo Rojas*. Buenos Aires: Instituto de Literatura Argentina "Ricardo Rojas." 1984.

Viñas, David. *Literatura argentina y realidad política: de Sarmiento a Cortázar*. Buenos Aires: Siglo Veinte, 1971.

"Violeta." *La Ondina del Plata* (16 April 1876): 185-87.

Wagar, W. Warren. *Good Tidings: The Belief in Progress from Darwin to Marcuse*. Bloomington: Indiana University Press, 1972.

Walker, Nancy. "Toward Solidarity: Women's Humor and Group Identity." *Women's Comic Visions*. June Sochen, ed. Detroit: Wayne State University, 1991. 57-81.

Weber, Alison. *Teresa of Avila and the Rhetoric of Femininity*. Princeton: Princeton University Press, 1990.

Weber, Oscar. "Resultados inmediatos." *El Album del Hogar* (29 December 1878): 202-203.

Willianson, Agar. "La emancipación de la mujer." *La Alborada Literaria del Plata* (18 April 1880): 114-15.

Woolf, Virginia. "Professions for Women." *The Death of the Moth and Other Essays*. London: Hogarth, 1981. 149-54.

Wuili, Matilde Elena. "La gran causa del bello sexo: educación de la mujer." *El Album del Hogar* (23 March 1879): 301.

Zoraida [Eufrasia Cabral]. "Jorge Sand." *La Alborada del Plata* (1 March 1878): 117.

Zubieta, Ana María. "La historia de la literatura: dos historias diferentes." *Filología* 22 (1987): 191-213.

Index